CALL ME PISHER

"Pisher" is the Yiddish equivalent of a reversed upraised middle finger. Whenever my father and I got into an argument about something he had done or said and I let him know that I didn't like it, he would respond with, "So you'll call me pisher." A pisher is a "young squirt" or an inexperienced person, someone of little importance. "Call me pisher" is something like "tough luck" but much more than that. You might have to be Jewish to fully understand it.

HOWARD MOSCOE

Copyright © 2018 by Howard Moscoe and Ed Shiller

All rights reserved. No part of this publication may be reproduced, stored in a retrieval system, or transmitted, in any form or by any means, electronic, mechanical, photocopying, recording, or otherwise, without the written prior permission of the publisher.

Published by
Yorkland Publishing
12 Tepee Court
Toronto, Ontario M2J 3A9
Canada
www.yorklandpublishing.com

ISBN: 978-0-9697127-5-6

Cover design and illustrations by Howard Moscoe
Typeset in *Athelas* at SpicaBookDesign
Printed and bound by IngramSpark

CALL ME PISHER

A Madcap Romp Through City Hall

Howard Moscoe

YORKLAND PUBLISHING

Thanks

Thanks to those who tackled the Herculean effort to make this book socially acceptable. John Cosway and Marg McAulay, my editors, who valiantly struggled to overcome my inability to spell and make some of my illiterate ramblings intelligible. Rosemary Sibenik and Ed Shiller, my publishers, who saved me from my penchant for outrageous hyperbole and outlandish verbosity. And Iryna Spica, the designer, who pulled it all together. Most of all I would like to thank the 139,995 people who voted for me. Without their support none of this would have been possible. I hope that I have been able to measure up to their expectations.

To my wife Gloria; it's been a wild ride... couldn't have done it without you.

Table of Contents

PART I. NORTH YORK

1. In the Shadow of Old City Hall 3
2. Sparring Partner 7
3. The Bad Neighbour Relations Committee 14
4. Halifax Ahoy! 19
5. A Line In the Stand (or 122 metres away) 22
6. Who Wants to be a Millionaire? 25
7. Flag Flaps 29
8. The Sky is Falling – It Could Be! 32
9. Pesticide Pest 35
10. Yours In Government 38
11. Not My Feet 40
12. Thief 41
13. Never Revenge: Well Almost Never 45
14. Golf Cart Welfare Bums 52
15. On Signs 57
16. Hair Aches 64
17. Blowing Smoke 66
18. Moscoe vs. Moscoe 73
19. Hindu Flames 80
20. The Polish Twin 84
21. Bylaw Absurdity 87
22. North York Council Revolt 89
23. Paisley 92
24. Super Kids 96
25. Cut to the Chase 100

26	Garbage Stinks – Some Garbage Contracts Stink More	104
27	Gender Neutral, or Gender Neutered?	109
28	Saturday Night Rip-Off	112
29	Wheel-Trans Not for Burning	116
30	Pays the Piper	121
31	Good Party, Great Cucumber Sandwiches	129
32	The Big Move	136
33	Furniture Brings Out the Bad Boy in Me	142
34	Over the Rainbow	148
35	They Can Take their Civil Liberties and Shove them NOW Mel Lastman...March 1, 1988	151

PART II. METRO

36	The Sad Tale of Who Runs What	157
37	Lost and Found	163
38	Picking Up the Pieces	166
39	Team Zero and the Midnight Ride	170
40	Bush League	173
41	Didn't Have a Prayer	176
42	Bafflegab	179
43	Could Bureau Business be Better?	182
44	Perfect Harmony: The Blue Box, or How Coca-Cola Conned Ontario	186
45	Taking the Elderly for a Ride	192
46	The Battle of Downsview	196
47	Desert Deadbeat	203
48	Jakobek	205
49	Better to be Disabled in Toronto than in Paris	211
50	Tow Tale No. 1: It's Sometimes Hard to Separate the Good Guys from the Bad Guys	217
51	Tow Tale No. 2: Scum-Sucking Bottom Dwellers	221

Table of Contents

PART I. NORTH YORK

1. In the Shadow of Old City Hall 3
2. Sparring Partner 7
3. The Bad Neighbour Relations Committee 14
4. Halifax Ahoy! 19
5. A Line In the Stand (or 122 metres away) 22
6. Who Wants to be a Millionaire? 25
7. Flag Flaps 29
8. The Sky is Falling – It Could Be! 32
9. Pesticide Pest 35
10. Yours In Government 38
11. Not My Feet 40
12. Thief 41
13. Never Revenge: Well Almost Never 45
14. Golf Cart Welfare Bums 52
15. On Signs 57
16. Hair Aches 64
17. Blowing Smoke 66
18. Moscoe vs. Moscoe 73
19. Hindu Flames 80
20. The Polish Twin 84
21. Bylaw Absurdity 87
22. North York Council Revolt 89
23. Paisley 92
24. Super Kids 96
25. Cut to the Chase 100

26	Garbage Stinks – Some Garbage Contracts Stink More	104
27	Gender Neutral, or Gender Neutered?	109
28	Saturday Night Rip-Off	112
29	Wheel-Trans Not for Burning	116
30	Pays the Piper	121
31	Good Party, Great Cucumber Sandwiches	129
32	The Big Move	136
33	Furniture Brings Out the Bad Boy in Me	142
34	Over the Rainbow	148
35	They Can Take their Civil Liberties and Shove them NOW Mel Lastman…March 1, 1988	151

PART II. METRO

36	The Sad Tale of Who Runs What	157
37	Lost and Found	163
38	Picking Up the Pieces	166
39	Team Zero and the Midnight Ride	170
40	Bush League	173
41	Didn't Have a Prayer	176
42	Bafflegab	179
43	Could Bureau Business be Better?	182
44	Perfect Harmony: The Blue Box, or How Coca-Cola Conned Ontario	186
45	Taking the Elderly for a Ride	192
46	The Battle of Downsview	196
47	Desert Deadbeat	203
48	Jakobek	205
49	Better to be Disabled in Toronto than in Paris	211
50	Tow Tale No. 1: It's Sometimes Hard to Separate the Good Guys from the Bad Guys	217
51	Tow Tale No. 2: Scum-Sucking Bottom Dwellers	221

52	Tow Tale No. 3: Cockroaches are Hard to Eradicate	226
53	Tow Tale No. 4: Scams Evolve	230
54	Whacking Yourself Over the Head to Feel Better is a Dangerous Game	235
55	Up Close and Personal	240
56	Politics Brings out the Stupid in Some People	242
57	We Stand on Guard for Something	245
58	Sometimes the Little Guy Wins	248
59	Federal Election Campaign 1993	253
60	Poof, You're Gone	258

PART III. BIZZARO

61	Bizzaro – No. 1	263
62	Bizzaro – No. 2	271
63	Bizzaro – No. 3	276
64	Bizzaro – No. 4	283
65	Bizzaro – No. 5	288
66	Bizzaro – No. 6	294

PART IV. TORONTO

67	What Was That You Said?	301
68	Ellis Island	308
69	Political Hack	315
70	Ultimatum	318
71	Brother Jeff	322
72	Gunn Fight	324
73	On the Verge of a Shutdown	328
74	Grafitti and Mississauga Buses	330
75	Kindergarten Coup	336
76	The 1999 Transit Strike	342
77	Backstabbing Mayor	349
78	The Chair and the Restless: The Soap Opera Continues	352

79	Early Signs of an Election in York	359
80	The Sleaze Factor	363
81	At War With the Army	366
82	Playground Dispute	372
83	Windrows Away	375
84	Subways and Art	380
85	Best Kept Secret	386
86	In Bed With the Lobbyists	391
87	How Many Nurses Does it Take to Change a Light Bulb?	393
88	Down to the Wire	398
89	How Much is a Politician Worth?	404
90	Thinking Inside the Box Outside the Box	409
91	Kicked in My Canadian Identity	412
92	RSVP	417
93	Big City, Big Snub	421
94	The Right to Tinkle	424
95	Reaching Beyond	427
96	To What End?	434
97	Sending the Wrong Signals	441
98	Traffic Congestion is a Hodgepodge of Vested Interests	447
99	Farewell	453
100	Eulogy	457

Addendum. The Moscoe Team 461

PART I

CHAPTER 1
In the Shadow of Old City Hall

My grandfather was a horse thief, my grandmother a bootlegger, my father a bookmaker and my brother a scalper, so there was nothing left for me but politics.

My maternal grandparents came to Canada in 1908 and settled in the Ward – the immigrant reception area of Toronto. It was an urban slum located between Queen Street in the south and College Street in the north; sandwiched between University Avenue and Terauley Street (now Bay Street), in the shadow of City Hall. It had previously housed immigrants fleeing from the Irish potato famine after 1840 and was the Toronto terminus of the Underground Railroad during the American Civil War. By the turn of the century, it was predominantly Jewish and, to a lesser extent, Italian. The Ward was populated by the same wave of immigration that had hit American cities and was identical to the Lower East Side in New York, with one major exception.

THE WARD,
TORONTO'S IMMIGRANT RECEPTION AREA

Because Toronto zoning bylaws prohibited the construction of high-rise residential buildings, tenements, the most prevalent housing for immigrants in New York City, were never built in Toronto. As a result, families were crowded into single-family houses and often several families shared a house. At times, a stable served as living quarters for a newly arrived family. Many homes were without running water or indoor plumbing.

Most residents of the Ward worked for the T. Eaton Company, which at that time made ready-to-wear clothing in sweatshops located on the east side of Terauley Street, where the Eaton Centre stands today. The history of the garment industry in Toronto parallels that of New York. The International Ladies' Garment Workers Union was the first female-dominated union. Two major strikes in New York in 1909 and 1910 were followed by the Triangle Shirt Waist Factory fire in which 146 garment workers, mostly Jewish and Italian girls aged 15 to 23, perished. Garment workers in New York were more successful than those in Toronto. The Toronto garment workers' 1912 strike against Eaton's failed. Rather than give in to the union, the company closed its factories and contracted out their garment production. Most of the residents were out of work.

T. EATON COMPANY SWEAT SHOP ON TERAULEY STREET (NOW BAY ST.)
CITY OF TORONTO ARCHIVES

Everyone did what they had to do to survive. Many of the Italian families picked up fruit from railway sheds on Wellington Street and sold it door to door. I can remember my mother buying fruit from a horse-drawn wagon that visited our street every day. Some fruit pedlars eventually opened small grocery stores, which became the foundation of today's large Italian supermarket chains.

Many of the garment workers opened their own shops and migrated west to Spadina. Spadina Avenue became the focus of Toronto's garment industry and its union movement, both mostly Jewish.

My grandmother became a bootlegger. She opened a small 'so-called' grocery store at 96 Centre Street near the corner of Elizabeth and Centre Streets in the Ward. It was across from where the bus terminal stands today. There she dispensed booze by the shot.

When my daughter, Vicki, was taking a history course at York University, her assignment was to interview her oldest living relative. My mother was a Toronto version of Edith Bunker. After two hours, Vicki came back bubbling with stories.

"Did she tell you that bubby was a bootlegger?" I asked.

"No."

"Go back and ask her."

"Was bubby a bootlegger?" she asked.

"Oh no," my mother replied. "Her brother Shmuel was a bootlegger, but he was very observant, so on the Sabbath, bubby took over."

Somehow, I knew I was destined for elected office. I grew up in an era when to be Jewish in Toronto was for the most part to be political and left wing. It's not that my parents had any political ideology. We lived downtown, as tenants, in a lower duplex at 121 Clinton Street (north of College Street). My father drove a taxi. My house was in Ward 5 and, until 1946, Wards 4 and 5 elected communists.

Our alderman was Stuart Smith, a communist who lived just up the street from us. His teenage daughter, Janet, used to baby-sit me. Stuart Smith later became a member of the Board of Control. Our provincial MPP was Joseph Baruch (J.B.) Salsberg. J.B. was one of the few Labour Progressive Party (communist) members ever elected to the Ontario Legislature. I admired Joe Salsberg. He was an eloquent speaker in both Yiddish and English. At the age of 14,

I used to bicycle to Queen's Park and sit in the balcony of the legislature in the hopes I would be lucky enough to hear him speak.

My Yiddish was limited. At times, after I was elected alderman and needed a translator to help me understand a Yiddish-speaking constituent, I would conference call with Joe who was always willing to help. J.B., by the way, left the party as most Jewish communists did when Stalin initiated the purge of Jewish doctors and intellectuals.

I was never a communist. My socialist ideology grew out of the Labour Zionist movement. As a teenager, I hung out at *Hashomer* Hatsair, a labour Zionist youth centre on Beatrice Street. We learned about socialism and sex, danced the Hora and vowed we would move to Israel to live on a kibbutz and save the world. I never did, although my daughter, Candice, spent a year at a kibbutz in Galilee.

It was the rivalry in the Jewish community between the socialists and communists that split the left vote in Toronto and elected conservatives like Nathan Phillips and David Rotenberg to Toronto Council.

My mother once took me to visit Toronto City Hall. I sat in the council chamber staring

THE SHOEMAKER FAMILY
MY MOTHER, BETTY, IS IN THE MIDDLE

up at the large football-shaped partition that separated the top of the chamber and the Aldermen's Lounge. I wondered what went on behind that partition. I was hooked. I knew then that one day I would be there.

CHAPTER 2
Sparring Partner

Mel Lastman, the long-serving mayor of North York and then Toronto, disliked me even before we officially met. I had an equivalent distain for him. I presume it was because of our public personae. As president of the North York Elementary Teachers' Union, I was a publicly outspoken left-winger.

The source of my discomfort with Mel was not so much his right-wing views but his public image. I cringed at the brash, fast-talking hustler stereotype he projected.

“ WE'RE BOTH STREET FIGHTERS, BUT I'M BETTER AT IT THAN HE IS ”

“ YOU DON'T EXIST AS FAR AS I'M CONCERNED. YOU ARE NEXT TO AN ANIMAL ”

We had both come out of the same Jewish immigrant community and it is somewhat ironic that we ended up as polar opposites. Mel's father was a staunch trade unionist. He was a shop steward in the cap makers' union – definitely left wing. Lastman was definitely right wing. During the lengthy 1987 North York garbage strike, to his credit, Mel understood union sentiment enough to not even consider bringing in replacement workers. Scab was a dirty word in his family household.

My father had dropped out of school in Grade 10. During the depression, everyone had to work to support the family. He was a sign painter by trade, a prizefighter and a taxi driver, and I am fond of saying my father trained me for politics. He had right-wing tendencies and we argued vehemently at every meal. My left-wing views grew out of the Labour Zionist Movement, not my family background.

My fiery relationship with Mel Lastman began in the basement of the North York Civic Centre at my first-ever council meeting. It was 1979 and the inauguration of council was to take place in an afternoon session. The inaugural meeting was traditionally a ceremonial swearing in followed by a reception where everyone sipped tea and munched on dainty sandwiches. There was no other business to be considered. Mel was very proud that day. He was going to add something new to that tradition, an inaugural address by the incoming mayor in which he would introduce his legislative program for the term; his version of a speech from the throne. The mayor's staff had been working for weeks on the address. Its contents were top secret.

That morning, councillors gathered in a basement committee room in informal session for the business of assigning committee memberships and appointments to community boards and associations for the coming term. Mel proudly outlined his aspirations for the coming term – a sneak preview of his inaugural address.

While council members were busily negotiating positions on committees, I used the telephone at the back of the committee room to dictate an inaugural rebuttal. That afternoon, when copies of his inaugural address where handed to the media, my secretary followed with copies of my rebuttal.

Mel was livid. Apart from his anger about the rebuttal itself, he couldn't fathom how it had been produced. This led to a witch-hunt in his office to find out who had leaked it. Of course, he had leaked it in the morning meeting. The relationship between the mayor and me was established on Day 1 of my first term.

That relationship was a flame that was fanned by the Toronto Star's circulation growth policy. At that time, the Toronto Star was experimenting with a way to build their readership by adding a weekly local news section. It meant assigning a reporter to cover each of North York, Etobicoke and Scarborough councils. That reporter had to fill half a page a week, which in itself was not a challenge, but the local news sections became so popular that they were expanded to two full pages a day. The Star established zone news bureaus. The North Bureau covered local news in North York, the City of York and York Region, but mostly North York. Now there were several hungry reporters scrambling for stories in North York to generate two full pages of local news every day. It was a made-in-heaven opportunity for a politician seeking a profile.

Every day, one or more of the reporters would pop into my office:

"Have you got a story for me today?"

I always had one or two in my back pocket, yet there were days when nothing happened in North York.

On those days, Warren Potter, the Star's North Bureau chief, would invent stories. He would stick his head into my office and say:

"Do you know what Mel Lastman said about you today? He called you a *%&^*."

"Well tell him "*&%^*," I would respond.

He would then run into the mayor's office and get a response from Mel.

Presto! He now had a story. One of the old-time reporters, Harold Hilliard, often used to invent my quotes and then asked me if I said them.

North York officially became a city on February 14, 1979, Valentine's Day.

When Mel unveiled a boundary sign with a big heart and a "City with a Heart" caption, I opposed it and brought a motion to have it removed from the sign.

Apart from the fact that council had never discussed or approved the slogan, and notwithstanding the fact that it was just plain hokey, it was a dumb thing to do. It masked the fact that the city had a lot of social problems. The Social Planning Council had just issued a report, *The Suburbs in Transition*, which illuminated the devastating poverty that existed in North York and the dearth of services available to assist new immigrants. Jane-Finch was a festering sore of neglect, and social services across the entire city were sadly lacking. I knew that time and time again, when residents petitioned the city or came before council, they would throw the slogan in our faces. Council backed Lastman and my motion lost, but it wasn't too long before the slogan quietly faded from the signs.

By this time, the war between Lastman and Moscoe had become endemic to the media coverage in North York. Mel's staff urged him to try and make peace. Vandalism was a problem in my ward and Lastman extended an olive branch by appointing me chair of a committee to study ways to combat vandalism.

The olive branch quickly wilted when Mel rushed off to the annual conference of the Federation of Canadian Municipalities

(FCM) in Quebec City the following month touting a motion to make parents pay for vandalism committed by their children. As a teacher, I knew children who had difficult home lives often committed vandalism. The concept he was promoting would put a powerful weapon into the hands of every dissident teen. Our system of justice is based on the concept that people ought to be responsible for their own actions. I was offended that almost immediately after establishing a committee to study vandalism, he was rushing off to Quebec City with the solutions before the committee had even met.

It was unusual for Mel to attend the FCM. He hated large conferences and particularly hated debating resolutions before large gatherings of delegates. I suppose the value he put on his public profile had trumped his fear of public debates. Dennis Flynn, the then-Metro Chairman, was president of the FCM and Mel had arranged through Dennis for his vandalism resolution to be the first one debated at the plenary session.

Mel rose to his feet and made an impassioned speech in support of his position. Just before he stepped away from the microphone, he clinched his speech with a definitive assertion: "Too many parents think all they have to do is give birth and walk away."

Loud applause!

He may have proved himself right. It came back to bite him twenty-two years later when two brothers who claimed to be his children born out of wedlock sued him for non-support. The media is unforgiving.

The next speaker was Alderman Howard Moscoe from North York, opposing the resolution. The third speaker was Alderman Mike Foster from North York, in opposition, followed by a speech by Alderman Pat O'Neil from North York, also against the motion.

Mel was livid.

The Globe and Mail reported: "The lively debate on deterring vandalism touched off a typical shouting match among North

York city fathers outside the meeting room later when Alderman Howard Moscoe tendered his resignation as chairman of North York's Task Force on Vandalism. 'You are more interested in generating publicity than solutions to vandalism,' Mr. Moscoe told the mayor. His resignation was predicated on 'your demonstrated lack of confidence in the task force' and 'a deliberate act of bad faith,' Mr. Moscoe said."

After the resolution session, the conference divided into two workshops. The plenary session continued with a speech from a Montreal professor on *Municipalities and the Canadian Constitution*. It was attended by most of the delegates. There was also a resolutions session attended by some 100 delegates. It was a dead-end workshop where resolutions that the organization did not want to reach the floor got debated. It was not expected to be covered by the media. Mike Foster and I drifted into this session. We were followed by a seething Lastman. Dennis Flynn again chaired the session.

The first resolution was a motion from the boondocks of Saskatchewan that called on the federal government to re-introduce capital punishment as a deterrent to crime. When it looked like the resolution was going to pass, I rose, tongue planted firmly in cheek, to make an amendment:

"Be it further resolved that the FCM support other deterrents to crime like, whipping and lashing, keel hauling, the dunking stool, castration, torture and killing of the first born," seconded by Alderman Foster.

Still smarting from the previous session, Lastman leaped to his feet: "I'm ashamed of Aldermen Moscoe and Foster. They're a disgrace to North York."

Dennis Flynn, red-faced, didn't quite know what to do. The amendment went down to defeat, the main motion carried and Mel dashed out of the room to tell all to Marina Strauss, a reporter for the Globe and Mail.

Marina interviewed me and said, "Of course, you were being facetious?"

"Yes."

But somehow, the story got twisted. Nobody paid any attention to the fact that the country's mayors were supporting re-opening the debate on capital punishment. The next day, all the media were focused on was some nut bar politician from North York, who was proposing castration and other horrors as a deterrent to crime. I was bombarded by requests for interviews from, it seemed, every media outlet in the country. The most disturbing thing about all of the media coverage was almost half of the calls that came into my office were in support of my amendment.

Lastman flew back to Toronto, and at the Board of Control meeting on the following Wednesday, controllers took turns taking shots at me.

Lastman swore, "as long as I'm mayor, Howard Moscoe will never again attend a conference representing North York."

He was wrong. I attended the AMO conference the very next month, but that's another story.

By then, the Moscoe vs. Lastman follies had erupted into all-out war.

I once said to Mel:

"You've made me famous Mel. Now when are you going to make me rich?"

CHAPTER 3
The Bad Neighbour Relations Committee

S aul Alinsky was my hero. He was an American social activist who grew up as an orthodox Jew in the slums of Chicago. He is considered the father of the community-organizing movement. Alinsky wrote *Rules for Radicals* in which he outlined principles for community activism.

Alinsky believed no system could abide by its own rules. When a Rochester department store refused to hire blacks, he organized a shop-in. Hordes of protesters from the black churches purchased goods and immediately lined up at the exchange window. The store quickly changed its hiring policy.

In 1979, just after I was first elected, the Canadian Imperial Bank of Commerce, now the CIBC – we called them the Canadian Imperialist Bank of Commerce – already had a permit to construct two office towers on Lawrence Avenue west of the Allen Road in my ward. It planned to shift a block of Commerce employees from Commerce Court in the downtown financial district to these new buildings. The bank claimed it would create 3,000 new jobs. That was baloney. It was simply moving those jobs out of Commerce Court in space that could be rented out for $45 a square foot to space in the new office towers, valued at $15 a square foot.

The buildings were less of an issue than the parking garage. The original plan called for parking to be underground. One afternoon, I received an anonymous tip from the architect's office that the bank was considering scrapping the underground garage and erecting instead a three-story parking structure that would overshadow the yards of the homes behind it on Dane Avenue. The area is largely Italian and almost everyone had a tomato garden at the rear of their yard. I contacted the bank and met with their construction officials at Commerce Court, where I was shown a model of the garage. They assured me the decision had not yet been finalized and they would consider my concerns. They also promised to notify me as soon as the bank had come to a decision.

If the garage had been built in the City of Toronto, it would have come under public scrutiny. The City of Toronto had a site plan control bylaw. North York, while it had the right to enact site plan control, had chosen, for whatever reason, not to do so.

About three weeks after that meeting, a resident called to tell me they were pouring footings for an aboveground garage. I immediately called an emergency meeting and fired off a letter to the bank asking that they attend a meeting at the Lawrence Heights Community Centre that night to explain their plans to area residents. The meeting brought the three ratepayers groups in the area together. About 90 residents attended.

The bank refused to come. They instead hand delivered a telegram to be read at the meeting in which they advised they were not prepared for a meeting until they had completed a scale model of the garage so they could adequately explain the structure to residents. I had already seen a model at their offices. They said they needed four weeks to complete the model after which they would attend a community meeting. Of course, by that time the superstructure of the garage would have been poured.

The residents were furious. The CIBC advertising strategy that year was built around a "Good Neighbour" policy. Remember the TV ads "Commerce Bank, a Good Neighbour" featuring Anne Murray? We immediately formed a "Bad Neighbour Relations Committee" and mapped out a strategy for dealing with the bank.

Our first move was to write to the bank and advise them we would be staging a "hold-up" on Friday of that week at the local neighbourhood branch, Dufferin and Lawrence. The branch was integrated into a supermarket. In those days, banks traditionally closed at 4 p.m. daily, remained opened an extra hour on Friday and were closed on weekends. Friday afternoon was bank rush hour.

Borrowing directly from Alinsky's book, 100 residents descended on the local branch carrying picket signs reading "Commerce Bank A Bad Neighbour." Those who had accounts withdrew 25 cents. They immediately went to the back of the line to re-deposit it. Others opened accounts and joined the bank-in. The line-ups stretched twice around the bank and into the attached supermarket. Customers who had come to do their banking were irritated. It was a new kind of bank hold-up. The media had a field day.

BANK HOLDUP

The protest committee then advised the bank it would be staging a hold-up the next weekend, but this time it would not tell the bank which branch they were going to hit. The next Friday, we hit the largest branch in the area, Yorkdale Shopping Centre. We knew Yorkdale didn't allow picket signs so we printed a run of shopping bags bearing the Commerce logo with a "COMMERCE BANK A BAD NEIGHBOUR" cutline. We stuffed them with crumpled newspapers to be carried by protesters. Yorkdale might be able to prohibit picket signs, but they could hardly ban shopping bags. By this time, the publicity had swelled our ranks to about 150. The bank countered by busing in a flying squad of extra tellers. Again, the media had a field day.

The Bad Neighbour Relations Committee then released a schedule of planned activities:

We would stage a hold-up event at a large downtown branch; one of our committee members was composing anti-bank commercials to be sung by our neighbourhood choir at a series of impromptu noon-hour concerts at Commerce Square.

The Lawrence Heights steel band was rehearsing.

We were planning an Anne Murray look-alike contest.

There would be a letters-to-the-editor campaign and we would invite other resident groups to join us.

We would be asking other municipalities to steer their banking business to more responsible banks. The City of Toronto, at that time, was doing some of their banking through CIBC.

We were arranging to have questions about the matter asked in the Ontario Legislature and the House of Commons in Ottawa.

We planned an extensive anti-bank sign campaign.

Several of us bought single shares in the CIBC so we could carry our fight to the bank's annual meeting.

I had a sign shop in my basement where I printed my own election signs. We did an initial run of 500 anti-bank signs, which we erected on the lawns of houses in the neighbourhoods surrounding the bank building on Lawrence near Allen Road. The signs extended as far north as Highway 401 and south to below Lawrence. The bank was beginning to take notice. They finally came to the table.

We weren't able to get the garage underground, but we were able to get some concessions. A berm was erected between the garage and the homes. The landscaping was upgraded, security provisions were built into the project, a low-level lighting plan was put in place, and the ventilation system for the garage was upgraded. We also had the city put in traffic controls that would direct cars leaving the garage away from local neighbourhoods and schools. The bank claimed they intended to do all of these things anyway. That assertion was as real as their "Good Neighbour" policy. You can bank on that.

So, apart from a few trees, what did we get out of all of this? In the first place, the neighbourhood felt empowered. The resident associations were community active for many years afterwards. This incident prompted North York Council to bring in site plan control, where the site plans of these kinds of developments had to have a public hearing and approval by North York Council.

Subsequently, I led the homeowners in an appeal of their property assessment to the Ontario Assessment Review Board. The board agreed the garage did depreciate the value of the abutting homes and 19 homeowners were compensated by a reduction of 15% in their property assessments.

The ensuing fuss over the lawn sign campaign touched off a review of the sign bylaw, which prompted a sign war that lasted for several years. I threw my share of CIBC stock into a drawer. It later became a weapon in an attempt to bring the Bank of Commerce to its knees, figuratively speaking. (More about that later.) We did Saul Alinsky proud.

CHAPTER 4

Halifax Ahoy!

In 1980, 21 delegates from municipalities within Toronto attended the Federation of Canadian Municipalities' annual meeting in Halifax. None of the mayors went, but Dennis Flynn, the Metro Chairman, did. That is because he was active on the FCM executive.

I was one of five who chose to go by train. It was not to save the city money, but rather because Mike Foster was afraid to fly. He didn't tell us that, but convinced us it was our patriotic duty to see the country from the window of a train. We gabbed, sang and made merry the whole trip and had so little sleep that we were completely exhausted by the time we got to Halifax. Patriotism be damned. I flew back.

FCM conferences were an opportunity for municipal politicians from across the country to gather in a major city once a year and talk policy, attend workshops, share ideas, debate resolutions and steer the organization. And, oh yes, we had a good time as well. The media, particularly the Toronto Sun, of course, used to bash us for going on "junkets" at "taxpayers' expense," but that's something you learn to take in stride. The Globe and Star thought enough of the FCM to send reporters to cover their conferences. They kept a close eye on Toronto-area delegates, and if we slipped up you were sure to read about it in the Toronto media. After a short while, I stopped being defensive about going, and used to say things to reporters like:

"It's a tough job, but somebody has to do it" or "I swore out an affidavit before I left that I would not have a good time, and I only smiled once the entire trip."

Thunder Bay on the north shore of Lake Superior would be hosting the Canada Games in 1981, and the mayor of Thunder Bay, Dusty Miller, attended with a troop of people from the Lakehead who came to promote the event. Dusty was a fellow lefty, a tall, enthusiastic person you couldn't help but like. She was the first female mayor of her city.

Just for the record, I don't drink. I get high on conversation and tomato juice, and so when I go to a hospitality suite at a conference, I'm there to meet and talk to people, not to drink. That doesn't mean my behaviour is always sober. I have a mischievous streak that sometimes gets me into trouble.

1980 was the year the Soviets invaded Afghanistan. We couldn't resist. Put it down to youth and enthusiasm, Foster and I drafted a resolution that the FCM urge a boycott of the Canada Games because the City of Thunder Bay had refused to close their port to Soviet ships. It was a joke, of course. We had no intention of actually submitting it to the resolution's committee for debate at the conference. Somehow, it found its way around the gathering, and on Monday morning an article appeared in the Halifax Chronicle about the proposed boycott resolution.

We should have quit there, but you know how it is! The enthusiasm of the moment spurred us on. There are three questions almost every local politician can answer.

What is the name of your local newspaper?
Which reporter covers City Hall?
What is his/her phone number?

We began to buttonhole delegates, wrote down the answers and left a flood of telephone messages with the hotel operator for Mayor Miller. As she returned the calls, she did a rash of interviews and the boycott story spread across the country. Tuesday, local newspapers everywhere carried it in some form or another. Then the CBC picked it up and it hit the national news.

The next day, staff from the Thunder Bay Harbour Commission flew to Halifax to do damage control. The Thunder Bay delegation did an excellent presentation. The resolution disappeared, but to this day, I can't help but feel guilty. Dusty lost the fall 1980 election by a handful of votes to Walter Assef, the person she had beaten in 1978 to become the city's first female mayor. You remember Walter. He's the one on the Royal visit in 1973 who introduced the Royal couple as "His royal highness and his lovely wife." He also gained notoriety as the mayor who was reputed to have patted the Queen's bum.

MAYOR DUSTY MILLER

Dusty Miller died in 2012 following a lengthy illness.

I don't know if she ever forgave me.

CHAPTER 5

A Line In the Stand
(or 122 metres away)

It bothers me when I encounter a bylaw that is obviously drafted to protect the economic interests of a powerful business interest. When I was 13, my brother and I used to sell football ribbons in front of Varsity Stadium. We would attach little plastic footballs to ribbons in the colours of teams playing that day, pin them to a sheet of cardboard and sell them for 50 cents to fans who wanted to display their team loyalty. That is, until the City of Toronto passed a bylaw that prohibited street vending south of Bloor Street. From that time on, we were hounded by the police and treated like we were peddling crack-cocaine instead of team colours. My dad had to go to court with me; I was convicted of "peddling without a license" and paid a fine of $2. There you have it. I have confessed to being a convicted soft-boiled criminal.

That's why I reacted the way I did to a 1979 Metro bylaw prohibiting the sale of tickets within 400 feet of Exhibition Stadium. The Jays were at the top of the league. Most Jay's tickets were sold to season ticket holders who had to buy tickets for every game. Now, if they were unable to attend a game they couldn't re-sell them anywhere close to the box office.

In May of 1984, I went to bat for fans that were being scalped by the bylaw and appeared before the Metro legislation committee to try to persuade them to rescind the bylaw. Scarborough Controller Frank Faubert joined me.

"This bylaw isn't aimed at scalpers," I told the committee. "The Ticket Speculation Act already prohibits what they are doing. This bylaw only applies to Exhibition Stadium and is aimed at protecting the economic interests of the Jays, the Argos, the promoters of special events and Exhibition Place against the interests of loyal fans. If I can't attend a game, why should I have to flush my tickets down the drain?"

Our pleas fell on deaf ears.

"Go tell them to sell them 400 feet away," quipped Chairman Paul Godfrey.

The crisis had actually been provoked by the Jays' organization. The bylaw had been on the books for five years, but had never been actively enforced. I was prompted by a complaint from one of my constituents, who was a season ticket holder. He had been fined for trying to sell his tickets for a game he was unable to attend. Apparently, the Jays had now begun hiring off-duty, plainclothes police officers on pay duty specifically to enforce this bylaw. I approached the Jays' organization, but there was no flexibility.

"Absolutely not," they said. "The tickets will fall into the hands of scalpers."

They could have ended scalping instantly by allowing season ticket holders to return the tickets for sale on consignment. Re-sell them at the box office and take a commission on each re-sale to cover any costs. They weren't the least bit interested.

That's why, on Sunday, June 4, 1984, I hustled down to Exhibition Place, painted a line on the road 400 feet from the stadium and set up a "Free Trade Zone" with a sign painted in my basement. I had re-designed the Jays' logo by replacing the blue jay with a vulture. The sign said, "No scalpers please." The Jays were in first place, the Yankees were in town and the stadium had been sold out for weeks.

The Free Trade Zone was an instant success. It became the spot to buy, sell and trade tickets for the balance of the season.

I learned later the Jays were preparing to lay charges against me for damaging the pavement, but they couldn't. I had used tempera paint. It was washed away by the next rainfall. It didn't matter. By that time, everyone knew where the Free Trade Zone was located.

CHAPTER 6
Who Wants to be a Millionaire?

I was raised on dented tins and Kraft Dinner. My mother, a child of the Depression, was known as "Bargain Betty." She attended every store opening and closing in the Junction and knew almost instinctively where to find marked-down sale items everywhere in Toronto west of Eaton's Annex. When I was growing up downtown, admission to a Saturday afternoon movie at the Pylon Theatre on College Street cost a dime, and for that you got to see a double feature, six cartoons, a newsreel and the regular weekly episode of Flash Gordon. An ice cream cone cost six cents. A million dollars was a lot of money. That's why Torontonians pursued their dreams of wealth by purchasing illegal Irish Sweepstakes tickets.

People have always been fascinated by the concept of a million dollars. While the concept doesn't have the same cache that it used to have, it remains an unattainable objective for most. When my daughter named her son Maximilian, I quipped "Why not Maxabillion? What's a million nowadays?"

From 1955 to 1960, one of the most popular television programs was a series called *The Millionaire*. Every Monday, John Beresford Tipton Jr., a wealthy benefactor, gave away $1 million to some unsuspecting recipient. A million was the equivalent of about $10 million today.

The rest of each episode depicted how that money changed the recipient's life. We never actually saw Mr. Tipton, only his right arm handing the cashier's cheque to his executive secretary,

Michael Anthony. Mr. Anthony, who presented 206 $1 million cheques during the series, was charged with the responsibility of delivering the cheques and reporting on the results. There was only one stipulation. The money was to be conferred anonymously, the name of the donor never to be revealed.

As an impressionable 16-year-old, I regularly watched the program dreaming that someday John Beresford Tipton Jr. would pick me. He did. In 1988, I received a telephone call from a developer who told me he was selling off his holdings and retiring. He had made his money in North York and he wanted to give something back to the community.

"Here's a million dollars to invest in a community project," he said. "I have two stipulations. The money has to be spent on something that will have lasting benefit to the community and my identity must never be revealed."

Wow! After I picked myself off the ceiling, I began to think about the responsibility. I have to admit I spent a few sleepless nights. How can anyone really be sure what the community needs most?

"Why don't you ask the community?" my wife, Gloria, suggested. "Put it out there and see what you get."

I convened an ad-hoc committee of civic officials to help guide the process. We threw the question out to the public: "If you had a million dollars how would you spend it to best help North York?"

Of the more than 60 proposals received, half pointed to the lack of services for newly arrived immigrants. It was not surprising. In 1980, the Social Planning Council of Toronto released a report, "Metro Suburbs in Transition." It hit Toronto like a tornado. We were in the throes of rapid change. Immigrants were settling in the suburbs in droves, but all of the infrastructure to support them was downtown. In the eight years since the report had been released, little or nothing had been done. The need was obvious; The North York Community House was born.

I remember how important the University Settlement House had been to my family when I grew up in the 1940s. My brothers played floor hockey after school in a league sponsored by the University Settlement House. Each child in my family took low-cost music lessons at the settlement house, and each Saturday night my mother dressed us up and took us off to Toronto Symphony Pop Concerts at Massey Hall on free tickets supplied by the settlement house music school. There we had an opportunity to listen to stars like Richard Tucker and a chance to go back stage to meet them.

With the help of staff from St. Stephen's House, we pulled together a board of directors from the community that broadly reflected the population it was serving. I remember setting up our first facility, a combination office and drop-in centre for seniors in a tiny storefront on Bathurst Street facing Lawrence Plaza. The board hired its first employee, Shelly Zukerman. I remember the first annual meeting. We made the mistake of putting out all the sandwiches before the meeting began. There was a run on the refreshment table and in short order they were gone. A number of seniors left the meeting with purses bulging.

As the organization established its presence and extended its reach, the involvement of my office diminished until it was limited to, like Michael Anthony, mailing out the annual report to the donor.

The North York Community House has become the lead agency for services to new Canadians in North York. That role won it the distinction of becoming the first new organization to secure United Way funding in many years. In 2016, under Shelly Zukerman's leadership, the North York Community House provided services to 13,357 newcomers to Canada, with programs like English classes, parenting skills, community kitchen, job search programs and civic literacy and democracy talks. They had settlement staff on a regular basis in 80 schools and provided service to 150 other schools. In 2016, they also directly assisted over 100 Syrian refugees to settle in Toronto.

Best of all, the North York Community House has not yet spent the original donation, which it holds in trust as a hedge against the future. Imagine all this from a single, anonymous donation.

CHAPTER 7

Flag Flaps

NORTH YORK

Canada, after what became known as the Great Flag Debate, changed its flag in 1964 to the red maple leaf we so proudly fly today. In September of 1979, North York began its own municipal version of the national flag debate about its own flag. I called it the "not-so-great-flag-flap." It began when Councillor Irving Paisley introduced a motion to replace the existing flag with a new one.

NORTH YORK FLAG   PAISLEY'S PROPOSED NEW FLAG

The existing North York flag showed 14 golden balls, each representing a ward with the name of the municipality across the centre. The flag was flanked by two vertical bands of blue. It was pretty hokey. Paisley's new flag would replace the golden balls and name with the city's crest. When he introduced it, he held up two heavy tomes on heraldry.

"It isn't a proper flag," he quipped. "There isn't a municipal flag in Canada that shows the municipality's name."

I had some flag ideas of my own and managed to throw the entire meeting into a flap when I introduced five alternative designs.

The first was a field of blue with a crowd of people on the left side and a lone flower on the right. It illustrated that the west-end (Jane-Finch) got all of the people while the east received all of the amenities.

The next flag featured a classic comedy mask topped with the words "NORTH YUK" in bold block letters. The mask bore the Latin motto, "sic transit decorum." At that point in the meeting,  some members of council who were obviously upset began to shout and boo.

Others were grinning. Barry Burton, chair of the committee of the whole, had trouble controlling the meeting.

The third flag featured a hand holding five aces. It needed no explanation. I never got to show the fifth flag because the fourth so enraged the mayor that he began to shout. It featured a three-dol-  lar bill with his picture on it. He demanded a full explanation.

"Why Mel," I replied, "everyone knows what a three-dollar bill means."

"It's a complete insult," he shouted.

At this point, Lastman demanded I be thrown out of the meeting. Barry Burton conferred with the clerk. They could find no rule of decorum that I had broken. In the interests of harmony, I hauled down my flags and withdrew the designs.

Paisley's motion was defeated. Unlike our country, North York never got its new flag.

In the end, it really didn't matter. North York has disappeared, absorbed by the city's amalgamation on January 1, 1998.

The mayor may be gone and the City of North York has faded into the pages of history, but the symbols of office carry on. A huge medallion displaying the city crest continues, to this day, to hang  behind the former mayor's chair in the North York Council chamber. It proudly bears the motto "economy with progress." I always said it truly captured the spirit of North York. It looked like bronze, but was made of cheap plastic. I interpret the motto to mean, "Cheap government on the move."

TORONTO

In August 1974, as the result of an open competition, the old city of Toronto selected a design by Renato De Santis, a 21-year-old George Brown College student. It  depicted the sleek lines of City Hall configured as a symbolic "T" for Toronto.

After amalgamation, a contest was again held to find a flag for the amalgamated city, but council in 1999 selected the De Santis design again.

The suggestion made by Councillor Brian Ashton at the time was that it be flown upside down at tax times because it depicted the image of a short taxpayer with big feet after he had paid his taxes.

CHAPTER 8

The Sky is Falling – It Could Be!

On September 16, 1981, the City of North York's Property Standards Department issued a work order to the Hudson's Bay Company, one of Canada's largest department store chains, to repair the roof on its Bay store in Lawrence Plaza. The work was to be completed by October 16. Most property owners, when they receive a city work order, act promptly to get the repairs done. This order had been stalled, delayed and appealed to the property standards committee, which had the effect of further delaying the order.

Around the time the work order was to be completed, a property standards officer came to visit my office.

"I'm really worried about it collapsing," he said.

The roof of the Bay store was underlain by a thick layer of insulation. Because of water leakage, the insulation had become sodden and he was concerned that the weight of the roof might bring it down. In July of 1980, the roof of a Kmart store in Etobicoke had collapsed. Fortunately, it had happened on a Sunday when nobody was in the store.

At the nub of the issue was a dispute between the Bay and the owners of the plaza. The Bay had a long-term lease at a fixed rent that was well below market rent for the time. Normally, the landlord is responsible for repairs, but because of the rental dispute they were wrangling about who was going to pay the repair bill.

I visited the store with the inspector, who pointed out the stucco falling from the east masonry wall as further evidence of water penetration. Winter would bring snowfall and add weight to the already weakened roof.

I fired off a letter to Donald McGivern, president of the Bay, demanding some evidence that the roof was safe and advised him that failing that evidence I would be recommending the store be closed unless the roof was repaired by the hearing date of November 24. I spoke to Rolph Huband, corporate secretary of the Bay.

"It's not our responsibility," Huband protested. "The landlord has to fix the roof."

"Every day that you and Lawrence Plaza bicker about who pays, the danger of a disaster increases," I told him.

The Bay must have complained to the mayor. Mel, who never missed the opportunity to leap on me from great heights wearing hobnail boots, fired off a statement praising the Bay as a great corporate citizen and denying the roof was unsafe.

"Moscoe's a liar. He creates disasters," the mayor quipped.

Given the mayor's response, I contacted the Bay and demanded a report from an independent structural engineer.

"If I don't receive written confirmation of the safety of the structure within two weeks I will be picketing the store with a sign that reads: Shop at Your Own Risk.

On Thursday, October 29, Lastman advised the media again that my comments were "untrue" and he would ask the Board of Control to issue an apology to the Bay. That night, I received a certified copy of an engineer's report, but the last page was missing and there was no signature.

On Friday, I had a frank telephone conversation with a senior official at the Bay.

"You can complain all you want to the mayor, but if I don't see any action by Tuesday morning I will be out with my picket signs and the media."

On Monday morning, repair people were crawling all over the roof.

A sad sidebar of all of this emerged later. Cecil Foster, the reporter who broke the story, went off to Jamaica with his pregnant wife for the Christmas holidays. While he was away, the Toronto Star fired him and other stringers to quell dissent at its bureaus.

Cecil, now a professor at the University of Buffalo, told me, "In retrospect, it was the best thing that ever happened."

The Barbados-born Canadian went on to a successful career in journalism with the Globe and Mail, the CBC and as senior editor for the Financial Post before leaving media for academia. He was professor of sociology at the University of Guelph when hired by the University of Buffalo faculty in the fall of 2013. He is now chair of transitional studies.

Cecil is also the author of several scholarly works and five successful novels.

The Bay at Lawrence Plaza? Long gone!

CHAPTER 9

Pesticide Pest

The Province of Ontario legislated a province-wide ban on the spraying of pesticides for cosmetic purposes on Earth Day, April 22, 2009. This followed a similar ban pioneered by the City of Toronto five years earlier. It is amazing to think that in 1980 city officials in North York were assuring everyone that spraying was completely safe.

In that year, a parent approached me. Her young child was seriously allergic to 2-4-D. She wanted to know when her local park was being sprayed so she could keep her children away. The parks department couldn't provide that information.

I took the matter to the commissioner of parks and recreation. What I wanted was the city to erect a sign two days before a park was being sprayed and remove it two weeks afterwards. That way, people could at least keep their children out of the park if they didn't want them exposed to the chemical. Doug Snow, the parks commissioner, assured me "when the chemical is applied properly no adverse effects will be encountered."

Not satisfied with his answer, I took the matter to the Board of Health, but the bureaucrats closed ranks. Dr. Marguerite Archibald, the medical officer of health, told the board: "It's not dangerous so why are we bothering to say anything at all? I think we'd be putting a negative piece of information into the community inferring the chemical is toxic. Why should we propagate fear?"

The board of health bounced the matter back to the parks department for a report to the parks committee. In his report,

Gord Hutchinson, the commissioner of parks, told the parks committee it would be an unnecessary expense. In typical bureaucratic fashion, he estimated it would cost $25,000 to print signs. He detailed the cost in his report and recommended no action be taken. When asked if they could simply tell people who called when a park was being sprayed, he couldn't provide that assurance because the spraying schedule depended on the "vagaries of the weather."

I was miffed. I went home, cut a silk screen and printed off 200 signs in my basement sign shop that night. They included a space where the date could be filled in with a felt pen. The next morning, I dumped them on his desk. "Here," I said. "They cost me 15 cents each."

My constituent came to the committee meeting with her 17-month-old daughter. She told the committee: "I spoke to a workman spraying a nearby park who told me he would not let his children play there for at least a week or 10 days. Then I saw a child run his hand through the grass and put his fingers in his mouth. I wouldn't be happy if my child did that."

The committee adopted my plan, but it was over the objections of Controller Bob Yuill, who told the committee:

"We have been assured that the herbicide 2-4-D Amine 80 is harmless. The representative from the chemical company even offered to drink a cup of the stuff and said that the worst that could happen would be a case of diarrhea."

Bob Yuill led the charge against the committee's recommendation at the Board of Control. He complained of the waste of money and staff time. Yuill was joined by Controller Esther Shiner, who piped in: "The damage has already been done in scaring people with 'unfounded fears' about spraying, because of the publicity it has received."

Mel Lastman agreed. He couldn't see any sense in alarming people. Only Controller Irving Paisley spoke in favour of the ban, but he too voted against it. The damage indeed had been done. The Board of Control killed the plan, which now had the approval of the Board of Health, the environment committee and the parks committee. It would now require a two-thirds vote at council to overturn the board's decision.

I met with a parks department worker the day before the council meeting. After being there for only a short time, he was assigned to spraying. He later went on workers' compensation. His body was covered in red welts that were extremely uncomfortable and unsightly.

When the matter came before council, I was ready for Bob Yuill. He rose to his full height, made his "you can even drink the stuff" speech and smugly sat down.

It was my turn to speak. I reached under my desk and produced a bottle of 2-4-D and read out the warning label on the back of the bottle. I then produced a shot glass, filled it with the vile stuff and reached out to hand it to Yuill. He sat there stone-faced.

"Put up or shut up," I said.

Council voted to overturn the Board of Control.

DDT use in Canada was banned in 1995.

CHAPTER 10
Yours In Government

Toronto Sun columnist John Downing published these two letters in his February 20, 1981 column entitled "OUR GANG COMEDY."

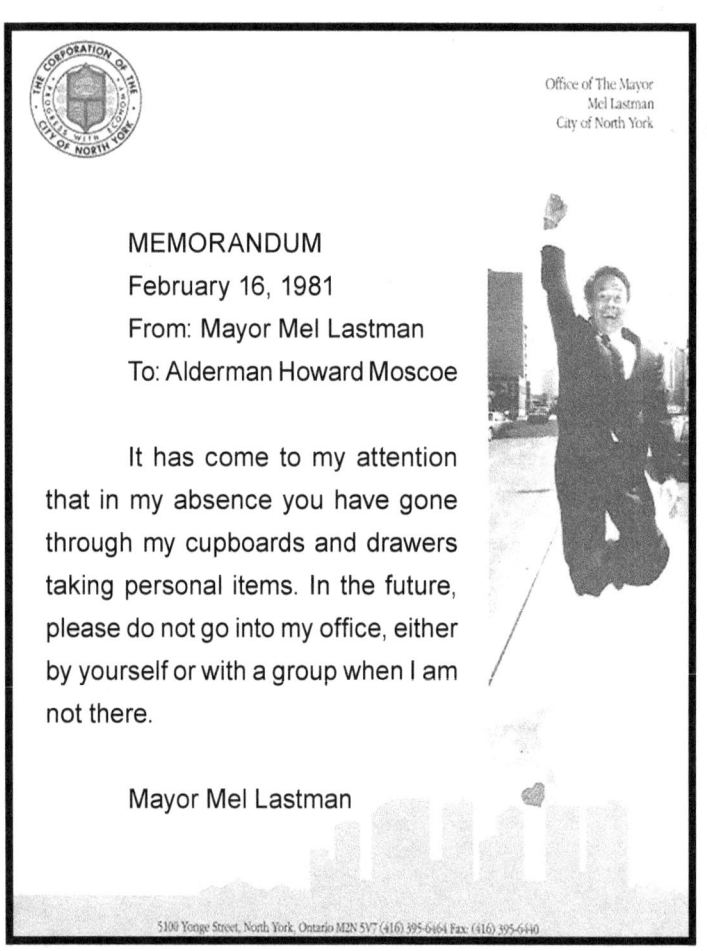

Office of The Mayor
Mel Lastman
City of North York

MEMORANDUM
February 16, 1981
From: Mayor Mel Lastman
To: Alderman Howard Moscoe

It has come to my attention that in my absence you have gone through my cupboards and drawers taking personal items. In the future, please do not go into my office, either by yourself or with a group when I am not there.

Mayor Mel Lastman

5100 Yonge Street, North York, Ontario M2N 5V7 (416) 395-6464 Fax: (416) 395-6440

ALDERMEN'S OFFICE

HOWARD MOSCOE
ALDERMAN WARD 4

CITY OF NORTH YORK, 5100 YONGE ST., NORTH YORK, ONTARIO M2N 5V7 TEL. (416) 224-6021

MEMORANDUM
February 18, 1981
From: Alderman Howard Moscoe
To: Mayor Mel Lastman

Thank you for bringing your concerns about student tours of your office to my attention. I don't recall ever bringing a group of students into your office, although on several occasions I did accompany student tours conducted by one of your official tour guides. I understand that it is common practice to include your office in guided tours of the civic centre, even when you are not present. On at least three occasions you were present and treated my students to a demonstration of your proficiency on either a bolo bat or your yo-yo. You also presented each student with a box of McDonaldland cookies. Your memo of February 16th must be referring to last week when I accompanied a guided tour of my students into your office. At that time our tour guide remarked that if the mayor were present he would give each student a box of cookies and a demonstration on his bolo bat. I sincerely apologize for any concern that I may have caused, and give you my word that in the future I will never again touch your cookies or play with either your bolo bat or your yo-yo.

Yours in Government
Howard Moscoe

CHAPTER 11

Not My Feet

The Editor, North York Mirror, November 28, 1979

SICK OF THE SIGHT OF HOWARD MOSCOE'S FACE

Is it really necessary to have Howard Moscoe's picture in every paper? I would think the other aldermen would demand equal exposure!

I feel your paper is a Socialistic biased one, bordering on sensationalism. In many instances the facts have been grossly overlooked! As a school teacher, I resent Howard Moscoe speaking as if he represents the teachers. He certainly doesn't represent me! Never!

M. Day,
Don Mills

The Editor, North York Mirror, January 2, 1980

NEVER IN PUBLIC

I am inclined to agree with M. Day when he or she writes to complain about the lack of variety in Mirror graphics. (November 28 letter: "Sick of the sight of Howard Moscoe's face")

BACK OF MOSCOE'S HEAD

Since I believe that all issues need to be viewed from a variety of perspectives, I am enclosing a photo of the back of my head. I want M. Day to clearly understand that this is as far as I intend to go. Under no circumstances will I bare my feet in public. Unfortunately, they are even more grotesque than my face.

Howard Moscoe,
Alderman, Ward 4

CHAPTER 12
Thief

*"The secret of life is honesty and fair dealing.
If you can fake that, you've got it made."*
GROUCHO MARX

The incident followed hard on the heels of a bid to contract out security services for the North York Civic Centre. The service had always been contracted out, and we were frequently changing security companies in successive contracts as the companies rushed to outbid each other in a race to the bottom. As a result, we had the lowest level of security.

Some of us wanted a permanent stable professional security service like they had downtown at Toronto City Hall, but couldn't win the debate. The Board of Control members seemed to be in a contest to "out cheap" each other.

When my secretary had her desk broken into one night, it was the last straw. I learned it was one of a string of thefts that occurred over the previous two months. I decided to run a test on the security service; so one night I taped the lock open on a rear exit door near our offices to see if security would detect it. When I checked the next morning, the tape had been removed and I was satisfied. That was the end of it, or so I thought.

A few weeks later, in a casual conversation with George Hardy, the commissioner of building services, he happened to mention the taping. I told him I had done it to test security and was satisfied the security company was doing their job. The incident was revealed by the mayor at a Board of Control meeting, and that's when Bob Yuill jumped at the opportunity to go after me. He proceeded to turn the incident into a major breach of security and a flagrant violation of the law of the land.

At council the following week, he rose to his full height of indignity: "The building was left open to theft and vandalism while the locks were sealed by Moscoe," he intoned. "It was a reprehensible act. Maybe his next step will be to dip into the till to check the treasury, or check the women's washroom to see if the staff was malingering."

Yuill managed to blow the incident into seven or eight tapings of several doors over an extended period.

"I freely admit that I taped one door to test security as is my responsibility to protect the taxpayers' investment. I have no knowledge of these other incidents," I responded.

At this point, Alderman Peter Clarke, his drinking buddy, jumped into the fray. Peter was on North York Council before I was elected. He represented "white bread" Willowdale. Peter was a thoroughly dislikeable little weasel.

"Moscoe is a liar," said Clarke.

Despite prodding from other council members, he wouldn't withdraw his statement. He went on: "Is this the North York Watergate or North York Gate?" Clarke added. "He showed a subversive disregard for the law. At no time can a politician put himself above the law – the laws he's been elected to protect."

PETER CLARKE

Mel and his stooges, one by one, joyously seized on the opportunity to personally attack me. The debate ramped up to heights of rhetoric, and Peter Clarke put the cherry on top of it by calling me a "break and enter thief."

Yuill tried to have a motion passed that would permit city staff to investigate laying charges against me, but the meeting was declared adjourned before a vote could be called. Yuill and Clarke told the media they would pursue the matter by demanding a complete police investigation. Clarke went on to repeat: "He's a break and enter thief."

Clarke's remarks were reported in the North York Mirror. I expected, and could take, a lot of abuse; it goes with the territory. But this was too much. My solicitor fired off a letter to Clarke advising him we were filing a libel and slander suit.

On the following Monday, the council meeting re-convened and the soap opera continued. After an hour of further debate, council adopted the Board of Control motion reprimanding me for my action. I remained unrepentant.

I suppose Peter got some good advice because shortly thereafter I received a letter of apology. That in itself did not give me a lot of satisfaction, but what followed did.

In June of 1982, Clarke was convicted of one count of fraud and five counts of theft in using $600,000 in Co-Operative Health Services of Ontario funds to finance land speculation, his election campaigns and the purchase of household furniture and appliances. Clarke was the former treasurer and general manager of CHSO. The company was now bankrupt.

In rendering his judgment, County Court Judge Hugh Locke said, "Clarke tapped the corporate till... with the same criminal intention as a common street thief."

Locke also found Clarke was "less than forthright... vague in his recall... shifty in demeanour... and evasive" while testifying under oath.

Clarke had misappropriated company funds to do two land deals, defrauding CHSO of $600,000. Evidence during the trial showed he was attempting to have the zoning of the land changed to allow high-density development. He was also convicted of theft by having the company pay $31,000 towards his election expenses while concealing it from his directors.

All this was happening while he was calling me a "liar" and a "break and enter thief."

Clarke was sentenced to 18 months on each of four counts, served consecutively. For me, it ended with a feeling that sometimes there is justice in this world.

By the way, it was later discovered that the thefts at city hall were being committed by nightshift employees of the contracted cleaning service.

The city terminated its contract with the cleaning firm. The voters terminated their contract with Peter Clarke.

CHAPTER 13

Never Revenge: Well Almost Never

I am not normally a vindictive person. I have always said you can't hold a grudge in politics or it will eat you alive. Forgiving and forgetting is a practical matter of survival. You might need your worst enemy on some future vote, and I've held with that view throughout my career; that is, most of the time. You can't, however, ignore a direct frontal attack, and I have to confess that something deep down inside of me thrills at the prospect of exacting political revenge.

There was a teacher shortage when I first started teaching in 1960. It was dictated by demographics. One year of Teachers' College after Grade 13 and, if you could stand in front of a class, you were a teacher. Not only that, your year at Teachers' College was tuition free – paid by the Province of Ontario. Move ahead 15 years and the post-war baby boom had rolled on through. What with declining enrolment and an increasing number of graduates lining up for teaching jobs, it was tough for a young teacher to find a job. Teaching now required a university degree, and it was almost as hard to get into teaching as it was to get into medical school. It was even tougher to keep a job once you had one.

In 1979, when I was first elected to council, I was president of the North York Elementary Teachers' Federation and represented teachers at the bargaining table. I was the staffing negotiator and it was difficult. We were in a period of declining enrolment so as the student population shrunk so too did the teacher population. That meant the board would hire teachers for September and as enrolment shrunk, lay them off in June. Layoffs were based on seniority. It was it hard for young teachers, especially those that were lucky enough to be able to find a job to end up unemployed at the end of each school year. It was also bad for the school system. Schools need a periodic infusion of new ideas and the new blood that was brought in by newly minted, enthusiastic young graduates.

There's nothing like scraping the bottom of the barrel to get the creative juices flowing. It was an era of unprecedented co-operation between the North York Board and its teachers. We came up with a plan that would save new teacher jobs and provide a break for some senior teachers at no additional expense to the board.

The average salary of a senior teacher was in the neighbourhood of $28,000. The average salary of a beginning teacher being laid off was around $18,000. The way the plan worked was a senior teacher could apply to take a one-year sabbatical for the difference between the two salaries, around $10,000. Everyone would benefit. We could keep a young teacher, give an older one a year of rest and it would cost the taxpayers nothing. After two years of discussion, the plan was put into effect as a one-year pilot project, and it worked. A total of $64,000 was paid to 19 teachers that applied. We saved 19 jobs. The board actually saved money on the plan because almost half of the 19 never came back. They started a business, moved away or found other employment so in the end the board saved money and nine jobs permanently. It was an excellent idea. I applied.

Applause! Applause! Not quite. You can always trust your enemies to put a negative spin on a good idea.

SERGIO   GENTILE   CHAPLEY   YUILL   CLARKE   LASTMAN

They wrote: Toronto Star, Saturday, November 29, 1979

"A recent article in the Star reported that one of our aldermen, Howard Moscoe, is getting paid $9,300 by the board of education for not working. Since it is not against the law for politicians to have moonlighting jobs, we, the undersigned, would like to have the opportunity to apply for these $9,300 non-working jobs. We feel that politicians are ideally suited for this kind of work. If the North York Board of Education is so free with the taxpayers' money we might as well have our slice of the pie."

There it was. Out of the blue, an unprovoked frontal attack. I'm not sure who orchestrated it. Gentile, Sergio and Chapley were all too dumb to have conceived it. I'm sure Mel didn't come up with the idea but would have been the first to sign up. Most of the members of this rogues gallery are like sheep that would gleefully line up to put their signatures on the letter. The gauntlet had been thrown down. It took but a few phone calls to organize a defence. The first shot was fired by Controller Barbara Green. She wrote this letter to the editor of the Toronto Star, titled "Ideally Suited for Non-Jobs":

"I am well able to vouch for their ability to not work. One has only to turn on their TV on Monday nights to see their non-performance. They ask questions though they know the answers, they refer, defer, seek further reports and when they do occasionally, by accident, make decisions these are either reversed later in the meeting, re-opened at another meeting or overturned by the Ontario Municipal Board."

Larry Crackhower, the trustee for Ward 13 and chair of the board, came to the board's defence. He wrote to suggest that the mayor did not understand the plan and was miffed that he hadn't taken the trouble to call and get the facts right. He pointed out that I was eligible to take the leave. Other writers wrote to express their outrage that I had benefited from a plan that I had negotiated.

Mrs. E. Gotlieb wrote: "These politicians requested that your newspaper find them positions for which they are paid to 'do nothing.' It seems to me that these gentlemen have already found these positions... their achievements this year have been few if any. The mayor's only distinguishable achievement this year has been to grow his own hair. It is certainly a relief to all the residents of North York to feel that as a municipality they have been saved from the horrors of baldness while social services continue to be overlooked. The other gentlemen's achievements pale by comparison."

The Yorkdale Ratepayers Association leapt to my defence: "Moscoe deserves every penny he gets.... It is not unusual for Moscoe to come to the aid of people at night after the meetings in North York are over and offer his sincere assistance. Moscoe stands up for the rights of the individual and should not be ridiculed by a few council members just because he 'won't play their game'. He has worked hard with an honest unselfish effort... we are delighted to have him as our Alderman."

(I couldn't resist printing this one. Call me vain, if you must.)

This leave plan had been carefully thought out. The board could not have adopted it without the scrutiny and approval of the Metro School Board. The North York trustees won considerable praise in education circles for their plan, a ray of hope in a dismal decade for education. Because of the political noise surrounding it, the plan became informally referred to as the "Moscoe memorial plan."

I tacked the strip of pictures of my detractors onto my office wall and exed out each as I got "satisfaction."

MARIO GENTILE

Alderman Mario Gentile was the first to cave. For some reason, he had an epiphany on the issue. He wrote an apology in a letter to the editor of the Star: "I would like to take this opportunity to apologize to Moscoe.... I am content with his explanation and do not have any further comments."

He should have stopped there, but he then proceeded to make a whole lot of further comments by launching an attack on Barbara Green for her remarks about his indolence. He concluded the tirade by telling everyone how hard he works.

"How come I happen to sit on seven committees, three of which are very active and powerful committees of council and she only sits on one committee?"

Dah!

MEL LASTMAN AND BOB YUILL

North York had approved the construction of a new stadium. It was a co-operative venture with the public school board. While financed by the city, it was being built on board of education land. Mel was desperate to build his legacy by having his name on some civic facility, but the rules were that you had to be dead to have something named after you.

He and Bob Yuill cooked up a plan. Yuill would draft a notice of motion to name the stadium "Mel Lastman Stadium," but before he brought the motion forward, he would hustle enough votes to make sure it would pass. Once he had the votes locked up, he would unveil the notice of motion. I was as determined that it not be named after him as Mel was determined that it should.

While Yuill was rooting around in the back rooms for votes, I fired off a notice of motion to name the stadium the "Terry Fox Memorial Stadium." Terry Fox was a national hero. He was a one-legged runner who started out to run across the country from coast to coast. His Marathon of Hope inspired the entire country.

"It's a sports-oriented stadium designed for young people," I trumpeted. "I can't think of a more appropriate person to name it after than Terry Fox. The most impressive speech the mayor ever gave was at the memorial service for Terry Fox."

By this time, everyone knew about Yuill's proposal. It had now become a political hot potato.

Lastman feigned surprise: "I didn't have anything to do with it – honestly. It's exciting, thrilling and something I never expected.

I'm completely speechless. I'm going to stay out of the debate. We should find something more important to name after Terry Fox."

The votes immediately lined up. Six members of council declared support for the "Terry Fox" name. They were Bill Sutherland, Mike Foster, Eleanor Caplan, Pat O'Neill, Marie Labatte and I. I wrote to Mel and urged him to withdraw his name and end the unsavoury debate.

Yuill accused me of "a contemptible display of cheap politicking. Never has a politician in North York stooped so low as you in your current campaign to humiliate the mayor."

"What a shame that Controller Yuill has chosen to drag the name of Terry Fox through the mud of North York politics," I responded.

It was clear Yuill and Lastman had their votes lined up, but then the public weighed in. The Toronto Star did an informal poll of people in the Sheppard Centre. They were overwhelmingly against calling the facility the "Mel Lastman Stadium." Only one person in 15 supported the idea. In the face of public pressure, his vote began to crumble. Yuill began thrashing around to find something else to name after Terry Fox. He even contacted the University of Toronto alumnae to see if they would sponsor a cancer research facility as an alternative venue to bear the hero's name.

There was little else to do. Lastman withdrew his name and Yuill withdrew his motion, but not very graciously.

"Moscoe is vindictive," Lastman said. "He has been playing politics with Fox's memory to get his name in the papers.... He's the most destructive politician that North York has ever produced.... He has a hit list. He is the smallest thing in my mind. I don't want to talk about him.... I don't want to see him re-elected."

I solemnly remarked: "I'm very pleased that the mayor has bowed to public pressure and withdrawn his name from the controversy. It's too bad he didn't have the good taste to do it graciously."

Inwardly, I was smiling like a Cheshire cat.

PETER CLARKE

As discussed in the previous chapter, Peter Clarke, the paragon of moral indignation, was convicted of fraudulently stealing funds from the company he ran. He went on to do jail time. His contract was terminated by the voters of Willowdale. It was a just reward.

IRV CHAPLEY

The aldermen's copy room had a fridge that was always well stocked with soft drinks. It was the building staff's job to keep it filled. I gave up on Irv Chapley when one night I caught him sneaking out of the room with two shopping bags filled with cans of pop. There is no satisfaction in fighting a duel with a man whose gun isn't loaded.

MARIO SERGIO

By this time my ardour for revenge had cooled. Mario Sergio was untouchable. That was only because he rarely said or did anything of note. It is hard to belittle a person's ideas if they have none. Mario went on to greater political heights when he was elected to warm a bench at Queen's Park and still later when he was promoted to be a token ethnic at the cabinet table. Most people don't know that he is still there. I do because I get a calendar from him every year.

"*Moscoe's nuts. He keeps a hit list.*"

Mayor Mel Lastman

CHAPTER 14

Golf Cart Welfare Bums

Sometimes there are issues that just have to be discussed. At their root is a kind of unfairness that gnaws at everyone's gut. It's like ripping a scab off an old wound. It will never really heal unless it is exposed to the air. Most people don't mind paying their municipal taxes if they believe they are being treated fairly. While the property tax system is probably as fair as any, the wealthy and well connected have managed to carve out areas of privilege where they are being carried by the rest of us.

In 1952, the Province of Ontario created the Municipality of Metropolitan Toronto. It was the first amalgamation that merged the 14 towns, townships and the City of Toronto into six municipalities. The boroughs of North York, Scarborough, Etobicoke, York and East York and the old City of Toronto handled local issues like local roads, parks and streets, fire services and libraries, while an overriding Metro government was responsible for regional issues like police, ambulance, social services and regional transportation. Buried in the legislation that created Metro was imbedded a sweetheart deal for golf clubs. Fred Gardiner, nicknamed Big Daddy, who became the first Metro chairman, had negotiated it with the province on behalf of the golf clubs. It gave the clubs inside Metro the right to negotiate agreements with their local municipalities that deferred property taxes.

The rationale went something like this. Golf courses provide green spaces. With the pace of rapid development accelerating, there was pressure on the clubs to sell their land for development.

Under these agreements, the clubs could defer a portion of their taxes, which would be owed to the municipality. It would accrue interest and it would become a liability on the club, which they would have to pay when the land was sold. It was touted as a disincentive to sell and would forever keep the lands green.

It was a boondoggle; a trumped-up deal to give tax breaks to these exclusive wealthy clubs. The media have portrayed Metro approaching the clubs to make a deal. That's not how it happened. The deal was lobbied by the clubs who approached Big Daddy. Metropolitan Toronto was coming into being (1952) at a time when Ontario had just enacted the Conservation Authorities Act (1946), and regional conservation authorities were being organized. This Act gave conservation authorities flood plain management control and the authority to limit development in valley lands. The large golf courses were situated mostly on valley lands. The danger of them being gobbled up for development was greatly exaggerated. Under the Conservation Authorities Act, nobody could build on valley land. It did, however, provide a convenient rationale for these agreements. For example, only 12 acres of the Rosedale Club's 132 acres located in North York is suitable for development.

The municipalities within Metro signed agreements with 12 golf clubs. Three have since been sold. (I guess the incentive didn't work all that well). Presently, there are nine clubs with agreements: Islington, Lambton, Markland Woods, Oakdale, Rosedale, Scarborough, St George's, Toronto Hunt Club and Weston. The agreements were one-sided deals in favour of the clubs, which then owed Toronto taxpayers $28 million in deferred taxes. They were agreements in perpetuity and could only be terminated or amended with the concurrence of both sides. Deferred payments accumulated at the rate of only 4%. The deferred interest rate for other taxpayers is around 18%. The clubs had the taxpayers by the throat forever.

In 1984, I uncovered these buried agreements when the Northwood Golf Club was sold for re-development. It was then I learned of the existence of agreements North York had with two other clubs, Oakdale and Rosedale. For members of council, it was the first they had heard of these all-but-forgotten gems. Rosedale, for example, at that time was paying taxes on only 38% of its assessed value. On assessment of $114,000, they had owed the city $900,000 in deferred taxes. If they had been paying at normal assessment rates, they would be $1.5 million in arrears. Each North York taxpayer had unknowingly contributed $9.60 to support green space owned by the Rosedale Golf Club to which they had no access. Nor could most of them ever have afforded the $10,000 annual dues paid by Rosedale Club members; if that is, they could get in.

"It's not as if they can't afford to pay their property taxes," I quipped. "All they have to do is raise the price of a martini by 50 cents, and I am sure they could pay what they owe in less than a year."

The agreements were unshakable. North York Council told staff to go back and try to negotiate a settlement. Staff went away and came back with minor concessions. I urged council to reject the deal. And they did on a vote of 8-7. The only thing left to do was try to embarrass the clubs into paying up.

I then took the show on the road. The Rosedale Club lands were partly in North York and partly in the City of Toronto. I appeared as a deputation before the City of Toronto Council, which was also owed similar amounts. Toronto Council voted to try and terminate their agreement. The next week, I scooted out to Scarborough to do a pitch to their council on the Hunt Club and Scarborough Golf Club agreements. Scarborough was interesting. Almost half the councillors declared an interest. I guess the clubs in Scarborough provided some council members with free memberships.

I then laid out a program for embarrassing the clubs in the media. First shot was to be fired at the Oakdale club. I would dress up in a tuxedo T-shirt and set up a bridge table and chair on the 18th green and be served a leisurely lunch by a uniformed waiter. After all, as a taxpayer, my property taxes were supporting the club, and thus I should be able to share its facilities. The cameras would have rolled as the police hauled me away. The next shot would be a deputation to Etobicoke Council on the taxes owed by their three clubs, Islington, St. George's and Markland Woods. The third shot would have been at the Lambton Club. I would hire local kids to collect used golf balls. I would then spend the day with a tennis canon firing the balls onto the fairways to screw up everyone's game.

This would be followed up with a presentation to York Council on the deferred taxes owed by the Lambton and Weston clubs.

All of this was pre-empted by the clubs agreeing to sit down and enter into negotiations with staff. The issue went underground not to re-emerge for another 20 years. By the next time I raised the issue at Toronto Council, the deferred taxes owing had grown to $37 million.

In 2004, the city was facing a $360 million budget deficit. I estimated that if the clubs paid the back taxes owed the city we could make every recreation program the city offered free. Again, I raised the issue and council asked me to meet with the clubs to see if the matter could be resolved. We met with a group headed by Herb Pirk, general manager of the Oakdale Club. Herb was a former City of Toronto parks commissioner. The clubs were reluctant to enter into any direct discussion because MPAC, the provincial assessment agency, was reviewing the entire issue of the way golf clubs were assessed, and it claimed it was in no position to negotiate back taxes until the assessment issues were resolved. The issue again went into remission for seven years, and it might have remained buried forever if Councillor Adrian Heaps hadn't raised it in 2009.

The result of the provincial review was that MPAC changed the way golf courses were evaluated to an income-based approach. The sale of the golf courses in Toronto revealed the lands were grossly under-evaluated. Since that change, 500 of the 850 golf courses in Ontario have appealed their assessments.

On December 13, 2010, the clubs and MPAC cut a deal for determining the value of golf course land. So what was the result of the deal? You may have guessed it. The nine Toronto clubs that had fixed assessment agreements had their assessments reduced by between 16% and 53%. It seems the upstanding citizens who own these clubs have Toronto by its "Titelists" forever.

Other than cutting off their water, there was little more the city could do. My parting shot at my last meeting of council was to get council's approval for yet another appeal of the assessments of the nine golf courses. At that time, they owed the city $37 million. With the new assessment, that has grown to $41.7 million in 2017.

Don't hold your breath while waiting to be paid. The Toronto Star was right in its March 19, 2012, editorial: It's time to "Sink this Tax Break". Unfortunately, unlike the Titanic, they really are unsinkable.

Fore!

CHAPTER 15
On Signs

I have always had a "thing" about signs. My father had been a sign painter by trade. When things were tough during the Depression, my grandfather pulled him out of Harbord Collegiate and apprenticed him to a sign maker so he could learn a trade. In those days, everyone in the family had to make some contribution to the family income. I learned the trade second hand by watching my father so by the time I was in high school I knew how to cut a silk screen, lay out a large banner and some exotic things like how to apply gold leaf to a bank window sign. In the summer, I would hang around my dad's shop. When he painted a sign on a transport truck, he would outline the letters and let me fill them in. Before long, I could handle a brush and a mahl stick with some skill.

Eventually, Berger's disease forced him to leave his trade. Berger's disease is a hardening of the arteries in the legs and is caused by breathing fumes from the lead in paint. He had to find a job that got him off his feet. He drove a cab. By that time, like the lead in his, signs were in my blood.

At election time, the basement of my house became a sign shop where we made all of my election signs. Elections were a home industry in my house. A crew of volunteers would print the signs from screens I had cut myself. Others would mount them for drying on clothes pegs hung from the rafters. A giant fan in my window would exhaust the fumes. During the "Commerce Bank a Bad Neighbour" campaign, we printed all the shopping bags and the protest signs in my basement sign shop.

That campaign taught me a valuable political lesson. One of our tactics had been to mount the lawn sign campaign against the Commerce Bank. We had erected some 400 in neighbourhoods around the bank tower. Controller Bob Yuill, either out love for the Commerce Bank or just plain mean spiritedness – I'm sure it was the latter – filed a complaint with bylaw enforcement about our signs. The sign bylaw was enforced on a complaint basis. Protest signs were illegal under the North York sign bylaw and we were ordered to remove our anti-bank protest signs. Our protesters were law-abiding people. The signs were taken down.

That's when I learned about the power of satire. North York's sign bylaw was exceedingly restrictive. The issue prompted me to put forward a notice of motion to review the sign bylaw. At the council debate on the notice, I prepared a series of signs to illustrate what the bylaw allowed and what it considered illegal.

I began by waving an illegal election sign posted by each of the four controllers and one by the mayor. The North York bylaw required that candidates remove all their election signs within 48 hours after the election. This was April – five months after the election. Yet it wasn't hard to find a sample sign for each that had not yet been taken down from an overpass or on a road allowance. Sign bylaw enforcement was as lax as the bylaw was tight. There was only one sign inspector for the entire city. Most of the signs for citywide candidates were erected illegally in the first place. Almost all of the main streets in North York were Metro roads and the Metro roads bylaw prohibited any signs. Under the North York election bylaw, a candidate had to have permission of the property owner to erect an election sign. You can be sure most citywide candidate signs were erected without permission. The mayor and controllers sat there grim-faced, with blood in their eyes.

I then revealed a number of signs that were either legal or illegal under the bylaw.

The mayor went bananas.

Real Estate signs are legal. The telephone number I used happens to be the number of a business owned by Controller Norm Gardiner.

Gay ads were highly controversial at the time. Bob Yuill turned green when he saw this one.

This one was directed at Controller Esther Shiner. She got elected on a "complete the expressway" campaign. The Spadina Expressway was cancelled by the Davis Government in the face of massive opposition by downtown residents. The Toronto Star dubbed Esther the "longest one track mind in Toronto politics". Esther had used lawn signs in her go Spadina campaigns.

"Protest signs will turn neighbour against neighbour," he shouted. "His motive isn't friendly. His motive isn't good. I'm shocked at his tactics."

Esther Shiner threw in her two cents worth: "The Commerce signs were abominable and fewer restrictions would lead to sign pollution," she quipped.

Butter wouldn't melt in her mouth.

My proposal to review the sign bylaw went down to flaming defeat with only Mike Foster supporting it.

I rushed back to my basement workshop with renewed vigour. That night, I cut a screen for a new sign. It consisted of a North York flag with the caption "A GREAT CITY."

After printing a small run, I pounded one into my front lawn. The next morning, I telephoned Foster, who also happened to be my alderman (I lived in his ward) and I asked him to phone the building department and lay a complaint about my sign. It took a while, but they finally issued an order to comply and gave me a week to remove the sign.

"I think it's a riot," said I. "Here I am, an alderman trying to boost the City of North York by putting a North York flag on my lawn and now I'm going to be busted for being patriotic. The current sign legislation is ridiculous. The prohibition of protest signs and non-controversial posters like this violate a citizen's right to free speech."

I vowed to take my fight to the Canadian Civil Liberties Association.

"I'm going to replace this sign with a Canadian flag. If I'm going to get busted for being patriotic at the municipal level, I might as well be busted for being patriotic at the federal level too. Posting a Canadian flag as a lawn sign is illegal in North York.

"Hopefully, the courts will display better sense than the council."

BOUNDARY DISPUTE

North York became a city on February 14, 1979 after the mayor petitioned the province for city status. It was an ego thing. He wanted desperately to be a big-city mayor. I pointed out that calling a place a city doesn't make it a city.

"Most North Yorkers who are more than 10 miles from home will still say that they are from Toronto," I said. "A real city has theatre, a real city has cultural centres, a real city has a heart."

Oops: big mistake. My remarks prompted the mayor to give it a "heart." He had "City with a Heart" put on all the boundary signs. It was the antithesis of sophisticated urbanity. I knew that slogan would get us into trouble. Every time we refused someone a grant, every time we toughened a bylaw, every time we refused a request it would be thrown in our faces.

I suggested other names we could consider:

"We could call it 'Emerald City' and re-name Yonge St. the 'Yellow Brick Road,' or call it 'Nirvana'. What developer wouldn't jump at the chance of building in heaven? When we called the mayor your worship we would really mean it. What about naming it 'Cativo Bambino (Italian for bad boy) City? We could then have a Bad Boy University."

Yuill wrapped himself in the flag. He deemed my speech "shameful."

A mail-in poll conducted by the North York Mirror showed 50% of the ballots in favour and 50% of them against. What it really showed, however, was nobody but the politicians cared. Only 12 ballots were returned.

The boundary signs became an ongoing source of irritation. I detested them. Apart from the bad design and the fact that "City with a Heart" slogan loudly proclamed "bad taste," North York had some serious problems. The Social Planning Council's recently released report – *The Suburbs in Transition* – showed North York had a lot of social problems; that it was a hostile environment for its growing poor and imigrant populations. The city had completely ignored social factors in its planning. Increasingly, the impression that the sign conveyed was "City without a Brain." Someone must have agreed with that assessment because the slogan quietly began to disappear from the signs.

Lastman's staff must have convinced him the signs weren't very attractive because I was approached and asked if I would be a judge in a citywide contest to produce a new design. Mel was extending a laurel leaf and I graciously consented to "give peace a chance." In "real life," I was a junior high school art teacher so I had some qualifications. Invitations went out to secondary and post-secondary schools in North York, and there were 52 entries. The prize was $500, but more importantly, the winner would have the satisfaction of seeing their design permanently on display everywhere in the city.

The prize for the winning design went to Ken Lackman, a York University student. As soon as he stepped off the stage after being handed the cheque, Mel began to put pressure on him to change the design. The mayor wanted him to include the words "fourth largest city in Canada." The judging committee, which included Sid Cole, the traffic commissioner, Lionel Lawrence, York's fine arts dean, and me, had already rejected several designs with "fourth largest city in Canada" as well as several designs with hearts or "City with Heart" slogans. The rules specified exactly what words were to be used.

Alas, peace was short lived.

I wrote to the mayor: "You have no right to interfere. The rules clearly indicated precisely what words were to be included. The contest would have to be declared null and void if you forced the change that you want to the sign."

Lastman's reaction hardly contributed to the armistice we had declared.

"Howard Moscoe is a horse's ass…. He has the morals of an alley cat; he lives a miserable life and tries to make everyone else miserable too. He's totally destructive and can throw a damper on everything…. I did not ask the artist to change the sign but merely to provide an overlay so council could see the winning sign both ways…. [i.e. my way.] The final decision is council's."

In an interview with the North York Mirror, the artist commented: "I didn't really want to put it (fourth largest city) on because I wanted to keep it as clean as possible. The impression that I got was that the city wanted something classy and I don't think this is."

He was right.

As it turned out, the matter was never brought to council and the new sign never made it to the street.

Is there an Olympic medal for fourth place? There seemed to be nothing holding back the egos of small-time politicians striving to be big-city big shots. I guess some people seek status wherever they can. Now a new slogan began to appear on the old North York boundary signs. They proudly proclaimed "Canada's fourth Largest City."

Then one day, about a year later, Statistics Canada came galloping to the rescue. The newly released census showed North York (now 555,791) had slipped from fourth to fifth place and Winnipeg (now 560,028) had inched ahead of North York to become Canada's fourth largest city. I pointed it out to the mayor.

"I don't believe the Statistics Canada figures....I want a recount," he said.

Mel looked the other way. So did everyone else. So I wrote a letter to Winnipeg's Mayor Bill Norrie asking if he was going to sit idly by and let Mel get away with this. I knew if he had any sense at all he would ignore it, and he would have had I not also sent a copy to the Winnipeg Free Press. It then couldn't be ignored and became an issue.

"I think obviously the signs should reflect the real stats," said the mayor. "I'll write a letter to them."

The story in the Winnipeg Free Press got the Toronto media's attention and the Globe did a story that went national. Mel isn't easily embarrassed, but the national coverage must have given him second thoughts because over the next year or so the slogan quitely slipped off the boundary signs. We were left with the original old ugly boundary signs. At last, there was peace – at least on the border.

CHAPTER 16
Hair Aches

I used to feel sorry for Mel Lastman at North York Council meetings. He was obviously suffering from some serious headaches. He would strain his eyes and struggle to maintain his composure, but was clearly distracted. I was trying to be empathetic, but he lost my sympathy when I learned they weren't headaches at all but hair aches. Mel was paranoid about going bald. He underwent a series of hair implants. His doctor would implant a plug of hair into his scalp. I am not sure where the plugs actually came from. His hair had always been naturally curly. Mel was fond of telling the media he became aroused when he saw a tall building going up in his North York downtown, but I gave no credence to the story that when he saw a tall building his head came to a point. There was no sympathy because the agony was self-inflicted.

One day, Gloria, my wife, called me at work to tell me she had purchased a wonderful gift for me. Skylight Theatre was the production company that gave free performances for the public in the open-air theatre in Earl Bales Park. It was holding a fundraising auction on Rogers Cable television and she had bid on, and won a toupee. It was Mel Lastman's rug, one of some 300 items auctioned off that week. He had donated it to the auction and she was lucky enough to purchase it. Gloria had bid on it under her maiden name, Gloria Green. It was the best $33 investment we ever made.

Mel, to say the least, was not a happy camper when he learned I had the rug in my possession, especially after I told the Toronto Star: "I've been after his scalp for five years."

"What are you going to do with it?" the reporter asked Gloria.

"We'll hold it for ransom and sell it back to him for $200 and donate the money back to Skylight Theatre," was her reply. "Or maybe I'll save it for when Howie goes bald."

Mel never took her up on the offer.

I now had a powerful weapon to deploy in the Moscoe-Lastman hostilities. I remember entering the council chamber for one of our regular meetings, putting my briefcase on the desk and pulling out the rug. I then made an elaborate show of using it to dust off my desk and chair. Mel turned red. If anger could grow hair, he could have abandoned the hair plugs and auditioned for the role of Sampson in the movie *Sampson and Delilah*.

I then took the show on the road and gave the wig a starring role.

The Toronto Sun came and took a shot of me spraying it for bugs. It became a feature on several TV shows. I remember taking the City TV show, Breakfast Television, on a conducted tour of the North York Civic Centre with the toupee tucked under my arm in a shoebox. I carefully lifted the hair piece out of the box, held it above my head and said:

"They say you can never be mayor of North York unless you own one of these."

I then received an offer of $800 for the hairpiece. It was from the doctor who was doing Mel's hair transplants. He wanted to mount it as a trophy on his office wall. Gloria wouldn't let me sell. When I retired, I offered it to the city archives, but they turned it down. It's not that it wasn't an important artefact. It is just they only have the facilities to store things that are flat. If it had been Flat Stanley's wig, they would have grabbed it.

So, what does the future hold for Mel's rug? In 2018, the lease expires on old city hall. The plan is to re-locate the courts into a new building and turn the building into the Museum of Toronto. I plan to donate it to the museum, where they can put it on display. It would be a fitting symbol of the Lastman years. Perhaps, they will have it bronzed. It will certainly last longer than the memory of both Mel and me.

CHAPTER 17

Blowing Smoke

My grandson, Max, was seven years old. I was telling him a story and used the word "ash tray." He stared at me blankly.

"What's an ash tray?"

Within a single generation, smoking has all but disappeared. It has gone from "cool" to "yech." That didn't happen by accident. It resulted from a hard-won fight led by people like Gar Mahood of the Non-Smokers' Rights Association and the Canadian Cancer Society.

I was a member of the city's environmental control committee. "Control" was a misnomer. The committee had been formed because it was the "thing to do." Most members of council had little interest in environmental issues. Consequently, the new members of council were appointed to the "expected to do nothing" committees. Usually, they consisted of one or two council members and a number of citizen volunteers who had a real interest in their topic. They were under the mistaken impression their participation would make North York a better city and their work would be valued. Wrong. Many members of North York Council belittled the work of these committees.

Unlike most of my council colleagues, I loved these kinds of committees; committees like race relations and the historical board because they gave me the opportunity to delve into issues that nobody else would touch and vault them to the forefront. There was no shortage of real issues to sink your teeth into if you were willing to grab hold of them. I saw them both as a challenge and an opportunity to make some significant policy changes.

I had been a heavy smoker (two packs a day and a pipe). Notwithstanding how many times I tried to quit, the pressure of elections had always "done me in." It worked something like this: During a campaign, I would attempt to knock at every door in the ward. I usually managed to hit about 75% of them. A short while into the campaign, someone would open a door with a cigarette dangling from their lips.

"Hi. I'm Howard Moscoe, your city councillor and I like to stay that way. How can I convince you to vote for me? [Pause]

Then it would hit me.

"Would you happen to have an extra cigarette?"

That was it. One puff and I was hooked. I had convinced myself if I bought a deck of smokes I would be a smoker again, so I spent the rest of the campaign going door-to-door bumming cigarettes. At the end of the campaign, I was a smoker again.

I haven't smoked for 41 years. How did I finally quit? My children saved their pennies and gave me a birthday present. It was a stop smoking course at Branson Hospital. I didn't have the heart not to attend, and every time the weed tempted me, I thought of that penny collection. Ironically, my youngest daughter, Vicki, who constantly lectured me on the evils of tobacco, struggled with her own smoking problem. (She finally quit in 2017 – hopefully.)

Some people who quit smoking tend to become evangelical on the issue of smoking. I wasn't, but I supported strongly the movement to protect non-smokers rights. It's not that I wanted everyone to stop smoking for their health as much as I wanted them to quit for mine. I knew that second-hand tobacco smoke would trigger another relapse for me. Throughout the entire exercise of attempting to build a no-smoking bylaw, not only was I struggling with the mayor and restaurant association, I was struggling with a tougher opponent – the devil weed itself. I chaired the sub-committee that would draft the bylaw.

Every environmentalist in the province was awaiting an Ontario Supreme Court decision. Hamilton had approved a tough no-smoking bylaw that, among other "places of public assembly," had prohibited smoking in restaurants. The bylaw was challenged by the Ontario Restaurant Association, but was upheld by the court. That gave the green light to many municipalities that were already drafting bylaws. The Toronto Restaurant and Foodservices Association (TRFA) was furiously lobbying behind the scenes to get North York to defeat the bylaw that we were drafting.

When I look back, our proposed bylaw by today's standards was insipid. It required restaurants to set aside a section for non-smokers. That's kind of like asking pool owners to set aside a no peeing section.

Even that small step met with hostility.

Cigar-chomping Mel bought the association's pitch completely. It was articulated by Robert Cowan, TRFA president, in a letter to the mayor:

HOSTILITY

"We are recommending that operators try voluntary no-smoking areas over a six-month period to give consumers a fair opportunity to try the concept."

The association continued: "To pass a bylaw, with the possibility of deleterious effects on North York's restaurant industry seems totally premature."

Mel fired off 500 letters to restaurant owners in North York urging them to establish no-smoking areas to avoid a bylaw.

Then he wrote to our committee to lecture them: "Government intrusion into the private marketplace should be reserved for serious cases where solutions cannot be achieved."

The rhetoric heated up. The mayor fired off another memo to members of council accusing me of attempting to *"destroy the free enterprise system."*

"Half the world is smothered by the dead hand of government-controlled economies, yet he persists in barging headlong into private affairs here. Moscoe is irresponsible."

I responded:

"The mayor seems to be unable to grasp the legitimate function of government elected by people to represent and protect their best interests. When it comes to protecting the health, safety and basic needs of North York citizens, I make no apology for interfering in the marketplace."

Why does history seem to always repeat itself? I was quoted as telling the committee "the restaurateurs could not be trusted and were stalling."

Voluntary efforts had been promised by the TRFA in Toronto. They were given several trial periods, and it never happened. Self-regulation could never work. I was confident that once patrons learned they could have no-smoking meals the demand would grow.

An outraged restaurant owner, Marvin Greenberg, who I had never met, showed up at the Board of Control to complain. He told the board my remarks were "cutting and injurious to me personally and totally ignorant of my profession and the services we provide satisfactorily to millions of people every day in this country." Lastman demanded I apologize. In fact, he apologized for me. (He had an annoying habit of doing that regularly). I made no apology. I announced we were proceeding with public hearings on the draft bylaw in the fall and Mr. Greenberg was welcome to share his opinions with the committee.

A month after Mel's letter went out, the Toronto Star did a tour of restaurants in the Yonge and Sheppard area. Of the seven restaurants they visited, only two had heeded the mayor's call and set up no-smoking areas. Several of the owners said they would not establish an area because they were too small. Others said they prefer to be legislated because then they would be on a level playing field with their competitors.

TRFA claimed membership of 35% of the 4,229 restaurants in Metro. There was a strong likelihood most of their members were downtown. I was tired of the finger pointing and name-calling, and I wasn't sure the association was accurately reflecting the views of the majority restaurateurs in North York. So I set out to survey every restaurant in North York listed in the yellow pages.

In my survey, I pointed out that a recent Gallup Poll showed 73% of people surveyed were in favour of smoking restrictions in restaurants; 59% wanted non-smoking areas and another 14% wanted smoking banned entirely. I also pointed out they would all have six months to experiment with a no-smoking area in any case because it would take at least that long to draft and enact the bylaw.

I told the media:

"There's nothing worse than sitting in a restaurant and having some insensitive jerk blowing smoke rings while you are trying to enjoy your meal. We don't want to take away the right to smoke. We just want the right to breathe fresh air."

Marie Labatte, who represented the Don Mills area, was the other councillor on the Environmental Control Committee. She was a feisty lady who was an ardent feminist and environmentalist. Marie was the one who spearheaded the push for non-smokers rights. Marie and I won the first round, which was pressing the committee to proceed with the bylaw in the face of resistance from the mayor. We lost the second round at council when the council voted 9-8 against holding a public hearing in the council chamber.

"That won't stop us," quipped Marie. "We don't need council's approval to hold a public hearing. We can get sponsorship funding from the Cancer Society."

Lastman said he would oppose both the bylaw and the hearing.

In January of 1984, the North York Board of Health came out in support of the bylaw. You might wonder why it took them two years to get to that position, but given the vehement opposition by the mayor it was a very courageous position.

The debate on this issue began in September of 1981. North York didn't get around to formally debating its bylaw until May of 1986. It had taken five years to get to the point of a vote on a comprehensive no-smoking bylaw. This wasn't our first. In 1973, North York had banned smoking in supermarkets. It was the restaurant provisions and the mayor that drove the controversy.

Mel began to realize he was on the wrong side of this issue. In the face of growing support for the concept of smoke-free areas in restaurants, the mayor began to back away. Etobicoke, three years earlier, and the City of Toronto now had bylaws that required restaurants with over 40 seats to provide 30% of their area as non-smoking. Mel put forward a standard that would require restaurants with 72 seats to have non-smoking sections. North York would have the weakest bylaw. Gar Mahood, president of the Non-Smokers Rights Association, called it a "joke."

There were about 45 people attending the public hearing. Only one spoke against the bylaw. Even the TRFA had given up, but not Mel. My amendment to adopt the Toronto standard size threshold to 72 seats lost on a vote of 11 to 6.

In the end, only two members of council voted against the watered-down bylaw, Ron Summers and Bob Yuill. Yuill said, "I don't support this intimidation by non-smokers – I'm not convinced that people smoking in restaurants will cause my death."

He may have been right. Bob died of heart failure in 2006.

Scan forward to 2003, two amalgamations later. In January of 2003, the new City of Toronto passed a tough environmental bylaw that prohibited smoking in all food service areas. In that year, public health inspectors conducted over 6,000 restaurant inspections and laid charges against only 156 premises for violations of the law. A year later, on June 1, 2004, all bars in Toronto became smoke-free without so much as a whimper, and soon thereafter workplace smoking was prohibited. The concept of not being forced to inhale second-hand tobacco smoke has become so much the norm that we all take it for granted. When I escorted a group of Polish mayors around the city, they commented on the number of women standing outside the doors of office buildings and bars smoking. They assumed we had a prostitution problem.

In a short 15 years, after the concept was introduced at the municipal level, public smoking had become socially unacceptable almost everywhere. In June of 2005, the Province of Ontario, reading the public mood, acknowledged the trail we blazed by enacting the Smoke Free Ontario Act, which prohibits smoking in all public places and enclosed workplaces.

I'm not surprised that Max didn't know what an ash tray was. That's our legacy to his generation.

CHAPTER 18

Moscoe vs. Moscoe

The 1982 election was shaping up to be a tough race. Population shifts in North York made ward re-distribution necessary. Ward 3 (Jane-Finch), represented by NDP Alderman Pat O'Neill, had grown to 53,000 residents. The mayor was reluctant to initiate a review of the wards because it would have eliminated Ward 6 (Avenue Road), which had shrunk to 24,000 residents. Ward 6 was held by Milton Berger, a staunch Progressive Conservative Party member and one of the mayor's allies. Berger had taken a strong public stand against re-distribution.

"Let's once and for all forget about those fancy notions, representation by population," Berger urged members of council. Representation by population, like "oil lamps and out-houses, became outdated with the Boston Tea Party," Berger said.

Lastman chose his loud-mouthed, cigar-chomping minion, Irv Chapley, to head a committee to recommend new ward boundaries.

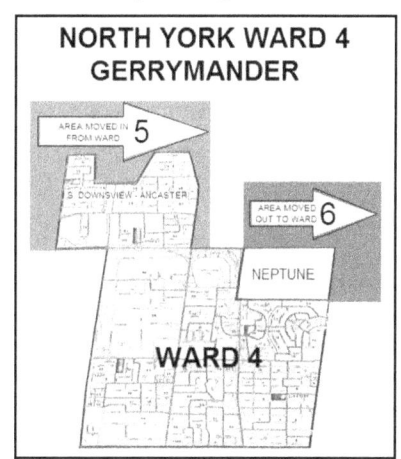

Chapley had two missions: keep Berger's ward from disappearing and get rid of Moscoe.

His solution was to take the Neptune area out of Ward 4 and move it into Ward 6. The Neptune area was largely Jewish and low income. It was one of my strongest areas. The South

Downsview and Ancaster neighbourhoods were almost exclusively Italian. There were to be 15 new polls added to my ward, where I had no presence whatsoever.

Now a nice neat, square electoral area was re-shaped to look like the state of Idaho.

The new boundary was sure to attract an Italian candidate and it did. Frank Di Giorgio jumped into the race. He was an affable, likeable candidate and I knew he would do well. He was also a good canvasser and presented himself well at the doorstep. It looked like it was going to be a tough election.

That month, the North York Council meeting had not gone well. The city was to consider a sweeping zoning amendment that would allow other commercial enterprises to share as-of-right occupancy on service station lots. That would mean a permit for a donut shop behind your house could be issued without notification and without any requirement to hold a public hearing or give you the opportunity to have a say in issues like the fencing and landscaping. The public hearing on the bylaw change was scheduled as the last item on the agenda. It came up just before midnight. It was moved by Alderman Ron Summers, the second speaker moved closure and the vote was taken immediately. It was a done deal. I rose to speak. Lastman shouted me down,

"You can't speak. Closure has been called."

I continued,

"I'm going to speak. You had no right to entertain a motion of closure. The issue is too important to my constituents and to the whole city not to allow it to be debated."

I continued speaking. Lastman tried to shout me down. I kept on talking.

The mayor was furious. He moved that if I did not sit down I would be ejected from the council chamber. It carried on a vote of 7 to 5. I just kept talking.

"I was elected to represent the people in my ward and I am going to do that. They are the only ones that can remove me from this council chamber."

The mayor slammed down his gavel and recessed the meeting. I just kept talking. He then rushed up to his office to call the police to come and eject me from the council chamber. They told him they didn't think it was a good idea. They wouldn't come. Next morning's headline read: "Lastman calls police to eject Moscoe from council chamber."

The next night didn't go much better. Fairholme Avenue is one block south of Lawrence Avenue and is a street of single-family homes. Abutting the rear of these homes are other single-family homes on the south side of Lawrence Avenue. Residents on Fairholme had been fighting a rear guard action to prevent the properties behind them from being re-zoned to permit high rises. Almost all of them were held by speculators. They had organized the Fairholme Residents Association to protect their properties. Eleanor Rosen, who was planning to run against me, was trying to organize a so-called "Lawrence Avenue Ratepayers Association" (I called it a Speculators Association). She called a public meeting at the local library.

Since it was a public meeting in a public building, I encouraged the Fairholme Association to attend as a group. Eleanor demanded we leave. The meeting was stormy.

The next day's headline read: "Ratepayer president calls police to eject Moscoe from meeting." The Progressive Conservative Riding Association in Wilson Heights was a problem for me. They detested the thought that the ward was held by a New Democrat and were determined to get rid of me. Their vice-president, Eleanor Rosen, had run against me in the 1978 election, my first attempt at a council seat. She had captured less than 10% of the vote.

Now with the re-distribution and the possibility of a strong challenge from Frank Di Giorgio, Eleanor had a plan.

One hour before nominations closed, a fourth candidate filed nomination papers for alderman in Ward 4, Sydney Moscoe. Sydney Moscoe (no relation) was a lawyer who also happened to be a past president of the Wilson Heights Progressive Conservative Association, the same organization Eleanor just happened to be vice-president of.

Sydney Moscoe was a credible candidate. He had served on the North York Board of Education and had been elected three terms as a trustee. He declined to run in 1969. It was because of public dissatisfaction over the Minkler affair, allegations of overspending on a lavish retirement party for Director of Education Fred Minkler. There was also public criticism of a trustee trip he and four other trustees had taken to Hawaii "to study Pacific music."

His nomination threw my campaign into panic mode. In the first place, I had printed my election signs without my first name. They read: RE-ELECT ALDERMAN MOSCOE. I had to destroy and re-print more than a thousand election signs.

On the new signs, the word "Howard" was almost as large as "Moscoe." The media predicted this election would be "the most confusing, and perhaps the meanest ward battle in all of Metro." They were right. Our campaign had to be totally re-vamped. We had a new prime directive: To make sure the voters knew the difference between the two Moscoes.

Sam Pazzano, my campaign manager, spent most of that day on the telephone. Next morning, we hit Sydney's downtown law office with a crowd of pickets with signs that read, HOWARD IS THE REAL MOSCOE and DOWN

WITH SLEAZY LAWYERS. We had to generate as much media as possible. We hyped the rhetoric and described his candidacy as "a sleazy trick to confuse the voters."

It really was a sleazy trick. The signatures on Sydney's nomination papers were identical to the signatures on Eleanor Rosen's nomination papers. Three of the signatures were from members of her immediate family and two were her campaign workers.

After the story broke, I received a telephone call from a lawyer who identified himself as a Progressive Conservative and was appalled and embarrassed by what they had done. He offered to help my campaign. That night, the two of us went out to interview the people who had signed the nomination papers. I was wired for sound and recorded the conversations. I needed the recordings to convince the media that my complaint was legitimate. That night, I played them to the night editor at the Toronto Star.

Seven of the 13 people listed as endorsing Sidney denied signing his forms. It appears that when Eleanor Rosen collected signatures for her nomination papers she asked nominators to sign duplicate forms. She then added Sidney Moscoe's name to the top of the second set of nomination papers and had them filed on his behalf. We took sworn affidavits.

When Eleanor Rosen was confronted by the media about the identical nomination papers, she said it was "only a coincidence."

Wednesday night was the first all-candidates meeting. It was at Caledon Village, a complex of four condominium apartments surrounded by town houses on Caledonia Road. The media were out in full force to cover what had become the only issue in the North York election. I carried a large sign that said, HOWARD. I don't believe Sidney had ever really intended to be anything more than a spoiler, but the publicity and media attention forced him into a real campaign. To try and maintain what little credibility he could salvage out of this, he printed signs and literature and had to throw himself into the campaign.

There were three candidates on the platform. Frank Di Giorgio, Sydney Moscoe and myself. Eleanor Rosen didn't even bother to show up. Poor Frank Di Giorgio, my only "real" opponent, the opponent I feared the most, got sidelined. The news articles mentioned him only in passing and the photo that ran in the Toronto Star the next morning showed only Sydney and me. Frank had been edited out.

On Friday of that week, my lawyer, Gary Farb, filed an action with the Ontario Supreme Court seeking to have Sidney's name removed from the ballot. It was supported by affidavits from people who had unknowingly signed Sydney's nomination papers.

Time was of the essence. The clerk was holding up the printing of the 25,000 Ward 4 ballots to the last minute, but they had to be printed for the advanced poll on October 30. A decision had to be rendered by Thursday. Sydney stalled by claiming he had not had time to consult his lawyer or prepare his case. The judge gave him an adjournment until Tuesday.

At that time, an affidavit was presented from Eleanor Rosen that alleged her neighbours had been coerced into swearing their affidavits. There was no time to call witnesses. They had run out the clock. The application was denied. The decision had to be left to the voters.

We had to keep the media churning. I filed a complaint to the law society about Sydney's unethical behaviour. Sydney struck back with a libel and slander suit for my allegation that he "crawled out of a sewer and put his name on the ballot."

My campaign team was looking for a couple of works department employees who could swear that they saw him crawling out of a sewer. The negative publicity was slowly eroding his candidacy.

The best thing about elections is they end on election night. The voters made their decision. The score was:

Howard Moscoe	4,000	46%
Frank Di Giorgio	2,923	34%
Eleanor Rosen	1,184	14%
Sydney Moscoe	500	6%

Frank Di Giorgio won 14 of the 15 new polls that had been gerrymandered into the ward, but lost the election. Eleanor Rosen and Sydney Moscoe were blown away. I was relieved. The voters had figured out who the real Moscoe was.

CHAPTER 19
Hindu Flames

During my first years on North York Council, I held two jobs. An alderman's salary was not enough to live on and was expected to be a part-time position. The reality was if you were going to do the job properly you had to put more than half your time into it. I straddled the line between a teaching job for the North York Board of Education and my council position. It became even more complicated when I was elected by the teachers as vice-president and later president of their union.

As a teacher activist, I was intimately familiar with the politics of the school board. I had attended every school board meeting for several years, often speaking on behalf of teachers. I knew all of the trustees and had developed a working relationship with most members of the board. That experience allowed me to easily step into my council role without having to spend a lot of time figuring how the system worked.

In 1980, I was approached by a Hindu Group, which was looking for a place to worship. Arya Samaj is a Hindu Reform movement with more than 10 million followers worldwide. In North York, they had a congregation of about 200 and had applied to the North York School Board for a permit to use a school gym one day a week for worship and cultural activities. North York School Board policy encourages the use of schools by community groups and many small congregations use school space for worship.

The Hindu Group was refused a permit. The reason: As part of their worship ceremony, they burn a few sandalwood chips and butter in an iron pot.

The board meets in committee of the whole once a month followed two weeks later by a formal board meeting when they confirm the actions recommended by the committee of the whole. We had asked, and were granted, an opportunity to appear before the committee to plead our case. It wasn't without some prior debate. Some of the trustees did not want to even hear the group. They had in their hands a letter from the board's insurance underwriter, Ivanhoe Insurance Managers, which stated:

"The use of a fire pot in a school would constitute a material change in the risk."

The company was not willing to entertain the matter even if a higher premium was paid. Furthermore, the board's solicitor had written that, "An open flame would leave the Board open to a charge of negligence if a fire occurred."

"The presentation is entirely unnecessary," quipped Trustee Ken Crowley. "I will not change my mind."

The chair, Peg Grant, ruled that they had been given an appointment to speak and they should be allowed to speak, but it looked like it would be impossible to crack the odds against a favourable decision.

The group proceeded to demonstrate how they would use the fire pot. It was the first time anyone, including the insurance company or the board solicitor, had seen it. The ceremony used five tiny wooden sticks and produced about as much flame as one would use to light a cigarette. Certainly not as much fire as the burner on the gas stove in the teachers' lounge.

I said the response from the insurance company and board solicitor was entirely bureaucratic. They had never examined the specifics, and use of the ceremonial fire pot would produce no more flame than any other flame already being used and should in no way increase the board's risk.

A few trustees changed their minds.

"It doesn't seem to be a fire hazard," said Trustee Sybil Darnell. "I'm inclined to agree with Moscoe. This is a bureaucratic response. It seems inconceivable to make such a to-do over a little thing."

Trustee Francis Chapkin added: "North York is multi-cultural.... I would hate to see that we turned away a religious group because of a custom thousands of years old."

Trustee Darnell moved to defer the motion and get a more detailed response from the insurance company and the solicitor. The board quashed the motion in a 7-3 vote. The next day, I fired off a package to the fire chief. It contained an alcohol burner that was commonly used in science classes. It was a glass container filled with methyl hydrate. I had a few of them in my art storage closet.

"Will you please evaluate the enclosed burner as a device to be used by elementary school students in North York classrooms under the supervision of a teacher."

His report was devastating.

We again appeared at the board. I carried a small box to the speaker's stand, reached into it, carefully withdrew an alcohol burner and lit it with a cigarette lighter. As I spoke, I tilted the burner to the side and a methyl alcohol flame dribbled down to the floor, but before it ignited the carpet, I snuffed it out with the heel of my shoe.

"I checked with our purchasing department. To date, there have been 2,565 of these devices purchased for use in elementary school science classes. They are fueled by methyl hydrate. Methyl hydrate is also used in duplicating machines. School regulations require concrete blocks to be installed under all duplicating machines.

"Here is a copy of a report from the fire chief evaluating these burners for use in elementary schools under the supervision of a teacher. I have forwarded a copy to your insurance company."

While the Hindus did not get permission to worship in a North York school that night, they left the boardroom smiling.

Their intransigence had cost the board more than $50,000 to replace the alcohol burners. If I really wanted to be nasty, I would have appeared at the next meeting with a Bunsen burner. Sometimes public agencies have to temper their reasoning with common sense.

CHAPTER 20

The Polish Twin

One of the favourite pastimes of cities, towns and villages in the '70s and '80s was twinning. The idea was to find a municipality of a comparable size in some exotic location and enter into some kind of agreement for a cultural exchange. I always thought diplomatic relations was the purview of federal governments, but that didn't stop my colleagues in North York, or Scarborough, or almost everywhere else, from wanting to twin. It gave local politicians an opportunity to travel the world at public expense and a reason to justify it.

One problem with twinning was once you selected your twin and exchanged visits, that was it. That limited travel opportunities, so someone thought up the bright idea of replacing "twinning" with "friendship agreements." A friendship agreement was a shorter term and not exclusive. That way, your municipality could spread warmth and friendship all over the world. They provided much wider travel opportunities.

When Toronto amalgamated and we were striking committees for the new council, my colleagues were falling all over themselves to be on the World City Committee. They all had visions of travel to exotic places flashing in their heads. I called it the Air Miles Committee. It became so obviously self-serving, the mayor, Mel Lastman, disbanded the committee. If a councillor wanted to travel, it had to come out of his office budget.

In my first term of office, North York aldermen were passionate to sign some kind of twinning agreement. The problem was they could not agree amongst themselves which country to select.

The two largest ethnic groups at the time were the Italian and the Jewish communities. The Italians on council wanted to select a city in Italy. The Jews wanted a city in Israel. So they struck a committee, an independent group of citizens to make the choice. That group reviewed the situation and diplomatically selected (according to Stats Canada) the third largest North York group of ethnic origin. That's how we managed to sign our first twinning agreement with Wroclaw, a city in Poland.

What the twinning committee didn't realize was that, other than technically, Poles were not the third largest group. Most of the Jews in North York at the time were of Polish origin. Statistics Canada counted them twice, once as Jews and once as Poles. My father, for example, was born in Lodz. He came here when he was nine years old. He never considered himself a Pole. In fact, most of the Jews came to escape Poland; its ghettos, pogroms, racial hatred and abject poverty. Most of us were trying to forget Poland.

A further complicating factor was that Poland was behind the Iron Curtain. It was a communist country. That made twinning all the more difficult. Nevertheless, the committee pressed on. Nobody who was Jewish on council, including myself, had the guts to squash the idea, so the agreement was signed and the mayor and a contingent of council members dashed off to Wroclaw (pronounced rotslav) to bring friendship and warm feelings. I don't know what happened on their visit. I had no interest in going, nor would I have ever, as a junior member of council, been selected to go.

About a year later, it was time for North York to host the return cultural visit. The mayor of Wroclaw, Poland, and three members of his council came to North York. You would think those who had gone on the Polish visit would have spent some time touring them around. Not a chance. Apart from the dinner and attendance at a council meeting, they went AWOL. So why was I assigned the dubious task of hosting the tour? My administrative assistant, Irene, spoke Polish.

North York is not exactly a tourist Mecca. Tourists are not lining up to spend their vacations in North York. If you have to showcase North York, where do you drag a delegation? The Ontario Science Centre was on the list. Beyond that and Yorkdale shopping centre what's left?

The Polish delegation was straight out of Mad Magazine's standard stereotype of Communist party officials. They were all older men, somewhat serious and, of course, because of the language barrier we had difficulty communicating. They wore black, shiny suits and were obviously on a low budget. The buying power of the zloty was so low they could afford to take little back. We had to find suitable gifts. It turned out the latest rage sweeping Poland at the time was darts. Their faces broke into wide grins when we presented each of them with a dartboard and a set of darts.

I spent their last afternoon with them touring our most important local tourist attraction, Black Creek Pioneer Village. At the end of the visit, I turned to the mayor and asked, "So what did you think about our pioneer village?" He looked at me and shrugged, "It's nice but we have 1,000 just like it in Poland."

CHAPTER 21
Bylaw Absurdity

Rule Number 4 of Saul Alinsky's *Rules for Radicals* was: Make the enemy live up to its own book of rules. No one can possibly obey all of their own rules.

I was called by someone who had purchased a new home in my ward. A bylaw inspector had just knocked at his door and told him he had to remove the walkway to his house. The house was on a corner lot, and the main entrance was on the side street. North York bylaws prohibited a walkway from terminating at a curb. If there was no sidewalk, the walkway had to be built to the driveway.

It wasn't a new house, but one that was at least 25 years old. I asked the inspector for the rationale behind the bylaw. It went something like this: "It's a safety measure. If a walkway ends at a curb there is a danger of someone stepping off the curb into the path of an oncoming car."

When I noted someone could just as easily step off the end of a driveway into the path of an oncoming car, he shrugged. I suggested that since the walkway had existed for at least 25 years without being noticed, perhaps it could not be noticed for a few more years.

"Absolutely not," he retorted, "I didn't write the bylaw. Council did. Once the matter has been drawn to my attention I am duty bound to enforce it."

My staff and I were busy for the next few days. We went out and photographed more than 120 similar situations. It was a common format because many of the older parts of North York had been built without sidewalks. We were careful not to visit any homes in my ward. I wouldn't want to bother any of my residents with a bylaw violation notice. We simply chose the four adjacent wards to do our hunting.

A week later, I walked into the inspector's office and dropped five addresses with photographs onto his desk. On Tuesday, I came by with 10 more. On Wednesday, I delivered another 15 and on Thursday, 25. The coup de grace came Friday when I delivered the remaining 65. I think he got the message. My constituent was never bothered again.

Incidentally, one of my staff suggested another solution, but this one was more fun.

CHAPTER 22

North York Council Revolt

How much abuse can you take? In 1984, a North York alderman earned $21,390 for doing essentially the same job as a member of the Board of Control. Some would suggest that the aldermen worked even harder because they carried the burden of local casework. Yet a controller was earning $44,442, more than twice as much. The controller salary included $12,000 for sitting on Metro Council. All controllers automatically sat on Metro Council. Controllers were also paid additional stipends for sitting on Metro boards and commissions. Only two aldermen got the Metro allowance. The mayor drew $52,005.

It was before Christmas in 1984. We had just settled with our unions for a wage increase of 4%. It was traditional to extend the union settlement to our non-union employees and to council as well. As the debate progressed, the aldermen were becoming increasingly irritated about the attitude of the mayor and the Board of Control. Aldermen had been complaining for a long time about the disparity in salaries. As each controller spoke, the temperature in the room increased a couple of notches.

Alderman Andy Borins rose to speak: "I move that the controllers and mayor be given no increase at all and the money budgeted for the controller increases be divided evenly among the aldermen."

That would have given each alderman an increase of 6.7% and the controllers and mayor an increase of 0%. Most members of council agreed with my comments: "I'm tired of working twice as hard for half the pay. The controllers don't have the constituency work that we do. The wage gap is being ignored."

The motion carried. The aldermen simply got tired of being told to move to the back of the bus.

The reaction from the controllers varied.

Esther Shiner had supported the Borins motion. Controller Barbara Green called it "blackmail." She went on to whine about how hard she works. Controller Bob Yuill, true to character, pulled yet another stunt by setting up a "poor box" outside his office and invited contributions. The only donations he got totalled 37 cents, mostly in pennies, two paper clips, a button and 15 cents in Canadian Tire money. Bill Sutherland said he would support some kind of compromise.

The issue was re-opened at the next council meeting. I brokered the compromise by putting forward a formula that divided the money evenly amongst all of the members of council so everyone got the same dollar increase, but aldermen ended up with 4.7%, controllers with 3% and the mayor with 2.5%.

I told the media: "Why shouldn't we gain a bit? We've been jerked around by the controllers long enough. All they do is run around with lampshades on their heads to get publicity."

"I think the message was sent," said Borins. "That was my basic intention. Maybe they'll have a Christmas now."

You might think the matter ended there. It didn't. Because of the seething resentment among the aldermen about their salaries, the mayor had earlier in the year struck a "Citizens Committee" or a "Blue Ribbon Panel" to review council salaries.

I have no idea why they are "blue." With regard to municipal salaries, these panels have become clichés. They are supposed to take the heat off municipal politicians who are obliged to set their own salaries. They can be blamed when councillors grab for gold.

Someone always says, "It's not our fault, we simply adopted the recommendations of the Blue Ribbon Panel."

If the panels were red, it would be more symbolic of the blood that is usually spilled on the floor of the council chamber during municipal salary debates.

The panel studies the matter with the help of personnel staff or a consultant and recommends significant wage increases. When the report of the panel is tabled at the council, the knives come out and the debate rages anew. It's kind of like a windup toy, unwinding. The pot-shots fly and the media have another go at pillorying politicians.

The report of the panel was ready a full month before the pre-Christmas salary rebellion by aldermen. The mayor sat on it, I presume for good reason. It was recommending a 20% catch-up for aldermen, but it wasn't released until after we had ratified the collective agreements and taken our salary increase. We were in the middle of bargaining with our unions, and it was safe to assume that if the report had become public, it would have had a significant impact on those negotiations.

The release of the Blue Ribbon Panel report once again re-ignited the debate about aldermen's salaries. It gave Barbara Green an additional opportunity to whine again about how hard she worked and how little she was paid. I was happy when it was passed to be put into effect after the next election. If unhappy, the electorate could toss us out.

"It's not a raise," I told council, "it's a job re-classification. At the moment those of us who are not on Metro Council earn less than their secretaries."

CHAPTER 23

Paisley

One feature of municipal government in Ontario that has disappeared is the Board of Control. London, Ontario, was the last city to dump its board (before the 2010 elections). The concept dates back to the days when municipal politics was largely a part-time endeavour. The only office that was likely to be full-time was the position of mayor. Unlike the alderman, who generally represented a defined ward, controllers were elected citywide. North York had four.

IRVING PAISLEY

The Board of Control, the mayor and four controllers functioned as a City Executive. It approved all financial expenditures and on matters of finance could only be overruled by council with a two-thirds majority. Controllers were sort of mayors in waiting. Being elected a controller automatically gave you a seat on Metro Council as one of the nine North York delegates.

Because they were citywide, the Board of Control positions attracted some bizarre characters. Your election as a controller depended almost entirely on one of two things: name recognition or social connection. For a controller, getting your name in the media was a prime directive.

When the voter stood alone in the polling booth and had to pick four names from a list of 20 candidates for Board of Control, you needed to have your name stick out. That's why clowns like Bob Yuill pulled a budget debate stunt every year at Metro Council. One year, he dressed in a sailor suit with the refrain; "You guys are spending money like drunken sailors."

Another time he brought a money tree to council: "You're spending money like it grows on trees."

Yuill was a little miffed when $10 bills began to disappear as the tree was being passed around the council chamber. The quest for name recognition explained why Bob also hosted the annual blood donor clinic dressed as Count Dracula.

Other controllers got their name recognition by espousing causes. Esther Shiner, who the Toronto Star once described as the "longest one-track mind in municipal politics," achieved notoriety by fighting for the completion of the Spadina Expressway. It was never completed, but Esther's name recognition went on forever.

Barbara Green was catapulted on to the Board of Control when she won a Supreme Court decision against the city. Three single women living together in North York were charged under a North York zoning bylaw that said unrelated people could not live together in a single family neighbourhood.

The bylaw, in a landmark decision, was ruled unconstitutional, the court deciding municipalities could not zone on the basis of personal relationships. Two of the bylaw challengers, Barbara Green and Katie Hayhurst, were elected to council. Katie became an alderman and Barbara was elected to the Board of Control.

Irving Paisley was the fourth controller. Fourth was always a tenuous position to be in. As fourth controller, you were in greater danger of being knocked off by a better-known candidate. Irv won his seat primarily through social connections. He was active in many fraternal, community and charitable organizations. Irv, a likeable guy, was an old-style glib politician with the gift of the gab. When the council chamber was filled with opposing groups, he had the unique ability to make speeches supporting both sides of an issue. In his quest for votes, Irv sucked up to everyone. One technique he used was to attend the fundraising events for other council candidates and make speeches saying nice things about them. He was gathering votes.

During the 1980 election, I had a fundraising breakfast at the Yorkdale Holiday Inn. Irv bought a ticket. He wasn't on the agenda, but during the speeches, without even asking, he pushed his way to the microphone:

"Howard Moscoe is the best councillor on North York Council," he said. "While I don't share his politics, I admire his dedication and the hard work and energy he brings to the job."

Loud applause.

Not missing an opportunity to harvest votes, Irv went on from there.

"I support Paul Adler. He will make a terrific Hydro Commissioner."

More applause.

Paul Adler was the treasurer of our riding association. He had put his name on the ballot for Hydro Commissioner. Adler, his family and friends were all at the breakfast. Irving knew full well that Paul had no real election campaign. There were no election signs. He went on from there.

"I want everyone here to know that wherever I have an Irv Paisley sign in this city, I want Paul Adler to put his sign right under mine."

After breakfast, I took Paul aside. Let's teach him a lesson. Bring six campaign workers to my house after 9 p.m. tonight.

As mentioned, my election campaigns were homegrown affairs. I had all of the equipment at home. The rafters were fitted with clothes pegs where we hung signs to dry. I rushed home and cut a silk screen, which read:

Normally, lawn signs were designed to fold down over a wooden stake but these were printed upside down so they folded up. By midnight, we had printed 300 signs. We then split into three crews and fanned out across the city affixing them to the bottom of Irv Paisley's large arterial signs so the message read: "Irv Paisley Controller supports Paul Adler for Hydro"

We met at 5 a.m. in the Country Style doughnut shop at Wilson Heights and Sheppard and each of us threw $10 into a pool. The winner would be the one who picked a time closest to the time Irv Paisley would telephone me.

At precisely 8:32 a.m., I was awakened from a deep sleep.

"Do you know what this guy Paul Adler has done? He has put signs all over the city saying that I support him. He stapled them under all of my signs. Do you know what this will do to my campaign? There are 20 hydro candidates and I am going to lose all their supporters' votes."

"But Irv, that's what you told him to do," I said. "There are 250 people who attended my fundraising breakfast that heard you say it."

"I didn't mean that he should attach them to my signs. He didn't have any signs. This is a conspiracy. It had to be pre-planned. These signs were made upside down to fit my signs."

Irv agreed to pay for and erect new freestanding Adler signs across the city. He spent all of that day tearing down Paul's signs. Paul now had a sign campaign. By that time, the damage was done.

Paul did not get elected, but neither did Irv. He had slipped to fifth place. Irv lost the Board of Control seat by 812 votes.

CHAPTER 24
Super Kids

I know the satisfaction my son–in-law gets coaching little league baseball because I have experienced it myself. I once coached little league politics.

My daughter, Vicki, 11, and her friends, Claudia, 9, and Carole, 11, were lolling around one hot summer afternoon looking bored.

"Why don't you go to the park?" I said.

That was met with no enthusiasm at all.

"The park is worse than boring," said Claudia. "The rusty old playground equipment has been there forever. It's no fun anymore."

"So why don't you do something about it?" I replied. "Get the city to put in new equipment."

Like many North York parks, Bratty Park had one straight slide, seven swings, a set of monkey bars and a few benches. When I came outside later that afternoon, Vicki and her friends were going door-to-door. They had drafted a petition to City Council asking for new playground equipment for Bratty Park. The petition had been signed by 12 children, including a 2-year-old and 10 adults. Vicki was busy drafting a letter to go with the petition. It said:

"We feel that it's a very dull and boring playground. I usually go to the park after school with my friends but now we are getting tired of it."

Claudia added: "I want an unusual slide – maybe a curved one and monkey bars shaped like a dinosaur. The swings we have need paint and the seats have to be re-done."

Vicki continued: "The kids in this neighbourhood want the playground to look a bit more lively; some things that are great to look at and play on."

I suggested rather than mailing the petition, they might want to appear before the parks committee and present it to them directly. I gave her the name and telephone number of the secretary of the committee and told her to request an appointment to appear before the committee to talk about Bratty Park.

"They don't listen to kids," Vicki said.

"You'll never know unless you try," I told her.

"That's a good idea," she said. "We could show them pictures of the park and tell them how we feel."

The day of the park's committee meeting arrived. Claudia's parents drove them to City Hall. I knew it was a tough task. The parks department budget for playground equipment for that year was only $18,000 for the entire city. That's barely enough to do two, perhaps three playgrounds. It had been a long-standing practice of the park's committee to ask communities to raise money for playground equipment before the city would match what they had raised. It was bad policy in that wealthy and middle-class communities had the wherewithal to secure nice playgrounds. Raising money was easy for them. The working class and poor neighbourhoods didn't, and as a result, you could measure the socio-economic status of a neighbourhood by looking at their local neighbourhood park. The west end of North York had the crappiest playgrounds.

The girls were nervous. They had spent a long time writing out their presentation. Kathleen Kenna, the Toronto Star reporter, interviewed them beforehand.

"What are you going to do if they turn you down?" the reporter asked.

"I'm not sure," said Vicki. "We might picket City Hall."

When they addressed the committee, you could feel most of the room was quietly rooting for them. Controller Bob Yuill responded.

"The committee will help if you help yourselves. Go raise some money and come back when you have."

The girls were undaunted. They went home and planned a sidewalk sale. After rooting around in their basements, they dug up old toys and books they had outgrown. Other kids in the neighbourhood contributed their cast-off toys and set up shop in my driveway. That weekend, they raised a grand total of $21.13. They then prepared for a return to the parks committee. I suggested they change the money into pennies and nickels and put it into a sock.

In September, they re-appeared before the parks committee. Vicki first reminded Controller Yuill of his promise to help if they helped themselves.

"There's a total of $21.13 there, which we raised at a sidewalk sale," she said. "We did the best we could. After 15 years of broken down and rotted things, our community deserves new equipment.... We know our community would appreciate it very much if you could help us in making Bratty Park a much more enjoyable, lively place to play in."

Carol then dumped the sock full of coins onto the boardroom table. They rolled everywhere. The TV cameras lapped it up.

The committee voted that $3,500 be put into the 1981 budget for playground equipment in Bratty Park.

Vicki was interviewed by reporters.

"I wrote the speech myself," she said. "My father didn't help, but he did make some corrections afterward."

In March, Vicki received a registered letter advising her that Carol, Claudia and she had been chosen by Owl Magazine as "Super Kids" and would be featured in the June edition of the magazine. Unknown to me, the girls had submitted a joint essay, which was selected from 300 entries across Canada. The letter advised that the award goes to children whose initiative and hard work helped to right an environmental wrong. They were invited to a Harbourfront ceremony on April 1 that would kick off environment week for 1982. Hon. John Roberts, Minister of the Environment, would present the awards.

How much did I help? Her effort was entirely unsolicited. I sort of just proudly watched from the sidelines. OK, so I coached just a little bit.

Reporters asked Vicki the obvious question.

"I've never really thought about entering politics when I grow up," she said. "That's a hard question."

Like a true politician, she never answered it.

CHAPTER 25
Cut to the Chase

Police Chief Jack Marks told the Police Commission: "We stopped 1½ million cars in 1989 with only 275 fleeing. We abandoned the chase in 50 of those cases."

The implication – what's the big deal?

He didn't get it. Perhaps we all watch too many movies. Why should a police officer be conducting a keystone cop's demolition derby on the streets of Toronto because someone has run a red light or a stop sign? I know the police feel their mandate is to get the bad guy, but at what costs? In Ontario between 1982 and 1985, 24 people died, including two police officers, as the result of police chases that had gone sour. In 1984 alone, 173 people were injured in 1,646 chases.

I asked the police for a copy of their chase guidelines. It was in response to a complaint from a constituent. His parked car had been hit by a police vehicle in hot pursuit of a drunk driver. They told me, in perhaps not so colourful language, "go stick it in your ear," the guidelines are confidential. That's never stopped me before. It made me more determined to pursue the issue. When I managed to secure a copy from an unnamed source, I discovered, for example, the guidelines frown on chases when children are on their way to and from school. Apparently, Metro Police felt it was okay to kill people as long as they are not school children. Somebody's grandmother was fair game.

The province had been sitting on the report of a special committee on police chases for more than a year. The committee, chaired by John MacBeth, former Ontario solicitor general, had recommended a policy of allowing a chase only when an officer suspected a criminal offence had taken place. Solicitor General Ken Keyes had promised to bring in guidelines on police pursuits, but nothing was happening.

When asked, his office spokesperson said; "It's too important a subject to rush ahead."

It seems the only things rushing ahead were the vehicles being chased and the police who were chasing them.

I asked Metro Council to push for action.

"The police are engaging in too many needless pursuits. 57% of reported police chases occur because of simple traffic offences while just 5% are the result of 'serious criminal offences.'"

In January of 1987, I appeared before the police commission and said: "Some will tell you that there will be chaos in the streets if we curb chases – don't you believe it."

Based on previous year's statistics, I estimated in the coming year there would be 389 chases resulting in 90 accidents with 40 civilian injuries, 11 police injuries and three deaths – at least one of them a police officer. I never really understood the logic. Why would anyone chase a drunk driver? By doing so, he is forced to travel at higher speeds thereby increasing the danger for everyone. Simply take his license number and meet him at home when he rolls into his driveway. Who benefits from chasing a stolen car? Certainly not the owner of the car when the vehicle is returned with a mangled body. Certainly not the insurance company that pays to repair the damage.

The commission voted unanimously to review the police force's car chase policy, but given the chief's obvious opposition, it remained unclear if the review would lead to substantial changes.

The chief's report appeared on the agenda in March, five months later. As I suspected, it recommended no policy changes:

"Limiting police chases to instances of suspected criminal acts also gives motorists the green light to speed away from traffic violations," Marks said.

Police Commissioner Clare Westcott threw in his two cents worth: "If bad guys are aware you're not going to chase them, it's a field day out there."

The report was received, meaning no action was taken.

It wasn't until 1999, a full 12 years later, that the Province of Ontario enacted province-wide police chase guidelines to which all police chase protocols must adhere. It took a change in government to allow it to happen. The McGuinty government brought down guidelines, which specified that a police officer may pursue or continue to pursue a fleeing motor vehicle that fails to stop only if the officer has reason to believe that a criminal offence has been or is about to be committed, or until the vehicle or driver has been identified.

How often do we read about Wild West police chases in Ontario today? Not surprisingly, the Ontario policy is credited with significantly reducing deaths from pursuits.

Have the police lost control? No. The increasing presence of surveillance cameras has done much to offset much of the need for police chases.

In his report, Marks stated, "The 292 pursuits in 1986 produced 360 criminal charges that had nothing to do with the chases themselves."

I'm not entirely sure what that means, but what he had conveniently ignored was a statement buried in the solicitor general's report: "The statistics further indicate that a felon is rarely apprehended either purposefully or unintentionally as a result of vehicle pursuit by the police."

Police vehicles run on fossil fuels – police forces run on testosterone.

CHAPTER 26
Garbage Stinks – Some Garbage Contracts Stink More

The temptations are huge. It is not surprising that some politicians are corrupt. What surprises me most is more of them aren't at the municipal level. Think about it. At the blink of a zoning amendment a municipal council can skyrocket the value of a piece of land. This phenomenon is particularly intense in suburban areas where raw farmland is being gobbled up by development. In growth municipalities, decisions about land use and big decisions about infrastructure are made on a weekly basis. It is conventional wisdom in the development industry that more than sewage flows out of the sewer system. As the sewer system grows, the land value flows.

It was a standing joke at City Hall that if a municipality had the word "York" in it you would find cockroaches under every rock. There was a progression outward from the centre; Town of York (Toronto), York Township, City of York, North York, York Region and so it goes. These places had some of the "best politicians that money could buy."

Municipal councils award billions of dollars' worth of contracts annually. Two notable ones that were subjects of scams when I was on council were the 1987 garbage contract in North York and the MFP Financial Services computer leasing scandal in Toronto. These were two that bubbled up to the public perception, but you can be sure there were others that did not.

On September 19, 1995 Metro Councillor Mario Gentile was sentenced to two years in prison and fined $92,000 for bribery and breach of trust. Temptation, combined with a colossal ego, was Gentile's downfall. Mario emigrated from Puglia, Italy, as an adult. He was not very well educated and began work as a welder in Canada. After selling insurance for a while, he opened his own travel agency. He was elected as the alderman for Ward 2 on his second attempt and was intensely proud that he had "made it." Mario was the first person of Italian heritage elected to North York Council and that added to his self-importance.

MARIO GENTILE   MILTON BERGER

Mario's problems began in 1986 when he and Alderman Milton Berger (both members of the North York works committee) accepted an all-expenses-paid trip to Las Vegas from Paul Reuter, who headed a company selling an automated garbage collection system. It was Mario's first taste of the good life. By the time of his conviction 10 years later, the court record showed Gentile charged everything, from sexy lingerie, expensive designer shirts, to posh hotel rooms and cases of custom labelled wine totalling $49,000, to Diners Club and Visa Gold credit cards paid for by developer Lou Charles.

Mario and Milton took it upon themselves to grease Paul Reuter's garbage collection system through the approval process in North York. It was my first lesson, Municipal Corruption 101, and it left a lasting impression.

The city put out a request for proposals for an "Automated side-loaded refuse pick-up system," which was mailed to 10 companies. Four proposals were received by the closing deadline and were opened at a March 11, 1987 meeting. There was no proposal from Reuter Inc. of Minneapolis. Sometime between March 11 and March 24, the documents disappeared.

On March 24, Paul Reuter wrote to ask for special consideration because his company had not received the request for proposals. He claimed it was sent to the wrong place. Another proposal was also received from Athey Products. They claimed it had been sent on time, but because of the strike in progress at City Hall the courier had refused to cross the picket line so it was not received.

The two additional submissions were accepted, replacement copies were obtained for the four that had disappeared and a comparison report was tabled at the Works Committee on April 8, and three companies were short-listed and invited to make submissions: Frink Canada, Rand Automated Compaction Systems Inc. and Reuter Inc. But after the others complained, all six were permitted to make presentations although two – Athey and Labrie – chose not to attend.

On May 6, the works committee met and awarded the contract to Reuter. Rand sought to appeal the decision and presented their proposal to the Board of Control on May 13. Reuter was present and made a verbal presentation. The Board of Control recommended the contract be split, with 50% going to each of Reuter and Rand.

Before the matter went to council, Rand complained to the mayor's office about five irregularities: Reuter responded after the deadline; Reuter was able to use a lower U.S. exchange rate; the Reuter report was opened later than the others; Reuter knew the prices quoted by the others when he made his submission; the original proposals were lost.

The mayor asked the city's auditor, Coopers & Lybrand, to investigate and report on the process. They did so in a report marked PRIVATE & CONFIDENTIAL on June 9, 1987.

That report stated: "We believe the deficiencies noted in the process are significant and are sufficient to question the fairness of the process to all suppliers."

The auditor's report was never shown to council; they were just told about it. (I have a copy, which was slipped to me privately much later.) I am convinced if council had been able to read that report they would have opted for the auditor's first recommendation:

"Consider only those suppliers that had responded by the official closing date."

Council instead opted to re-bid the contract for a third time. Between that council meeting and the re-bid, I did some investigation of my own. I asked George Hardy, the official in charge of the building, to provide me with a copy of all of the telephone records from Gentile and Berger's office during the period of the bid process. What I discovered was Gentile made regular calls to three different numbers in Minneapolis and as many as 12 calls to Reuter's head office as the process unfolded. The telephone logs became key evidence in the police case against Gentile. Berger escaped prosecution. He cut a deal and gave evidence against Gentile.

Needless to say, it was no surprise when Reuter was awarded the contract. The lobbying by Berger and Gentile was an inside job. North York was stuck with a garbage system that was inferior. These ugly, disgusting oversized bins became a blight on our arterial roads and a major source of complaints from constituents. It took me more than five years to get rid of them.

Project 80 was set up by the Ontario NDP government of Premier Bob Rae to investigate municipal corruption. Project 80 brought some interesting facts to light.

An inactive heavy machinery importing company owned by Mario Gentile shared the same municipal offices on Ingram Drive as Reuter of Canada Inc., the Minnesota parent's subsidiary. The only business operating out of that office was a body shop owned by Mario Menna, Reuter's Canadian rep and a friend of Gentile hired by the company around the time bids for the contract were first received. Mario had never disclosed his business relationship with Reuter.

The company never met its warranty obligations, which included a satisfaction-guaranteed, buy-back clause and a promise by the company to open a manufacturing plant in North York. Residents just didn't want the bins. More than 1,575 of the 2,740 bins purchased were never used. Only five of the nine trucks purchased from Reuter were ever sent out on the road.

Just prior to Mario's conviction, two of his friends who were members of York Council, pleaded guilty to municipal corruption and breach of trust for their part in the Fairbank Park land scam. That project resulted in six of the eight members of York Council losing their seats in the 1991 election. Jim Fera got 18 months and was fined $25,000 for accepting more than $340,000 in bribes, including $219,000 in cash. Deputy Mayor Tony Mandarano got 15 months. In addition to his involvement with Lou Charles, he pleaded guilty to accepting a payoff from Paul Reuter. Apparently, the next part of the grand plan was to extend the automated garbage contract to the City of York. It never happened. By the way, both Paul Reuter and Lou Charles were also convicted for offering bribes and both did time.

After his conviction, Gentile had the arrogance to proclaim he would run again.

"Let a jury of 35,000 [the number of people in his ward] judge me!"

They did. When he ran for councillor in Ward 12, he finished third. They were a lot smarter than he was.

CHAPTER 27
Gender Neutral, or Gender Neutered?

After an eight-year-long battle, Councillor Marie Labatte won her fight to change the title "alderman" to "councillor." It happened on January 20, 1986, the first business meeting of North York Council after the municipal election.

Her attempt in the previous year, at the July 3, 1985 meeting of council, was a disaster.

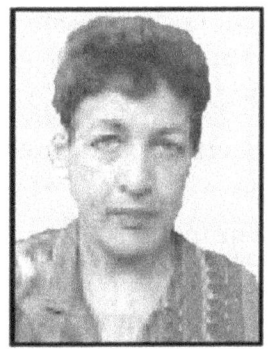
BEV SALMON

JUDY SGRO
[ONE OF THE BOYS]

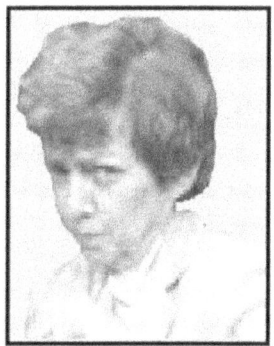
MARIE LABATTE

"Women want to be included in the English language," she said.

The men in council were stubbornly holding on to their masculinity. They argued vehemently against the change citing tradition and status. Bob Yuill, the resident Neanderthal, argued the term councillor was not appropriate for big city use. It was only for "hicks from the sticks."

Milton Berger, never one to be outdone by Yuill, was heard to quip, "Those members of council who are supposed to be women don't act like women."

Labatte's motion went down to defeat.

The resistance to change was intense. Between 1922, when North York Township was carved out of York Township, to 1967 when it became a "borough," members of council had been called "councillors." After 1967, they were referred to as "aldermen," a term that posed some considerable difficulty for female members. The '60s and '70s was a time of awakening gender consciousness, the age of feminism. The feminist movement, led by women like Gloria Steinem, was fighting to change the inherent bias in everyday life.

Nowhere was male bias more pronounced than in the field of politics. Women in Canada didn't gain the full right to vote and hold office until 1919 and not until as late as 1940 in Quebec.

Gender-specific language was a significant skirmish in that fight for equality. It was during this era that women began to insist on keeping their pre-married names after marriage and that "Miss" and "Mrs." be replaced by "Ms." The term "chairman" was replaced by "chair," which is the official term used in Toronto's procedural bylaw today.

The 1986 meeting was no less raucous. The motion to change the title was put forth by Councillor Bev Salmon and raged on until midnight. Mario Gentile, the alderman representing Ward 2, was a macho six-footer who was full of his masculinity. I kept goading him by referring to him as "Alderwoman Gentile" (pronounced Gen-tee-lay). As the meeting proceeded, he became increasingly agitated. He began pacing behind his seat all the while shouting: "I'll show you who's a man."

At this point, I wasn't quite sure whether he would pull down his pants or use his water jug to turn my head into a pizza.

"You seem to be upset," I replied, "Is it because you object to being referred to as a woman?"

"Yes." he yelled.

"Perhaps then you can understand how the women on this council feel about having to be referred to as a man."

It was as if a light bulb went on. Gentile apologized and then quite surprisingly voted to support the motion. The motion carried. His vote was the swing vote.

Was this a happy ending to a long shaggy dog story? Not quite yet.

Those members of council who had lost began to lobby to reverse the vote. They managed to convince Judy Sgro, a newly elected member of council, to sponsor a notice of motion to revert the title to alderman. Judy was elected in a by-election when Mario Gentile was appointed to the Board of Control. She was "one of the boys." Her first official act as a North York Councillor was going to be an anti-feminist move against the women on North York Council. The boys had the votes.

Luckily, it didn't happen. Whoever had framed the provincial legislation that allowed for a name change had anticipated such a move. They had wisely written a provision into law that limited the change to only once in a council term.

Marie Labatte was happy. I was happy on two counts. Firstly, I supported the change as a matter of principle. Secondly, I was in the sign business. They all had to re-print their election signs for the next election.

CHAPTER 28

Saturday Night Rip-Off

Maybe it's a character flaw, but I just don't like being ripped off and, by extension, I don't like seeing others being ripped off either. Call it the Ralph Nader Syndrome if you wish, but I have spent much of my political career trying to end scams. Apart from the fact nobody else wanted the job, it's probably why I have spent much of my political career in licensing, including stints as chair of the Metro Licensing Committee, chair of Licensing and Standards for the City of Toronto and quite a few years on the Metro Licensing Commission. I've tackled such diverse issues as ticketing schemes, tow truck scams, phoney charities, clothing drop boxes, sexploitation, rickshaw rip-offs and sundry other low-life schemes people invent to make a fast buck.

It started in 1979, shortly after I was first elected. I took my two young daughters to the Canadian National Exhibition. The CNE began as an agricultural fair in 1879 and morphed into an agricultural/industrial exposition where innovations like automobiles, electricity and electric streetcars were introduced to the people of Ontario. It is housed on a 192-acre lakefront site, Exhibition Place, which is owned and operated by the City of Toronto. It now includes a trade centre, hockey arena, soccer stadium and a number of exhibition buildings. It is operated by a board of directors and is partially funded by the City of Toronto. The CNE was then the summer holiday adventure of almost every kid in Toronto. It ended summer and signalled the fall return to school. Then, most teens in the city at one time or another spent the last two weeks of their summer working at the CNE.

The most important part of the CNE adventure for most kids is the midway. It was Saturday night and the midway was crowded. I bought $10 worth of tickets and gave my daughters three tickets each to ride the Wave Swinger. I had just turned around and they were behind me.

"Why aren't you going on the ride?" I asked.

"We've already been on it," they replied.

I looked around. All the rides seemed to have long lines and short times. Just a few turns and the passengers were dumped out. The next week, I came back with a stopwatch and began to clock the rides at different times. On Saturday evening, a 75-cent ride on the Wave Swinger lasted 55 seconds. The same ride on Sunday afternoon lasted 70 seconds and on Monday morning 99 seconds.

I ran checks on five rides. It turned out the average riding time for the five rides was 45 seconds on Saturday night, 57 seconds on Sunday afternoon and 102 seconds on Monday morning. On the basis of this sample, patrons of the CNE on the average got 56% less for their money on Saturday night than on Monday morning. I don't like people being taken for a ride.

I wrote to the board of the CNE association: "Many young people save all year to attend the Ex. Others work hard at summer jobs. The variable prices of midway rides are a blatant rip-off and I am asking the board to review their contract with Conklin Shows to ensure that patrons of the CNE get a fair deal."

I calculated that it was less expensive to fly Air Canada to Vancouver than it was to ride a midway attraction on a Saturday night and I urged the board to establish and post a minimum ride time for each attraction.

This was my first shit-disturbing adventure outside of the tight circle of North York politics. The timing couldn't have been better. The CNE happens during the doldrums of late summer.

No political body is in session and the newspapers are hungry for news, any kind of news. The CNE gets big play, much more play than it deserves and management at the CNE knows and depends on it to build attendance. That's why the Saturday Night Rip-Off Story got such big newspaper play.

Bill Mallatrat, general manager of the CNE, was miffed that I had broken the story to the media.

"Why didn't you come to me first?"

I knew better. I spent several years as president of the North York Elementary Teachers Federation. I had to deal with a host of school board officials and I knew how bureaucrats grind potential controversy into pablum. I'm sure if I had come to him first he would have brushed the matter aside or attempted to explain it away. For that exhibition, at least, he had to do something to adjust the ride times.

Later, when I became a Metro councillor, I was appointed to the board of the CNE. That, in itself, is no great accomplishment. Most of the rookie councillors get assigned to lesser civic bodies like the CNE. For me, it was a great thrill. I loved the Ex. At one time, on the last day of school every child in Toronto was issued a free pass to the Ex. As a youngster, I landed a job selling ice cream at the grandstand. I got to see all of the shows free. Later, as a teenager, I graduated to the midway hustling balloons or working one of the midway games. It was a great place to pick up girls.

The board of the CNE was as geriatric as the fair itself. It was a board of some 50 members, which meant very little of substance ever got decided at a board meeting. Some of the members, it seemed, had inherited the post from their grandfathers. Because I was under the age of 50, I was automatically considered an upstart radical. Board members were issued badges that looked like military medals and directors wore them on their chests during the fair. It puffed up their importance. I referred to mine as my Victoria Cross. Along with the post came free admission to the grounds for my car and all its passengers, plus access to a free dining room every night of the fair. Even Rob Ford (Mr. Stop the Gravy Train) enjoyed the gravy at the Ex.

The solution to the midway rip-off was easy. Establish a one-price wristband that would admit the purchaser to all of the rides. It didn't matter how long a ride lasted if you could ride it as many times as you wanted.

I learned some valuable lessons that summer. If you want to get anything done in politics you have to develop a healthy disrespect for authority. If you want real change, the normal channels don't usually work. Don't be afraid to challenge the norms. Secondly, people like politicians who are "in your face." They want political representatives who are willing to fight against things, big and small, that they know are wrong and are willing to speak out about them. I never forgot that during the 32 years I was in office.

CHAPTER 29
Wheel-Trans Not for Burning

The '60s was a period when minority groups became aggressive in asserting their rights. The Viet Nam War sparked the protest movement in the United States and one of the spin-offs from the war was the fight for disabled rights. That era saw thousands of disabled veterans returning to a nation that was ill-equipped to accommodate them. They had sacrificed their health and limbs for their country and rightfully demanded their country give something back to them. That era of protest culminated in the Americans With Disabilities Act, 1990, which laid down some basic rights of access for disabled Americans.

In the face of intense political lobbying, American cities began to provide for the disabled by adapting their transit systems to accommodate disabled riders and establishing separate transit systems for those they were unable to fit into the regular system. In Canada, the spill over of those efforts resulted in the establishment of the Wheel-Trans system by the TTC in 1975.  Wheel-Trans was operated by a company called All-Way Transport under contract to the TTC and provided service for about 5,200 passengers a day. It ran a fleet of some 62 Mighty-Mite buses that provided a door-to-door service for the disabled community.

I first became interested in the Wheel-Trans system when on New Year's Day, 1987, one of their Mighty-Mite buses burst into flames. One of my constituents, who was on the bus, called me to complain. I wrote to the TTC urging them to take the remaining 47 vehicles off the road and have them inspected by the Ministry of Transport. The response I got from Alf Savage, the chief general manager, was that the fleet was in good condition and there had only been a minor incident on one of the buses. This was contrary to a tip I received from one of the drivers, George Robitaille. He called to advise me that six of the buses had burned to the ground and the others were falling apart.

"George, if I am going to pursue this issue with any credibility I need to have hard evidence. I can't just go around calling Alf Savage a liar. Without hard evidence, we have no case."

"No problem," he replied. "I will pick you up at your home tomorrow night at 8 p.m."

Under cover of darkness, we snuck into the All-Way compound in Scarborough armed with a flashlight and a camera. On January 23, George and I appeared before the commission waving photographs of deteriorating buses, including photos of faulty wiring, loose insulation, rusting bodies, broken door latches, bald tires, broken windshield wipers, frayed seat belts and faulty emergency brakes. George told the commission of having to refuse to take out two buses one morning until he found one that was safe to drive. The first had a broken emergency brake and a cardboard panel that had been installed behind the brake pedal 15 cm behind the firewall. Behind the cardboard panel was a huge conglomeration of wire held together with tape. The second bus had a broken emergency brake.

Before we attended the commission meeting, I had asked the North York fire chief to advise me if there had been any Wheel-Trans incidents. His report confirmed that fire vehicles had attended six fires on Wheel-Trans buses. There was a seventh fire the day before the commission meeting.

Under the All-Way contract, awarded in 1980, the company was to replace the vehicles every six years. The contract was in its seventh year and they were running the same worn out buses.

The very next day, Rhona Mickleson, a paraplegic university student, had to be rescued from a Wheel-Trans bus after the lift caught fire. She agreed to appear with me before the next commission meeting. Ms. Mickleson told me Raymond Hould, the manager of All-Way, had telephoned her and toward the end of a bizarre, hour-long conversation, had offered her a position as a "consultant." She said he told her if she would co-operate "they would be willing to make it worth her while." We appeared before the commission and demanded the operation of disabled transit system be taken over by the TTC.

It wasn't the first time. Several years before these incidents, there was widespread dissatisfaction in the disabled community about the reliability of the Wheel-Trans dispatch system. The community was so unhappy they organized a protest march down Yonge Street to TTC headquarters at Davisville. The dispatch system was brought in-house. It was now time to end this public/private partnership (I called it a public/pirate partnership) and bring the entire system under TTC operation. The Transit Commission passed the issue over to Metro Council.

Politics is like theatre. "The willing suspension of disbelief" is a dramatic device that playwrights employ. Once you have convinced the audience that something absurd is possible then all things that follow from that are also possible. In politics, it is used to ignore the obvious. Most politicians view the world through glasses that are coloured by their ideology. Councillors on the left would look favourably on the prospect of a municipally run service. Those on the right would be pre-disposed to a contracted-out service and then there were all those in between.

The company hired lobbyist Jim Fleming to win the hearts

and minds of the mushy middle. Fleming had been a Liberal Member of Parliament representing the riding of York West between 1971 and 1984. For a brief period, he served as Minister of State for Multiculturalism in the Trudeau Cabinet. He was good. You could see his work reflected in some of the speeches made by mushy middle members of council. Allan Tonks, the mayor of York, spoke eloquently about the fine service record of this company.

"The contractor has been doing an excellent job," said Tonks, who had the benefit of a two-hour meeting with All-Way officials.

Never mind that by this time we had fire department reports of 12 fires on the buses and that six of them had burned to the ground. Never mind that the buses were falling apart from lack of maintenance and that you wouldn't be allowed to operate them in a mountain village in Colombia. Never mind that the company had tried to bribe Rhona Mickleson.

"Bribe? Not at all," averred Richard McGraw, company president. "We were trying to debrief her because we wanted to know what went on in the interests of our commitment to safety. It's very easy to get dramatic about issues dealing with the disabled. They get blown out of proportion."

Some of the mushy middlers tried to have the issue deferred, but Al Leach, the TTC's new chief general manager, would have nothing to do with it. He said a decision in principle was required now because any delay would force them to negotiate an extension to the present contract and the TTC would be at a considerable disadvantage. An amendment to get a study of the cost and benefits of TTC takeover was passed, but the takeover was adopted in principle by council by one vote.

Once that decision was made, there was no turning back. The lobbying continued, but the TTC staff position began to shift. Wheel-Trans manager Alan Hewson, who had previously defended the safety of the Mighty Mites, began to muse about taking them off the road. By the time the final reports hit the transportation committee four months later it was a foregone conclusion. Yes, we would have to build a $25 million service garage and yes, Wheel-Trans operating costs would go up, but the committee voted unanimously to approve the takeover. It was a major turning point. At last we could assure the disabled a safe ride in Toronto.

CHAPTER 30
Pays the Piper

There's no question the outcome of political decisions create wealth. Governments award contracts, determine land use and make the rules within which businesses operate. It's not surprising then that more than a desire for "good government" motivates financial support for candidates. The snap of an official plan amendment can turn a vacant lot into a high-rise. In the '60s, the decade before I was elected, North York was the Wild West in terms of campaign contributions. They were all under the table because there were no rules and the temptations were huge. If you want to find municipal corruption, look at any municipality where urban sprawl is gobbling up farmland. The value of land in those municipalities is often determined by the route of a municipal trunk sewer. Municipalities that are rapidly developing often have cockroaches under every rock and some of the best politicians that money can buy.

It was common to find people like real estate and insurance brokers seeking public office. Hey, if you can underwrite a builder's insurance policy on a new subdivision you might feel warm and fuzzy when that subdivision comes up for approval. Who's to know? You want stakes to hold up your election signs? One telephone call to a builder will bring you a truckload. North York Councillor Irv Chapley used to brag to me that after an election campaign he had enough money left over to buy a new Lincoln Continental.

I don't want to overstate the extent of the political rot. The majority of civic politicians were honest, sincere people doing their utmost to serve their community. In my seven years on North York Council, only two North York councillors were jailed for municipal corruption. One was tossed off council for corrupt practices and one civic official, the planning commissioner, Bruce Davidson, was fired for accepting a questionable loan from developer Lou Charles to purchase his $530,000 home in Thornhill. Lou was later jailed for bribing civic officials. That represents a total of only six people; that is six people who were caught red handed. We, of course, don't know how many went undetected.

The provincial government brought in election financing reform for provincial elections in 1984. Under that legislation, the financing of provincial campaigns was overseen by an election expenses commission. Bernard Nayman, a North York chartered accountant, was the most experienced election finance auditor in the province. He was the NDP appointee to the commission and had been for 10 years. Unlike the other parties that allowed their ridings to select their own auditors,

BERNARD NAYMAN, AUDITOR

Bernie was engaged to do every NDP riding in the province. The provincial reforms were so successful that we were determined to bring them to the municipal level as well. Bernie approached me and we worked together to design a municipal election finance package that could be made to work at the municipal level.

In 1984, we brought the proposed municipal election reform package to the North York legislation committee and, to my great surprise, the committee agreed to forward the plan to North York staff for review. The plan included: property tax or cash rebates for contributors to municipal campaigns, complete disclosure of contributors over $100, municipal financing for candidates who garnered over 15% of the vote, and a $500 limit on donations to any one candidate. For the first time, a system that bought accountability to municipal election campaigns was proposed. In July of 1984, council debated the controversial legislation. The only parts we could actually legislate by local bylaw were the disclosure clauses.

There were three members of North York Council who spoke against them. The fiercest opposition came from Alderman Andy Borins who argued:

"All you're going to be doing is giving ammunition to a political enemy to come at you in a very unsavoury way," he told council. "By forcing disclosure of campaign contributions, North York politicians are leaving themselves open to charges of conflict of interest should they vote in favour of proposals made by contributors."

He was right. On April 16, 1985, a divisional court judge stripped Borins of his seat on North York Council finding him guilty of conflict of interest charges.

Councillor Esther Shiner opposed the disclosure. She claimed her list of contributors would become a "hit" list for other politicians.

North York only had the power to legislate the disclosure provisions. In order to give tax credits to contributors and for the public funding component we needed provincial legislation. Alderman Berger argued that we should wait for the province. Notwithstanding the objections, council solidly endorsed the proposal.

It was a real turnaround. Why? The endorsement came in the shadow of the firing of Planning Commissioner Bruce Davidson and the city was facing an upcoming consultant's probe of the planning department. There's nothing like a spotlight to sharpen your sensitivities.

Former Toronto Mayor John Sewell wrote in the Globe and Mail: "I think the political tenor of North York is beginning to change, to climb out of the pro development mood that has hobbled it for so long. That's something many North York councillors can sense and they are unlikely to abandon this bylaw now that they know the public is watching."

The 1985 election was the first time candidates in North York were required to file their election spending and contributions. It was revealing in several ways. The highest spending aldermanic candidate was Mario Gentile, who spent the most – $28,496 – even though he was acclaimed. The law specified that candidates who failed to file their list of contributors and expenses within the 90-day period following the election could be charged with corrupt practices and fined up to $2,000. An incumbent could also be removed from office. While all of those who had been elected filed returns, 27 of the 64 candidates who had run for office failed to file returns. When the matter came before the Board of Control, the controllers and mayor lined up to demonstrate the depth of their commitment to campaign disclosure.

Robert Yuill; "They feel badly enough as it is about losing without the victors bringing them more misery by trying to run them into court over an expense account. Mr. Moscoe is kicking them when they're down."

Esther Shiner wrung her hands in sympathy for the losers, whom she had just spent three months bashing on the campaign trail.

"I can't go along with going after these poor losers, many of who ran on a pittance, and may not even realize they have to file reports," she said.

As it turns out, a major flaw in the bylaw was that it was written in a way that put the duty on "electors" to enforce the bylaw and not the city to take them to court. It was unenforceable.

Another problem was what to do about campaign surpluses? Mel Lastman had raised $108,160 but had only spent $95,249. He had the difficult problem of having to find a home for a $13,000 surplus. There were no rules. He could have, if he wished, used it as a down payment on his next Cadillac. The bylaw had to be fixed, but clearly, that wasn't going to happen in North York.

In 1986, the Ontario Minister of Municipal Affairs struck a special advisory committee on election reforms. It was co-chaired by Anne Johnston, a former Toronto councillor, and Gerald Parisien, former mayor of Cornwall. After two years of consultation and discussion, the draft legislation that resulted from this report made the reporting of municipal election contributions mandatory, and it adopted the tax rebate scheme that Bernie Nayman and I had proposed earlier. Suddenly, many of the same North York politicians who had supported election reform under the spotlight of the Bruce Davidson investigation and firing weren't so sure about public financing of municipal elections.

The rules were introduced in a workshop at the Association of Municipalities Ontario (AMO) conference in August.

"I'm hearing things today that I've not heard before," said an irate Hazel McCallion. "This is going to cause a lot of problems."

"I think the legislation is far too complicated," quipped Nancy Porteous, a councillor from Brampton. "We're lay people but you are trying to make us into lawyers… or accountants."

Nancy became neither a lawyer nor an accountant. She went on to become a lobbyist for the waste management industry. I pointed out that every politician who ran for office had to learn the rules of the game. There's nothing new in that. If you can't understand the election rules, how could you possibly grapple with the complexities of a municipal budget? The public should know who is funding the election campaigns of their elected representatives.

Municipal government is close to the people, but it's also close to the development industry too.

The legislation that emerged provided for mandatory disclosure of contributors, but it offered the choice to municipalities of opting into Part III of the Act, which is the section offering tax credits for contributors. Under Part III, donors who gave $100 to a municipal candidate received a $75 rebate either on their property taxes or as a refund cheque from the municipal clerk.

North York was the first municipality in Metro to wrestle with the decision to opt in or out. Council's decision to opt out earned it a dart from the Toronto Star:

For rejecting a sensible proposal to give property tax credits of up to $350 to people for contributing to municipal election campaigns.

"If you can't get money, don't run. If you need money, go to your relatives," says Councillor Milton Berger. Unfortunately too many local politicians are turning instead to wealthy developers with a clear self-interest in getting their candidates elected. The only way to prevent that – and to stop giving the advantage to incumbents with huge ward chests – is to encourage small donations from the public with a tax credit system.

In the 1988 elections that followed, only two municipal bodies opted into Part III. They were the North York Board of Education and the Oakville Hydro Commission."

After the dust had settled on the election of 1988, the resulting data it generated hit the media fan. The legislation had more loopholes than a piece of lace. In the first place, the maximum of $750 that a single donor could contribute to a candidate didn't, for one moment, limit development money. Most developers build each project under a separate numbered company. A developer could give a $750 donation from each numbered company. A Globe and Mail review revealed that in growth municipalities more than 74% of the contributions given to incumbents was from the development industry. Furthermore, while there were restrictions on the funds a candidate raised during the campaign period, there were no restrictions on fundraising outside of the campaign period.

The legislation was an open-ended invitation to corruption.

While there were restrictions on what you could spend, there were no restrictions on what you could raise. As a result, candidates racked up huge surpluses, which they were free to use at their own discretion. In this election, Mel Lastman had a surplus of $26,000. Many developer-friendly mayors and councillors throughout Toronto and the GTA racked up equally impressive amounts. It left them scrambling to explain to the media what they were going to do with their extra cash. Allan Tonks, the Metro Chairman, said he would use his $14,641 surplus to "sponsor a sports team, buying trophies and pay for raffle and anniversary tickets." The most honest answer was given by Fred Beavis, a long-time Toronto councillor. He told the Globe and Mail he was going to use his $14,987 surplus to buy a used car and travel to Florida.

What did he care... he was defeated.

I told the Toronto Star in an interview: "I had a $6,000 surplus that I used to clear up my debts from the previous election, but I don't feel good about it, and I would gladly endorse a requirement that forced all councillors into Part III so the money could go to support the electoral system rather than the candidates.... The only way to make it fair is to force all councils in larger centres into Part III."

In the face of the wave of public criticism, the Ministry of Municipal Affairs and Housing struck a task force to review the legislation. As the chair of the Large Urban Section, I represented AMO on the task force. We managed to close most of the loopholes: All municipalities were forced into Part III of the Act; campaign surpluses were to be held in trust by the clerk and returned to the candidate to be used in the next election; if the candidate did not run, the funds were absorbed by the city.

Later, the Act was amended so that unused contributions were retained by the city to help finance the rebate program.

It became illegal to raise funds between election periods.

Donations from associated companies were considered to be

a single donation with an overall maximum of $5,000 to all candidates. If a candidate failed to disclose contributions, he was automatically disqualified from running in the next election.

Campaigns were subject to audit, and arm's length audit committees at local councils could audit a campaign and were required to lay charges for violation of the Act. Politicians found guilty of violating the provisions of the Act could be removed from office.

The amended legislation became the basis for all future municipal elections in the Province of Ontario. Is the Act perfect? Not by a long shot, but at least the system is now open and transparent. If you go to the City of Toronto website you can track every contribution made to each Toronto candidate from your home computer.

In the last decade, Councillor Michael Walker led the fight against corporate and union donations. In 2006, the City of Toronto Act was amended to give Toronto the authority to ban them. Subsequently, the city amended its election bylaw to prohibit donations to candidates from corporations and unions.

Does the development industry still have influence in municipal elections? They will always find some way to weasel their way around a legislative barrier. While Walker's amendment was well intended, what it did was drive corporate donations underground. Industry donations are now given in the names of individuals who are the owners, directors and lawyers for development companies. Now, in order to track developer contributions you have to know who they are. It kind of muddied the transparency.

The Toronto media were happy. Their crusade to close the loopholes succeeded. But the happiest of all was the guy who started it – Bernie Nayman. He had thousands of new campaigns to audit.

CHAPTER 31
Good Party, Great Cucumber Sandwiches

The "Bad Neighbour Relations" fight with the Canadian Imperial Bank of Commerce (CIBC) happened in 1980, shortly after I was first elected. As part of that campaign, I bought a single share in the CIBC. The plan was to carry our neighbourhood fight to the bank's annual meeting. After our settlement, I tossed my share into a drawer.

In 1982, Canada was hit by double-digit inflation. Mortgage rates soared to 18% and people were losing their homes and farms as the banks began to foreclose on defunct mortgages. Every day, the media reported on some related event, like the time a group of farmers in southwestern Ontario deposited their dead cows on the doorstep of their local bank. I received a number of pleas for help from constituents who were losing their homes or just couldn't afford to pay their property taxes. While I could get the city to forestall action on property taxes, there wasn't really much I could do about the mortgages.

As an advocate for my constituents, I was becoming increasingly frustrated. In one case, I spoke with the local CIBC manager on behalf of a resident who was about to lose his home. She really was in no position to do anything that would put her at odds with bank policy.

That same day, as a shareholder, I received at my home a mailing from the CIBC inviting me to attend the annual shareholders meeting on Thursday, January 21, at Commerce Court. I noted that in the prospectus there were two propositions before the meeting that annoyed me. The first was a proposal that Russell Harrison, Commerce chair and chief executive officer, be advanced a loan of $225,482 at an interest rate of 6¼%. This compared to the prevailing rates of 17% at the time. J.A. Hillier, vice-chair, had a mortgage at 5.61%. The second proposal before the meeting was to increase the remuneration for bank directors by 37.5%.

I fired off an open letter to Mr. Harrison: "I question the morality of these transactions at a time when the bank is standing by and watching its customers lose their homes, businesses and farms. Bank profits ballooned last year by more than 61%. How can a responsible bank profit so much from the same high rates that rob people of their homes?"

I went on to add: "At a time when average Canadian wages increased by just 10.8% – less than the rate of inflation – how can a 'responsible' bank allow its directors to vote themselves a 35.7% wage increase?"

Garth Turner, business editor of the Toronto Sun, ran a column based on my letter. His message was, if you are not happy with what the banks are doing don't gripe to me. Buy a share, attend their annual meeting and exercise your right to tell them yourself.

"Like teacher and North York Alderman Howard Moscoe, for example, who is bound to make a large smell at the Bank of Commerce gathering later this month. Moscoe owns some shares. [It was actually only one share.] He also is a disturber.... He is alleging that the Commerce has walked all over a commitment it made last year to be socially responsible."

I hadn't actually intended to go to the annual meeting, but Garth Turner's column – Bank Hater? Strike Back. HIT 'EM

WITH YOUR BEST SHOT – forced me to hit the mattresses. I would have been too embarrassed and lost too much face not to go.

I had some heavy-duty preparation to do. I had never attended a shareholder's meeting, but I was nervously confident. In the past, I had been a delegate to a lot of my teacher union annual meetings. I was fairly conversant with parliamentary procedure and had even been deputy speaker at the last teachers' annual assembly in Hamilton. Besides, three years of sparring with Lastman at North York Council meetings had taught me something about parliamentary procedure, even under the convoluted rules that North York used.

I bought a copy of the Bank Act and spent a couple of nights marking and tagging it, the same kind of preparation I usually did for a council meeting. I even went down to Commerce Court to pick up the copy of the bank's bylaws, which I studied.

After reading the Bank Act, I thought I might need a seconder for my motions. That meant I had to find another shareholder willing to aid and abet my efforts. I talked my so-called "radical" colleague, Alderman Mike Foster, into joining me. Foster was not a member of this shareholder club, but after telephoning around I found a Dr. Philip Berger, who ran an AIDS clinic in Riverdale and was willing to give Foster his proxy. We were all set to go.

On the day of the meeting, I donned my best blue suit, tucked the legislation and bylaws into my briefcase and ambled down to Commerce Court with Mike Foster in tow clutching his proxy. The media were gathered at the entrance to Commerce Hall in droves. (Cameras were not allowed inside.) When we checked in at the desk, we learned Foster had forgotten to register his proxy. Oops! Not only had I lost my seconder, but Foster, my undaunted partner, lost his courage. He wouldn't sit with me and slunk off to the back of the room where he tried to make himself inconspicuous. Without a seconder, would I be able to put motions?

Picture this. The bulk of the audience was made up of some 300 men in blue suits; the annual meeting was a command performance. Managers from across the city were expected to attend. Sprinkled amongst them were some 60 matrons with blue-rinsed hair sporting grey mink stoles. I sat beside one of them near an aisle next to a microphone. Scattered about the room, but mostly at the back, were about 50 or 60 ordinary shareholders, some of them there for the refreshments served at the conclusion of what would normally be a 40-minute event. Towards the west end of the auditorium were some 20 activists, including nuns and clergy who had come to the meeting to raise issues of social responsibility.

The front row of the middle section was made up of the bank's directors. That included such notables as Iron Ore president Brian Mulroney; Argus Corporation's Conrad Black; grocery mogul Galen Weston, former Ontario Treasurer Darcy McKeough, Jack Gallagher of Dome Petroleum, and Alf Powis, president of Noranda. Presiding over the meeting, on stage, was Chair Russell Harrison. He called the meeting to order.

I rose to my feet.

"Point of order Mr. Chairman," I said. "Which rules of order will we be using at this meeting; Sturgis's, Bourinot's or Robert's?"

He snapped back: "We are going to use the same rules of order that we have been using for the past one hundred and sixteen years."

Zap! Gotcha!

"Looking for a motion to approve the minutes of last year's meeting," he said.

"Point of order Mr. Chairman," I said. "I call for a recorded vote."

"By what authority?"

I reached into my briefcase and pulled out my copy of the Bank Act, turned to tab 1 and replied:

"By Article III, Section 5, subsection ii (c) of the Bank Act" (or something like that.)

He turned to the three solicitors at the tables to his right on the stage. They sagely, somewhat sadly, nodded their heads up and down.

"Point of order Mr. Chairman," I said. "I note in the minutes that all motions have a mover and a seconder, but there were no seconders to the nominations for director positions."

"We don't require a seconder for nominations to the board," he retorted.

Presto: I could now nominate Foster and myself for election to the board. I didn't require a seconder.

A word about the Bank Act: The section that allowed any shareholder to demand a recorded vote (whatever its real number) was a protection for the bank. It was enacted to prevent the minority shareholders from taking over a meeting. For me, it meant I had the right to a written ballot on every vote. A 40-minute meeting suddenly became a 2½-hour extravaganza.

After some routine business and several recorded votes, we came to the matter of deciding on the directors' remuneration. The motion was put and I rose to make the following amendment:

"Be it resolved that the motion be amended to limit the increase in director remuneration to the same percentage increase as other bank employees in 1981. Be it further resolved that the increase be only given to directors who actually attended meetings."

Then, with my heart in my mouth, I added: "Looking for a seconder."

Without Foster's proxy, I had no other choice. It seemed that five minutes went by. I'm sure it was only a few seconds, when someone at the back of the room rose to his feet.

"Herman Zilch, from Guelph, seconds that motion."

The room groaned. It was apparently one of the shareholders who had been inspired by Garth Turner's column to attend the meeting. He was adding his voice to the chorus of people across the country that was fed up with the arrogance of the banks. I now had a seconder for all of my motions. I then proceeded to speak calmly and dispassionately for "ordinary Canadians."

Harrison couldn't resist asking: "Do you consider yourself an ordinary Canadian?"

The grey-haired lady in the mink stole who sat at my left looked up at me and asked me if I held any stock in other banks. From that point on, the debate was spirited with a number of the small shareholders and social activists joining in. The bank, for the first time in a couple of decades, had a lively annual meeting.

The bank's public affairs department was stymied. Never once could they mention I owned a single share. That would have implied they placed no value on the contributions of small shareholders. They sunk to a real low when they quietly circulated to a few selected journalists the suggestion that my salary as an alderman had increased by 40% over the last five years. It looked plausible, except that I had only been an alderman for two years.

When the nominations for directors came up on the agenda, I nominated Mike Foster and myself. That forced a written ballot. Needless to say, we were not elected.

Garth Turner, in his follow-up column, was quick to point out: "Moscoe didn't succeed yesterday in the Great Commerce Hall of the Great Commerce Court West Tower in changing one hair of bank policy. And neither did other shareholders made bold by the alderman's brashness."

Actually, it was Turner's column that made them bold. But they did force Harrison into disclosing the purpose of his own low-cost bank loans and into revealing the lobbying practices the bank used with Toronto politicians.

Did I expect to win any of the votes? Not a chance. There are presently some 400,000,000 common shares issued in the CIBC. I knew the bank had millions of shares in proxies and could have voted down any proposal. Heck, the front row alone could probably have voted down the room a thousand times over. The point we made, loudly and clearly, was that banks are abysmally unresponsive. They are run like private clubs.

How important is public opinion to the bank?

If it wasn't important, why do the CIBC and other banks spend so many millions on advertising? Why does the CIBC go to the bother of hiring Anne Murray to sing about what a good neighbour they are?

Turner goes on to say: "On the surface, nothing much has changed but underneath I'm not so sure."

I'm pretty sure not much has changed.

The meeting adjourned and I stepped outside into the biggest media scrum of my political career. Everyone else moved into the adjacent hall for tea and cucumber sandwiches. The sandwiches were delicious; the tea was cold.

CHAPTER 32
The Big Move

Boards of Control were an anachronism that dated back to the early part of the 20th century. They arose at a time when most municipally elected councils were part-time. Boards of Control acted as a check on the power of the mayor. The Board of Control oversaw money matters and could only be overruled by a two-thirds majority of council on financial matters. They functioned like a council executive. As councillor positions grew into full-time jobs, Boards of Control were abolished. The last one, in London Ontario, was dissolved in 2010.

In Toronto, election to a Board of Control automatically gave you a seat on Metro Council. Because controllers were elected citywide, voters tended to elect people who had enough money to fund an expensive citywide campaign, or had high profiles. Two North York politicos elected directly to the Board of Control were Mel Lastman and Barbara Green. Mel was a salesman whose public profile was built on a series of publicity stunts designed to sell appliances. He would dress in a mini-skirt and create a riot on Yonge Street by standing on a corner and selling $5 bills for $2. He once sold a refrigerator to an Inuit. His high public profile catapulted him into a seat on the North York Board of Control in 1969. The publicity stunts and the Lastman hustle continued until he became mayor of North York in 1972 and beyond.

Barbara Green's profile was built on a challenge to a North York bylaw that said it was against the law for two or more unrelated people to live together in a single-family neighbourhood. Barbara and two other single women were busted by North York because they had rented a house together. Their much-publicized fight against the city landed Barbara a seat on the Board of Control in 1974, and Katie Hayhurst, another of the three women, was elected as a ward alderman in the same year. Their case went all the way to the Supreme Court, which quashed the North York zoning bylaw restriction in 1979 and along with it, every similar zoning bylaw in Canada. Barbara kept fighting, but this time it was Mel Lastman instead of a zoning bylaw. She quickly became a pebble in Mel Lastman's shoe. She spoke out for tenants, low-income people and the downtrodden in North York and was constantly at odds with other controllers.

The 1985 election in North York was the year of the big shuffle. Barbara Green got tired of waiting and decided to challenge Mel's grip on his Lastmanship's position. That left a vacant seat on the Board of Control. I was contemplating a run for controller, but before I could announce, Mike Foster, my friend and fellow NDP councillor, jumped me and held a press conference to announce he was seeking a seat on the Board of Control. I was pissed off, but bit my lip and prepared for my re-election campaign as alderman in Ward 4. I did my fundraising, printed my "re-elect Alderman Howard Moscoe signs" and prepared my first election brochure.

Two weeks into the campaign, Bill Sutherland announced he was retiring, leaving another seat on the Board of Control vacant. It was agonizing. Should I risk what was probably a safe seat as the alderman for Ward 4 or take a flier on a Board of Control shot? Should I take the financial gamble? There was no time to raise funds for a Board of Control campaign. If I lost, I would be heavily in debt. Gloria and I agonized about the decision all day. That night, along with some of our campaign team, I went out for a late dinner to Kwong Chow Restaurant in Chinatown. Kwong Chow was a popular hangout upstairs at the corner of Elizabeth and Dundas Streets, just north of City Hall. A lot of political decisions have been made there over a cup of tea and an egg roll. At about midnight, I cracked open a fortune cookie. It said:

That was it. I was at the Teachers' Credit Union when it opened the next morning. I walked in and borrowed $15,000, went to my campaign office, trashed my signs and campaign literature and announced my run for a Board of Control seat.

"I'm running because there's a vacancy on the board and when I look at some of the people on the board I see that they too have vacancies.... If there is anything that the board lacks now it's a social conscience. There needs to be someone who will put the heart back into North York."

Mike Foster wasn't happy, but he had no cause to complain. There were two vacancies on the board; it was a legitimate run. Yes, I hadn't consulted him, but neither had he consulted me before announcing. We had a tense peace conference that afternoon and agreed we would run as a team (sort of). We wouldn't go after each other on the campaign trail and my sign crews would erect some of his signs in the east end while his would put up some of mine in the west. I kind of got the feeling there were more Foster than Moscoe signs in some parts of the city west of Yonge Street.

I announced the first plank in my campaign platform. I would work to abolish the Board of Control.

"If you want to abolish the Board of Control why are you running for it?" I was asked.

"It's the only game in town; the only way for me to get a seat on Metro Council. If reform is going to take place, it has to be orchestrated from downtown. Besides, if both Mike Foster and I get elected you can be sure that North York Council itself will vote to abolish the Board of Control and Lastman will lead them on the issue."

As first-time controller candidates, we were at a distinct disadvantage. Incumbents, over time, build up lists of sign locations on private property where the owners are willing to allow them to place their signs. Except for arterial road locations in your own ward, a new candidate starts with a blank list. Mike Foster solved that problem by buying billboards. It was the first time a Board of Control candidate had used billboards in a North York campaign. Billboards are a very expensive undertaking, but there had been enough time for Foster to raise campaign donations. I hadn't.

You can't now, but at that time a candidate was allowed to place election signs on public property. I wouldn't. It was a wasted effort. The minute you erected one of your campaign signs at an intersection your opponents and everyone else immediately surrounded it with their own signs. Every intersection sprouted a forest of signs. There was so much sign static that nobody could read any of them. Instead, we resolved to only erect signs on private property, where we had exclusive access. That prompted us to develop a fast way of building a presence on arterial roads. How I managed to get so many arterial sign locations on private lawns still has my opponents mystified.

It requires two cars, a van, me and three other people. The truck is filled with election signs, wooden stakes and sign equipment. Sheppard Avenue is about 20 kilometres from Weston Road to Victoria Park. I would park my car on the first residential block and work my way door-to-door asking each house if I could put my sign on their lawn. When I found my first location, the second driver would join me on the doorstep and fill out a location slip with the name, address and telephone number of the householder. I would stop working that block and quickly drive to the next one and repeat the process until I had the next sign location. The record keeper would wait until the sign crew arrived to erect the sign and would drive ahead to join me in the next block. That way, we would hop skip our way from east to west across North York and develop an instant sign presence on Sheppard Avenue. We also had a Sheppard Avenue location list for the next election. When Sheppard Avenue was finished, we would tackle a north-south street.

Within two weeks, we had a highly visible sign presence all over North York. During the campaign, a volunteer would telephone each of the locations to ensure the signs were still in good shape and we were able to dispatch repair crews to repair or replace them. You knew you had a winning sign campaign when your opponents began tearing down signs at night. It was annoying, but I had an advantage over other candidates. I could easily replace my damaged signs. We were printing them ourselves in a sign shop in my basement.

The election results were as shown.

North York Board of Control (four members elected)

Candidate	Total votes	% votes
(x) Esther Shiner	67,345	19.47
(x) Robert Yuill	53,709	15.53
(x) Norman Gardner	51,137	14.78
(x) Howard Moscoe	42,303	12.23
Mike Foster	35,838	10.36
Frank Esposito	21,365	6.18
Bruce Davidson	18,926	5.47
Sonnee Cohen	12,822	3.71

Bernadette Michael	12,764	3.69
Angelo Natale	12,416	3.59
Cora Urbel	7,791	2.25
Arthur Zins	4,961	1.43
Ayube Ally	4,571	1.32
Total valid votes	345,948	100.00

Why did Mike Foster get 6,400 fewer votes than I did? I don't think it had anything to do with our platforms or our profiles. When a voter has four votes to spend, they cast them for a variety of reasons. Name recognition is a significant factor, but ethnicity is also a consideration. North York has a significant Jewish population. Four of the candidates were Jewish – Shiner, Gardiner, Moscoe and Cohen. Foster was not. If you break the vote down on a geographic basis, you can see that the Jewish vote made the difference.

I had another ethnic edge – one Chinese fortune cookie.

CHAPTER 33
Furniture Brings Out the Bad Boy in Me

GREEN WITH ENVY

So, there I was victorious; now a controller. The aldermen's offices were cubbyholes grouped around an open office area at the front of the political section. I had finally made it to the Board of Control, which meant I had scored one of the four spacious controller offices in the "executive suite" at the rear of the building. Along with his job, I had also inherited Bill Sutherland's office. I strode proudly into my new office and stopped dead in my tracks. It was filled with furniture that would have been refused by the Sally Ann thrift shop.

The vultures (my fellow controllers) had swooped down, carted away everything useful and had filled my new office with junk. The couch in Bob Yuill's office looked suspiciously like the one that had previously occupied the Sutherland office. The desk was gone and I could swear there were faint drag marks in the carpet leading to Norm Gardiner's office. Who knows where the lamp and the other furniture had gone?

I ordered staff to remove everything in my new office to the basement loading dock and spent the weekend putting together a budget of $5,000 to properly furnish the office. It was presented at the first Board of Control meeting. Talk about indignation. You would think I had proposed a massive property tax increase to furnish my digs. The board indignantly refused and each controller in turn lectured me about the need to be frugal with "taxpayer's money."

Undaunted, I launched into Plan B. For my desk, I used a bridge table and chair. The couch was fashioned from a row of upturned milk cartons and orange crates were enlisted to hold files and books. The lamp was a single bare bulb that I hung on a cord from the ceiling. I then gave media tours of my new office and invited them to visit my furniture in the other offices. When questioned about the couch, Bob Yuill mumbled something about Bill Sutherland having given it to him before he left. Sure thing! At the next board of control meeting, they were shamed into voting me money for furnishings, but instead of the full amount, they would relinquish only $3,500.

"This is not a luxury operation," said Yuill.

That initiated Plan C. I was determined to have an office with flare. After all, I was an art teacher and knew something about design. I spent the rest of the week shopping and designed the office around a plush rose-coloured loveseat with oak trim. It was the one expensive item. I purchased it at the Bad Boy store on Finch Avenue. At the back of my mind, I hoped Mel, who owned the Bad Boy stores, might have to declare a conflict of interest. I found lovely neutral grass wallpaper on sale at a discount outlet, some oak moulding on special at a lumber yard, loaded my car with brushes, paint, wallpaper paste, my mitre saw and other tools and snuck into City Hall. I spent Saturday and Sunday painting, papering and installing an oak chair rail and wainscoting around the perimeter walls. I probably violated two collective agreements that weekend. On Monday, I gave media tours of my new décor. The other controllers were blue from anger and green with envy.

ROSE-COLOURED LOVESEAT

In 1989, three years later, the system of governance in Toronto was changed. Metro Council became directly elected and Boards of Control were recognized for the dinosaurs they were and were disbanded. That election set up a seething resentment of the Metro government by North York Council. North York councillors not only lost the hand they had in determining the larger services, but the salary that went with it. They had all but declared war on their Metro colleagues, who were considered persona non grata at official events in North York. North York staff was specifically directed to grant no favours or assistance to Metro councillors.

Metro established temporary offices for the new Metro Council in a building at 390 Bay Street at the corner of Queen Street. We used the Toronto City Hall council chamber for meetings until Metro Hall was constructed. I had worked so hard to get my rose-coloured couch that I wanted to take it with me for my new office. I wrote to the North York treasurer: "I am very fond of the rose-coloured loveseat that I picked out for my office in North York. I would like to have it for my Metro office. How much money will you take for it?"

I believe he took the matter to the North York executive committee.

He responded: "Unfortunately, I am not able to offer you the loveseat. The furniture is required at the North York Civic Centre. It is North York's property and is not for sale."

I replied: "Thank you for agreeing to sell me the rose-coloured loveseat from my office. You neglected to specify the price. How much do you want?"

He responded: "You misunderstood. The loveseat is not for sale."

That weekend, I borrowed a truck and a friend and I backed it up to the North York Civic Centre and threw the loveseat onto the back. We hauled it downtown and dragged it up to my Bay Street office.

My reply: "Thank you for agreeing to sell me the loveseat. I have installed it in my Metro office and it just fits the space nicely. I am puzzled that you are reluctant to name a price so I have enclosed a cheque for $149.00. This would seem to be a fair price for used furniture of this type."

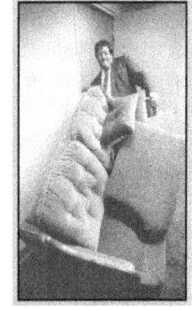

Response: "Send us $387.04."

My reply: "I'm thoroughly offended. First, you agree to sell me a loveseat. You refuse to name a price until it is installed in my office and after I go to the trouble of having it delivered, you attempt to gouge me on the price. I have changed my mind and cancelled my cheque. Please make arrangements to pick up your loveseat. It would look better in Councillor Milton Berger's office since it has an extra wall."

The last dig was too much to bear. Among the 14 politicians in North York, Berger was stuck with the worst office. In a closed-door meeting, the executive committee told staff to pick up the loveseat. Some of the councillors were furious.

"This guy takes furniture without authority and now has the gall to tell us to come and pick it up," snapped Berger.

"It's lost its cache," I replied. I've decided that it doesn't quite match the décor in my office. It's a bit too dusty rose."

Almost every grade-school pupil at one time was taught by a Miss TUD. TUD stands for title, underline, date. It is a classroom where form triumphs over substance. In 1993, councillor offices had moved to the second floor of Metro Hall. Mine was on the north side of the building overlooking King Street. It was at the end of the hall between Olivia Chow's and Miss TUD's office. In this case, Miss TUD was Scott Cavalier, the councillor from Scarborough-Agincourt. Scott was chair of the member services committee. It was largely composed of other TUDs, who for the most part had pickles up their tillers.

I grew up with a healthy disrespect for authority. I love to tweak TUDs. The Princess of Wales Theatre, directly across the street from our offices, was playing Miss Saigon, and Roger Hollander, who represented Don River, posted signs in his office window protesting the racist content of the musical. David Mirvish, the producer, complained to Chairman Tonks and the TUD committee swung into action. They issued an edict prohibiting signs in Metro Hall windows. Roger stood firm, but council forced him to take his signs down. Then, in sympathy with Roger, I posted a sign in my window showing an American flag with the slogan "Welcome to Toronto." Alas, the TUD edict prevailed. Imagine chastising me for having the audacity to welcome American visitors to Toronto. It was almost enough to cause me to resign my seat on the Toronto Convention and Visitor Bureau board.

ORANGE HAVEN

Drunk with power, the TUD committee issued further directives, like "clean up the coffee room" and "THERE IS TO BE NO FURNITURE LOCATED IN THE SECOND FLOOR HALLS."

EAST YORK ART DECCO

I am very fond of pop art. I am inspired by artists like Clause Oldenburg and Michael Snow. With the concurrence of Olivia Chow, who shared the cul-de-sac at the end of our hall, I set up a pop art ensemble outside our offices. A rummage through the Metro Hall furniture "graveyard" yielded two orange plastic-covered loveseats. They were straight out of the '60s and had once graced the decor of one of our welfare offices. We placed these on either side of a NOW Magazine rack and finished it off with a painting entitled "Landfill Monster." We called it our "pop art haven."

We were hauled before the TUD, aka (member services committee) where a furious debate erupted over our pop art ensemble.

Scott Cavalier called it a fire hazard: "That it's a fire hazard is a concern, but it also looks like something from a free clinic." Maureen Prinsloo said they were "crappy."

I defended my art: "I don't think this is a police state, and I don't think the art police should be out trying to control the appearance of my furniture. Sure they're tacky, but I like tacky."

Andy Warhol would have been proud. Nobody else seemed to be until two unexpected heroes came to my rescue, Humble Howard and Fred Patterson of CFNY-FM radio. The morning "goof troop" built a radio show around the couches, auctioning them off for charity. They even threw in some Neil Diamond tickets. CFNY/192.1 radio called itself the "leading edge" and they certainly were first to the couches. The pair dressed up as movers and mugged for the cameras as they hauled my treasures away.

We labelled the auction "Relics of East York Art Deco." I refused, however, to move the NOW Magazine rack even though some unknown person (or persons) kept moving it back into my office.

"I don't consider a NOW Magazine rack to be furniture." I quipped. "I've never met a street person who has tried to sleep in one."

Hey, there's something about furniture that inspires me. Not enough, however, to go into the business. I'll leave that to Mister Nooooobody.

CHAPTER 34

Over the Rainbow

I ran for Board of Control in 1985. It was my first shot at a city-wide council seat and I was determined to do it differently. We had the best sign campaign. Most candidates for Board of Control banged up their signs illegally on Metro roads. I determined that I would erect all of my signs legally, all on private property, with only one exception. I just couldn't resist the Don Valley rainbow, which is at the entrance to a pedestrian underpass that runs parallel to the northbound lanes of the Don Valley Parkway.

I had a fond affection for the rainbow. It was painted by Berg Johnson, one of my students when I taught art at Don Mills Junior High in the 1960s. Berg was a Swedish immigrant kid who grew to love Canada. This was his way of giving something to make his adopted community a better  place. When Metro discovered the rainbow painted on an underpass, they treated it as an act of vandalism. It was painted out three times by Metro parks crews. Eventually, Berg was arrested and charges were laid against him. The public outrage that followed prompted Metro officials to back away. They eventually adopted the rainbow as part of the city's public art portfolio and took responsibility for its maintenance. It brings a smile to the face of harried commuters on their dreary plod home up the Don Valley Parkway.

Thousands of commuters drive by it every day. The DVP is the main route to the east end of North York. It is the best sign location in the city. During the campaign, it became our one and only illegal sign. Even though vandals destroyed it several times, that didn't matter. We kept climbing the bank and putting it up again.

GLENCAIRN AVENUE

Chris Sikora was my sign chairman for the 1982 elections. He was young and enthusiastic. In those days, we used cardboard signs folded over a wooden stake. The 1982 election was a particularly nasty one. The Wilson Heights PC Association was galled that the ward was held by a New Democrat. They fought dirty.

I told Chris, whatever you do, do not destroy their signs. Tell all of our volunteers not to destroy any signs. Every day, someone called to tell us our signs had been smashed. One night, we spotted the culprits. They were with the Rosen campaign. I guess Chris's frustration got the better of him because as I drove up Glencairn Avenue the next morning, this is what I saw. Someone had turned the Rosen signs inside out and stapled them back onto their stakes. He followed my directive completely. He did not destroy her signs.

SIGNS OF SPRING

The North York sign bylaw was very specific. You cannot erect an election sign more than 30 days before an election. In the 1997 election, voters had to pick two councillors from newly enlarged wards. In the spring of that year, I wrote my name in six-foot letters across an embankment along Allen Road. I wrote it in fertilizer. As the season progressed, the name appeared traced in the dead grass. Was it an election sign? The legal department didn't know. In any case, nobody knew how to get rid of it or me.

VOTE HOWARD MOSCOE – THE BETTER WAY

I was chairman of the TTC. The TTC's slogan was "The Better Way". Why not use it in my campaign? One of my opponents complained bitterly to the TTC. It held the rights to the slogan, and I had no authority to use it in an election campaign. He was right, so we changed the slogan.

CHAPTER 35

They Can Take their Civil Liberties and Shove them NOW Mel Lastman… March 1, 1988

Somebody noticed the "dirty ads" in the back pages of NOW Magazine. The publication had been available in North York City Hall for more than a year. Shades of Sodom and Gomorrah. The building services manager pulled it out of the lobby and rushed it onto the agenda of the building services committee with a recommendation that it be banished from City Hall. The committee had a field day falling all over each other to defend the morals of our citizens, each one trying to be purer than their fellow guardians of public decency. The committee, after much teeth gnashing and hand wringing, recommended a ban. Never mind that you can pick up a copy of the Toronto Sun and see the same ads, or purchase the services of a prostitute (errr, sorry, an escort) from the want ads in the Toronto Star. Bell's Yellow Pages, also available at City Hall, offered the same escort services. Perhaps it wasn't so much the content of the ads but the way they were worded. In any case, the committee's recommendation had to be ratified by council and their next meeting would not take place until March 23.

I promptly announced that until North York Council reviewed the committee's recommendation I would be distributing the publication from my City Hall office to anyone who wanted it.

Then the unthinkable happened. I became mayor. (Well, not exactly, rather acting mayor.)

It was March break and the council bylaw specified that in the event the mayor was absent, the first controller (the one who had been elected with the highest votes) acted as mayor. Next in line was the second controller, followed by the third and the fourth. Lastman flew off to Florida and Esther Shiner, the first controller, was out of town. Bob Yuill, the second controller, took his traditional March break trip to Myrtle Beach. I am not sure where Norm Gardner had gone, but I knew he wasn't in town either. I was the fourth controller. This put me in the mayor's chair.

You have to remember this was March break. Politically, nothing ever happens during March break. The media are hungry for news and I gave it to them.

My first act as mayor was to issue a proclamation declaring March 14 to 20 "Freedom of the Press Week." This was entirely within the jurisdiction of the acting mayor. Almost every week had been declared something. Declarations ran the full gamut, from National Pet Your Dog Week to Be Kind to your Grandmother Week.

I then invited Alice Kline, NOW's publisher, to come to the mayor's office to receive a Mayor's Award for Excellence in

Journalism. During the award ceremony, I reflected on some of the things some governments, like Mussolini's fascist government, had done in the name of guarding our morals: "First you burn the words, then you burn the books and then you burn the people. The one thing that is more offensive than sexually explicit ads is the people who protect us from them."

I have to admit, the rhetoric was in full flight. Who could blame me; after all, it was March break, the media well was almost dry and I just couldn't resist filling it up and tweaking my colleague's noses at the same time.

A politician giving out an award in itself wasn't unusual. Members of council had given out thousands of them. Every rinky-dink corner cigar store and eatery had some kind of official North York scroll that had been presented to them when they opened. There were scrolls for 50th wedding anniversaries, special birthdays and retirements. The mayor and controllers, who had to run for election across the entire city, splashed them everywhere. They knew that every scroll they awarded returned at least two future votes and besides that, their names hung on the walls forever.

It was predictable. At the March 23 meeting of council, NOW Magazine went down in flames. I think Alderman Paul Sutherland got it right when he said, "Just because you don't like some of the ads, doesn't mean that you have to ban the whole paper. This is a witch hunt that has gotten out of hand."

His proposal to allow NOW to be distributed outside the south door of City Hall was defeated. Ironically, it was still available just outside the north door of City Hall in the public library. To its credit, the library board refused to follow the council's lead. Jo Stoh, acting director of the library system, articulated the library board's position.

"NOW is considered the best of its kind in terms of information about entertainment and the arts in Metro. NOW... is part of the library's magazine collection in every branch because it meets the board's material selection guidelines, which include criteria dealing with relevance and quality of information. The library distributes extra magazines free to the public."

Needless to say, I never again became acting mayor, not only because the council changed the bylaw to prevent it from happening, but also because both North York and, for that matter, Boards of Control disappeared when the province created the directly elected Metro Council that same year. North York is gone.

PART II

CHAPTER 36

The Sad Tale of Who Runs What

From time to time, a fierce and often confusing debate rages about the best way to deliver municipal services. Should they be delivered by elected politicos or appointed citizen representatives? The Toronto Transit Commission's day-to-day operating budget is about $1.3 billion. The term "citizen appointee" conjures up the impression that on Tuesday morning Mrs. Jones hangs up her apron and ambles over to the TTC meeting to contribute a healthy dose of common sense to its policy deliberations. Not so.

These are powerful and fiercely sought after patronage appointments that control millions of dollars of public funds. Some of them come with significant perks. The chair of the City of Toronto police services board, for example, gets $91,000 and the "citizen" chair of the TTC, in addition to a salary, gets free transit for life and, in those days, (I've never been able to figure this one out) a chauffeur-driven limousine. Many members of these boards and commissions are defeated politicians, the party faithful and friends of politicians – not exactly a cross-section of ordinary citizens.

Supporters of "citizen" governance often suggest they have special skills, talents and experience to contribute. That may be so, but that argument reflects some confusion about the role of a public board of directors. The last thing the TTC needs is another lawyer, engineer or technocrat. The commission already has a huge bureaucracy that presumably has all these skills and is paid well for them. Its role is to provide the board with options and manage the day-to-day operations of the transit system.

The role of the staff is to manage, the role of the board is to set policy. In a democracy, if people are unhappy about that policy they have the right to "throw the bums out." That's why boards and commissions like the TTC ought to be made up of elected officials who have to be accountable to the public.

In 1987, the TTC consisted of one appointed member of Metro Council and four citizen members. The council representative was City of Toronto Councillor Tom Jakobek and the chair of the commission was "citizen" appointee Jeff Lyons, otherwise known as "Uncle Jeff," dubbed so by the commission investigating the MFP Financial Services computer licensing scandal. Lyons and Jakobek were a dangerous duo. Madam Justice Bellamy referred to Mr. Lyons as a "lawyer, influence peddler, rainmaker and lobbyist." She had a lot more to say about Tom Jakobek, whom she described as "an audacious slippery operator" and a "strategic liar." The team of Lyons and Jakobek shared duties at the TTC, which Jeff chaired between 1987 and 1989. Other "citizens" included Gordon Chong and Carole Kerbel. Gordon was a Progressive Conservative who was defeated by Jack Layton in the 1982 municipal election. Gordon served as the vice-chair of the commission. Carole Kerbel was the owner of a marketing and public relations firm and was a friend of Paul Godfrey, the former Metro chairman. She, incidentally, was related to my sister-in-law. I later served with her on the Metro licensing commission.

Shortly after "Uncle Jeff" was appointed chair, the TTC through its subsidiary, Gray Coach, secretly bought an airline. It was incorporated as Vacationair Inc. in January of 1987. I can't imagine why they thought they should go into the airline business. How happy would their customers be if they knew they were attempting to service Tampa when they couldn't even provide decent bus service to the outer reaches of Scarborough? The whole thing smelled as bad as the tailpipe of an old GM-Newlook bus. Because Gray Coach was a subsidiary company owned and operated by the TTC, its activities were not subject to public scrutiny; they were hidden from view.

Under the Lyons leadership, Gray Coach purchased a one-third share of Vacationair in partnership with Regent Holidays Ltd. and Conquest Tours Ltd. with the object of flying passengers into Florida and the Caribbean. It was a jerrybuilt company with rented planes, rented office space, rented furniture, rented ethics and 70 employees. Gray Coach had no authority from the TTC and no authority from Metro to purchase an airline.

In 1988, I received a "deep throat" telephone call about the purchase. Metro Council, at that time, had a bylaw that gave members of council the right to file a written inquiry seven business days in advance of a council meeting. Officials were required to table a written answer no later than an hour before the council meeting that could be distributed or read to council. I dashed in a list of questions. The responses were evasive. They hid behind Gray Coach's claim that this was a private business deal and its terms could not be disclosed. The bus line is technically a private company, but it has been owned by the TTC since its incorporation in 1926. Its board consists entirely of all of the members of the Toronto Transit Commission – Tom Jakobek and four "citizens." Undaunted, I filed a new set of questions each meeting.

According to the Metro auditor, Gray Coach claims to have won its mandate from a vague "mission statement" that came up at an in-camera meeting of the commission on May 17, 1988.

"(c) To assist the TTC to reduce its operating costs and subsidy requirements by maintaining Gray Coach contributions and dividends through a combination of initiatives internally and new business associations in the transportation, tourism and travel-related areas."

Not exactly a solid runway from which to fly an airline. The auditor could find no specific reference in the commission minutes to authorize the purchase of Vacationair. Jeff Lyons was defensive and responded by attacking me.

"What's Howard Moscoe doing going around saying this wasn't a good deal?" asked Lyons. "He's a teacher. I don't think the guy could run a pop stand."

The press began to probe. They couldn't keep a lid on the facts forever.

Metro Council members were livid. Public outrage forced Gray Coach to sell its interest and Vacation Air Inc. ceased operations. To this day, the losses have never been made public, but estimates suggest they were around $2.4 million of public money. Other rumours suggest Gray Coach was the only partner that actually put money into the partnership, with the other companies having only to supply passengers. If that is true, the losses were much higher.

A year earlier, on the old Metro Council, we had had the same debate about "citizen" representation. At that time, I reminded the council that the TTC budget was one of its largest.

"Do you want to continue to farm out your major responsibilities?" I asked. Apparently they did. After a 2½-hour debate, my proposal was defeated.

Roll forward to December 15, 1988 – a watershed moment. This was the first business meeting of the new directly elected Metro Council. I rose to move that the three citizens on the TTC be replaced by Metro councillors. Allan Tonks, the newly chosen Metro chair, attempted to have the motion referred. His referral lost. I knew if ever there was a time to make real change it was there and then. The smell of the Gray Coach debacle had just wafted its way through the media. More importantly, the newly elected Metro councillors were starting their new government with a determination to make a difference. The business of governing Metropolitan Toronto was now full-time and they were eager to take control. That feeling was shared by people on both the right and the left of the political spectrum. One of my staunchest allies was Chris Stockwell, who later became a cabinet minister in the Mike Harris government and the Speaker of the Ontario Legislature. My motion carried. If there ever were any doubts about the worth of what we had done it was wiped away when the Toronto Sun (run by Jeff Lyon's friend, Paul Godfrey) published an editorial calling us "Urban Gorillas."

Was this the end of the debate? Not at all. Jeff Lyons went into high gear exercising his skill as a lobbyist. Pressure was being applied by the chairman and the displaced board members to reverse the decision in a desperate attempt to maintain the status quo and keep their positions. They had a lot to lose. Both Lyons and Chong had come under public criticism for their handling of the Canada Square-TTC land deal where the TTC conferred considerable benefits on a private land developer at bargain basement prices. It was revealed that Lyon's firm had acted for the developer. Chong was fingered by the media for using his membership on the TTC to promote his "professional services" at a conference in Hong Kong. It was also revealed that Gray Coach had purchased a bus line in Alberta.

In order to re-open a decision of Metro Council, the rules required that two members who had supported that decision had to sponsor its re-opening. The lobbyist's efforts went into high gear and they managed to turn some members of council around. Before the end of the month, a notice of motion sponsored by Brian Ashton and Anne Johnston to re-open and reverse the decision was filed with the clerk. This re-opened the debate, which raged anew at the February meeting of council, but by that time the idea that Metro Council could and should actually govern had taken hold. The motion to reverse the previous decision lost in a 15–15 tie vote. In a less than decisive victory, the new Metro Council limped into its first term.

CHAPTER 37

Lost and Found

The town of Chelm (to pronounce it, clear your throat and add 'elm') was situated somewhere in the pale of settlement between the Polish and Lithuanian boarders.

Wikipedia pegs it precisely: "It is located to the south-east of Lublin, north of Zamosc and south of Biala Podlaska, some 25 kilometres (16 miles) from the border with Ukraine."

Because the Tsar had decreed that Jews could only live in this area, the town was mostly Jewish. In Yiddish humour it was the "town of well-meaning fools." If someone did something foolish, people would say, "What do you expect? He's from Chelm." It was popularized by Isaac Bashevis Singer, the Yiddish writer who wrote *The Fools of Chelm and Their History*, which was translated to English in 1973. Chelm wound its way through Jewish folklore. It was part of the Yiddish psyche.

When the provincial government created a directly elected Metro Council, councillors wanted to have distinctive names for their wards. They asked the province to amend the legislation to allow the wards to have names instead of numbers. The province refused. We could have names, but they had to have numbers as well. It was their way of diminishing the status of municipal politics.

Numbers were problematic. They would clash with the locally numbered wards, adding to people's confusion. Besides, councillors were tired of being just a number.

Each councillor was given the task of developing a list of candidate names that reflected their ward. For some, the task was easy. Their areas had traditional names that were easily recognizable, like Scarborough Malvern or Seneca Heights. Some had distinctive geographic features that were natural identifiers, like Black Creek or Scarborough Bluffs.

Wrack my brain as I might, I just couldn't find a suitable name for my ward. Sure there were the historic villages like Fairbank around which the ward had grown, but because of the geography and immense size of the ward each one had no association with any other area in the ward. The only geographic feature common to all parts of my ward was the Allen Road (The Allen). William Allen had been Metro chairman, but he had no direct connection to the ward so I opted instead for two names.

The first was North York-Spadina. The Allen had been constructed as the Spadina Expressway. Residents could relate to Spadina Avenue, the heart of the Jewish district where many of their parents had first settled. The second was "Chelm."

"Chelm" sat on the council docket for three meetings. At the public hearings, nobody from my ward showed up to speak. None of the media picked it up and nobody telephoned me to express an opinion; nobody noticed. When the final decision had to be made, when the time came for me to move the motion naming my ward, tempted as I was, I lost courage and proposed 'North York-Spadina'. I thought the Jewish community would never forgive me if they woke up the next morning and discovered they were living in Chelm.

In 2003, I visited my daughter who lived in Brooklyn. The New York and Toronto Jewish communities have a parallel history, and my ward, like Brooklyn, has a huge Jewish population. While Gloria and Candice went shopping, I went to the courthouse to watch a murder trial and later drifted over to the Borough Hall and talked my way into the office of Marty Markowitz, borough president. New York City has an odd form of amalgamation. The presidents of its boroughs are directly elected but are not part of the New York City government. They are among the most powerful in the city, yet they do not have a seat on New York City Council.

Marty was very gracious. He toured me around Borough Hall and the Borough Square farmer's market. We spent more than an hour trading stories. I told him my "Chelm" story.

A few weeks later, my daughter called.

"What did you do to this guy?"

An article had appeared in the New York Times that Marty had proposed erecting a sign on the Brooklyn Bridge, which read:

I guess he found Chelm.

CHAPTER 38

Picking Up the Pieces

What were they thinking? In the 1960s, the world was on the brink of collective madness. The Cuban missile crisis had taken us to the edge of nuclear war. I was a young teacher at Franklin Horner Senior Public School in Etobicoke. In October of 1962, I remember the school board issuing instructions about what to do with your class if a nuclear bomb fell; as if there was anything that you could do.

The '60s were the years of the Diefenbunker. After the U.S. Bay of Pigs invasion, the Canadian government began to prepare in earnest for governing the country, or what was left of it, from underground fallout shelters. Canada was to be run from a four-story underground bunker at the Canadian Forces Station in Carp near Ottawa, which was built to house 565 people. The official manual specifies "political leaders, the most important federal civil servants and senior military officials." Just who were in each group I am sure remains "classified." Given that there are 308 members of the House of Commons, you can be sure being elected to Parliament would not be enough to admit you to the Carp shelter. Who then would be governing Canada?

The shelter at Carp had 286 "hot beds," meaning beds that could be occupied in 12-hour shifts. The prime minister was assigned a single bed. Would his wife be admitted? You can see what I mean by madness. Imagine being on the committee that mapped out who could enter the Carp Diefenbunker or the seven smaller regional bunkers across the country.

Most people don't know this, but the government of Metropolitan Toronto had its own Diefenbunker, paid for, I might add, without federal government funding. If they wouldn't spend the insane amount required to house all members of the Commons, how could they be expected to pay to house a few thousand municipal governments.

DIEFENBAKER

DIEFENBUNKER

Metro's nuclear fallout shelter was located at 220 Old Yonge Street (part of Lot 85, Concession 1, east of Yonge Street) in Aurora. It was hidden under an old farmhouse built in 1871, and its emergency entrance was disguised to look like a garden shed.

I knew the property well. When I was dating Gloria, her sister was engaged to one of the Caplans. The farm was owned by Jack Caplan, father-in-law of Elinor Caplan, MPP and later MP. Gloria and I spent several weekends there. I was shocked when I visited the bomb shelter to discover it was the Caplan farm. Metropolitan Toronto bought the site for $31,250 in 1962. It was supposed "to house city politicians and an emergency service headquarters in case of a nuclear attack."

Think about how absurd that idea is. Consider the difficulty of fighting your way through traffic to Aurora today. Now imagine the difficulty of getting to the Metro Toronto Emergency Preparedness Centre with the threat of a nuclear bomb hanging over the city and everyone rushing to leave town. So who was entitled to be housed in the centre? Who was essential to the governance of Metropolitan Toronto in the event of nuclear war? Who would want to be there and leave their families behind?

I became aware of the centre one night as I poured over the details of Metro's budget in preparation for our budget debate. What was this expense; $18,000 a year for the upkeep of an "emergency preparedness centre" in Aurora? It was called the Aurora Readiness Centre. I asked around. Nobody seemed to know. After some digging, I was told it was under the jurisdiction of the chief of police and it had been used as a training centre by the Toronto Emergency Task Force in the 1970s and '80s. It was now locked away with who knows how many other secrets.

Police budgets had always been sacrosanct at Metro. Nobody ever questioned them. When it came to their budget, the police circled the wagons to defend every dot and tittle.

I wrote to Chief Bill McCormack: "At a time when we are talking about laying off staff and cutting back on services, its outrageous that we are pouring money into this hole in the ground."

I asked if perhaps it wasn't time to de-commission the centre and sell the property. His response, as bizarre as it seemed, referred to the Soviets still being in Afghanistan and it would be prudent to retain the centre; "It might yet be needed." I had already learned that the property had been mothballed for some time and was in all likelihood useless as a command centre. McCormack told the land management committee, "The facility is still needed and I intend to include funds in the 1991 budget to refurbish it."

I made repeated requests to tour the site, and it was only after I tipped the media to its existence was I given a key and a map. The house looked like a typical Ontario farmhouse, white with a circular driveway around a flagpole. In reality, it was anything but typical. Below the existing basement – an additional underground concrete, reinforced nuclear bomb shelter 10.6 x 18.3 metres including a control centre, electronic equipment and a sleeping quarters. The shelter extended out under the lawns of the house. Nicholas Ionides described it in a Globe and Mail article as a scene straight out of Dr. Strangelove:

"The garage stores pillows and cots – dozens and dozens of them wasting away without ever having been used.... As you enter the house, you see a cosy, if dusty, place, with cobwebs on the ceilings and hardwood floors that creak with every step.... Open another door and there's a staircase leading down to the basement.... It's like being in a cave. It's cold and dark with the echo of water drops hitting the floor. Go down another small flight of stairs and there's the heart of what would be an emergency operation-command room. There's a platform with what looks like a set from a television news show. Take a closer look and it's a map of Toronto, hand-drawn on glass with one section that reads 'Casualty Counts.'"

It took me four years to pry the facility out of the police budget even though it was completely useless. Toronto offered it first to York Region as a possible location for an affordable housing site, but the region turned it down and ultimately it was advertised as: "1.4 acres in town. Here is a unique opportunity in the Town of Aurora, 3750 sq. ft. in need of renovation. Solid Structure, 3-car garage. $349,999."

They could have added "great wine cellar."

I never learned the actual cost of building it, but the cost of maintaining it for three decades was substantial. It's a bit scary when you think about the mistakes governments make and pour millions of dollars into. We don't usually make little mistakes, only big ones. What are the things that we're pouring money into now going to look like in the future?

CHAPTER 39
Team Zero and the Midnight Ride

The 1995 Metro budget was shaping up to be another major dustup. It would be excruciatingly painful. Ironically, some of the meanest budget hackers were the ones who called themselves "Liberals." They seemed to be falling all over themselves to out-Grinch each other. Scott Cavalier, the cavalier councillor from Scarborough, dubbed himself Captain Zero. Scott was determined to lead the charge for a 0% tax increase. Many of us considered him to be a zero.

Judy Sgro, a rookie councillor from North York who had also been elected under a red and white banner, was seeking to make a name for herself as a budget slicer. She proclaimed the Toronto Transit Commission should step up to the plate and cut $5 million from its budget. The chief general manager of the TTC had produced a confidential paper indicating that if faced with a $5 million budget cut, the poorest performing routes would have to be chopped and 30 routes were identified for closure. Two of those routes were in Judy Sgro's ward, The Maple Leaf bus and the Culford bus.

Most people in public transit know the last thing to do to save money is reduce service. It is far better to raise fares than cut routes. The success of public transit depends on its viability as a network. People have to be able to rely on their transit system. Chopping routes cuts holes in the transit network and causes a transit system to lose far more riders than raising fares does. When a transit system raises fares, the riders it loses eventually come back. When a bus route disappears, people buy cars and they seldom come back. Politicians, on the other hand, don't like to raise fares because they affect all voters. When a route is cut, people blame the transit system. When fares go up, people blame the politicians.

I was determined to teach Jumping Judy and Captain Zero that budget slashing could be dangerous. We had to teach them Newton's third law: "An action results in an equal but opposite reaction." We drafted up signs, and that night, Ben, my executive assistant, and I went out to Judy's ward and posted one on each bus stop along the Maple Leaf route. The signs had little tear-off tabs with her telephone number so people could remove them and call when they got to work. The next morning, Ihor Wans, her executive assistant, dashed into our office.

"Our telephone is ringing off the hook. Somebody posted signs on the bus stops in our ward. Did you guys have anything to do with that?"

"Sorry Ihor, but I won't confirm or deny that we had anything to do with the signs."

Judy was livid. She confronted me in the hall: "I'm going to distribute notices in your ward that you are in favour of a tax increase."

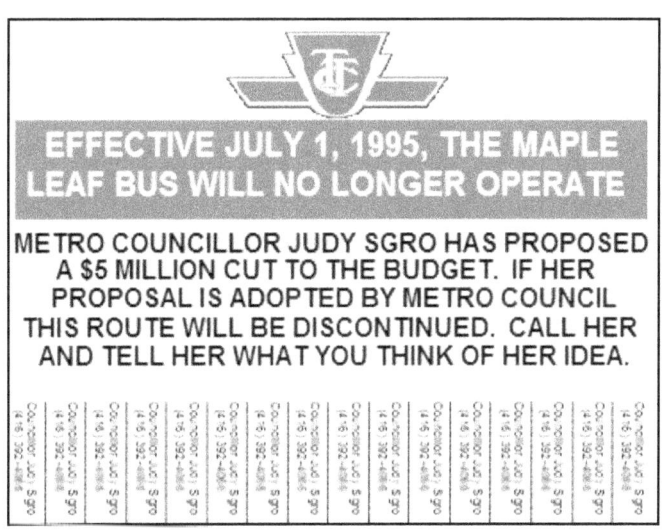

"Go right ahead," I replied."

The next night, Ben and I went out and posted signs on the Culford bus route. Both of these routes run through Italian working-class neighbourhoods where people depend on them to get to work. Strangely enough, Judy never talked about cuts to the TTC again.

The Huntington bus route slashed across the width of Scarborough from west to east north of Highway 401. It crossed three wards, Scarborough-Agincourt, represented by Scott Cavalier, and two Scarborough-Rouge River wards represented by Norm Kelly, a member of Team Zero, and Raymond Cho. This route was on the endangered species list. The next week, we placarded the bus stops along the Huntington route. The reaction was different from each councillor.

Scott Cavalier rose to his feet in the transportation committee meeting, turned red and gave a blustery speech complaining about how some unknown assailant had posted signs on the bus stops in his ward. The signs had lied and to make matters worse, the villain had used the TTC logo without any authority to do so. (Obviously, a capital offence.)

Norm Kelly walked into my office and asked to see me in private. He looked me in the eye: "Did you have anything to do with those signs?" he asked.

"I won't confirm or deny that I did," I replied.

"Come on Moscoe, you put them up didn't you?"

"Perhaps."

"That's great! Politics is a blood sport," he asserted as he turned on his heels and walked out.

While rumour has it that he got, by far, the most telephone calls, Raymond Cho remained stoic. He never uttered a word. There was no more talk about cutting the TTC budget that year and the endangered bus route list was quietly retired.

CHAPTER 40
Bush League

OK. I admit it. Sometimes a situation just cries out to be spoofed. Some things are just too delicious to ignore.

Baseball's 1991 All-Star game was to be held in Toronto's SkyDome on Tuesday July 9. President Bush (Sr.) was scheduled to pay a short visit to Toronto to attend the game and throw out the first ball. One of the reasons for any success I have in my job as a councillor is I read everything in council and committee agendas. Sometimes it gets me into trouble. We were in the midst of struggling with a tough  budget. There was talk about having to make some serious cuts in social services. Then I happened to read the cost of providing policing for the last game Bush attended in Toronto. I was miffed.

This would be the second time the president had visited Toronto to watch a baseball game. That short visit in 1990 cost us $60,000 in police overtime alone. At that time, he had come to watch the Houston Astros, owned by his son, play in the SkyDome. So I politely wrote to the White House.

"I want you to know how honoured we are to have you visit our city: However, the last time you attended a baseball game in Metropolitan Toronto it cost the taxpayers $59,140 in special costs to protect you. Our hostels are overcrowded and there are many more people sleeping in the streets. The food banks, for lack of government support, have had to ration out meagre supplies. In view of this and the possibility of having to close some of our daycare centres for lack of funding, I am writing to ask you to enjoy the game on television."

I advised the president I would be happy to kick in for a case of beer and would even throw in a couple of bags of chips and pretzels.

In an interview, the Buffalo News asked me if anyone else in Toronto agreed with me. I told them I wasn't sure, but I thought there would probably be several hundred thousand commuters who would. Bush was to land at Pearson Airport at 5:30 p.m. The police wouldn't, "for security reasons," reveal the exact route, but it was a pretty good bet it was going to be the same as last time. Then they had closed Highway 427 and the Gardiner Expressway to traffic so he would have a clear route downtown. Imagine the effect of closing two of the four major highways out of the city at the height of rush hour. Police did, however, issue a traffic advisory for westbound motorists. "Try to get home by 5:00 p.m."

Great advice: "Excuse me boss – I have to leave early tonight. President Bush is coming to watch a baseball game."

I asked the president to, "Suppress your urge to attend an All-Star game until the 1992 game next year in San Diego."

The story went viral. It didn't take long for the political spin-doctors to rush in to try and mitigate the uproar that ensued. The White House wisely disavowed any knowledge of the letter. Last time Bush attended the game, then-Prime Minister Brian Mulroney had joined him. Ottawa successfully turned it into a summit meeting. They spun it as the "Hot Dog Summit." Now at the All-Star game, Bush and Mulroney were going to have "Important discussions about the upcoming economic summit." Perhaps they were going to settle the difficult question of whether to serve ballpark franks or chateaubriand.

Some of my colleagues on Metro Council got really serious about the matter. Metro Chairman Tonks called it a, "large step over the line" and claimed, "it could damage Metro's hard-earned reputation."

Tonks promised he would write to Bush and set the matter right. The Toronto Star awarded me a dart.

Metro Councillor Peter Oyler angrily claimed it was "an insult, not only to the president, but to the people of Toronto."

I hasten to point out that most of the people of Toronto who were footing the bill couldn't afford a ticket to the All-Star game. Perhaps that was why they were insulted.

Councillor Roger Hollander wrote me from somewhere in the United States where he was vacationing: "I can't even escape the shmuck when I'm on holiday – good work Howard!!!"

There was even a letter to the editor blasting the Toronto Star for its dart.

David Garrick, vice-president of the SkyDome, whom I attended high school with, wrote letters to the editors of the Star and Sun: "Howard Moscoe has proven he is strictly Bush league by writing to the White House about Toronto incurring security costs during the President's visit."

I replied: "Howard Moscoe Bush League? How can anybody take seriously a guy who has managed to leap from the tallest, most successful freestanding structure in the world into the world's biggest financially doomed stadium?

Garrick had just left a job managing the financially successful CN Tower to take over management of the financially troubled SkyDome.

After all that pummelling, I was humbled and now ready to compromise. In an interview with the Los Angeles Times, I provided the president with an alternative option.

"If Bush wants to sneak into town wearing a fake nose with a moustache and glasses that would be all right with me. Heck, I would even buy him a hot dog and a beer at the game."

CHAPTER 41
Didn't Have a Prayer

Toronto was a different place when I attended Clinton Street Public School in the 1940s. My mother was born in Toronto. I had three uncles fighting overseas. My uncle Joe, captured at Dieppe, was in a German prisoner of war camp and my grandmother, who lived across the street from us at 123 Clinton Street, proudly displayed two silver stars in her front window. She had immigrated here in 1908, yet somehow we were made to feel we didn't quite belong.

One of the primary roles of the school system was to "Canadianize the heathens." We sang patriotic songs praising the virtues of the British Empire; songs like The Maple Leaf Forever and Pomp and Circumstance. Every morning, we opened the school day by standing to attention, singing God Save the King and reciting the Lord's Prayer.

The Lord's Prayer dug deeply into my psyche. I was Jewish. It wasn't my prayer. It made me intensely uncomfortable. Yet I would rather have died than ask to stand in the hall until the end of opening exercises. Most of us were the children of Jewish or Italian immigrants, but none of us wanted to single ourselves out. To this day, I regret that the school system made me ashamed of my grandmother, who spoke English with a heavy Yiddish accent. That's why I've always disliked the Lord's Prayer, and I was determined no other kid should ever be made to feel the way I had.

Later, when I became a teacher, I was active in my union, the Ontario Public School Teachers' Federation. When I was first elected to council, I was also president of the North York Elementary Teachers. I had, for many years, been a delegate to my union's annual assembly where we debated policy issues affecting teachers and education. That's where I learned parliamentary procedure and honed my debating skills. The North York District sponsored a resolution against public recitation of the Lord's Prayer. At that time, every classroom in Ontario opened its day with the prayer. It took us three annual assemblies, but with the help of the Toronto, North York and Ottawa districts, we did it. It was tough slogging. Most of the delegates were from small towns and rural areas and were fairly conservative.

It always seemed odd to me why the reciting of the Lord's Prayer should start every municipal council meeting. It is almost as if a public display of piety was pre-requisite to spending the next couple of days hacking at each other's throats. I can't imagine Jesus could have condoned the reciting of the Lord's Prayer at any municipal council meeting. In fact, he would have been appalled at the public recitation of the prayer anywhere. Anyone who doubts that should read Mathew 6:5-7 and the verses that precede the Lord's Prayer, which are found in Mathew 6:9-13.

I paraphrase: Don't be like the hypocrites. They like to pray standing in the synagogues and at the street corners to be seen. When you pray, go into the closet and close the door and pray secretly to G-d and say, "Our father..."

Mathew 6:5-13, including the Lord's Prayer, was specifically written to condemn public displays of piety.

I brought the resolution to North York Council. It should have been easy. North York was, by this time, becoming very multicultural. The second largest religious group was the Jewish community and the North York public school board had already replaced the Lord's Prayer so that every classroom in the North York Public School system opened each day with a different prayer from one of the world's religions. They already had compiled a list of some 300 different prayers that they were happy to make available to us.

It didn't happen. Apparently, prayer often brings out the worst in politicians. The bible thumpers on council had a field day. They rained down fire and brimstone. It was a nasty debate. Unknown to me, four years before I was elected some unknown alderman had the temerity to propose the idea. At that time, the public backlash was intense. Even Lastman, who you would think might have some sympathy, voted against it. The motion was cast aside.

When Metro Council moved into the new Metro Hall in 1993, I decided to give it one more try and brought the resolution to Metro Council. I knew it would not be easy, but times were changing. The Toronto population was being enriched by an influx of new immigrants from around the world, many of them not Christian. North York Council was largely conservative. Metro had a more cosmopolitan council with the centre and left well represented. Many of the rednecks had been left behind on the local councils so it seemed worth the try.

It wasn't easy. I'm not exactly sure what I said, but I was so immersed in the topic that several of my colleagues said I had given the best speech of my career. It appeared to be of no avail. The motion seemed destined to go down to defeat until Art Eggleton, who was then the mayor of Toronto, rose to speak. I have an enormous respect for Art and his political acumen. He proposed an amendment.

"That the Lord's prayer be replaced by a moment of silent reflection."

It was an elegant solution. The amendment carried. From that time on, Metro Council and later the Toronto Council that succeeded it began the first day of its meetings with a moment of silent reflection.

Roger Hollander, a friend and colleague on Metro Council, remarked to me: "I didn't think you had a prayer."

When North York disappeared, the public municipal recitation of the Lord's Prayer disappeared with it. My grandmother, Bubby Gittle, would have been proud. At least I could now face her in eternity [if there is one]. I think also that Jesus, the rabbi from Nazareth, would have been pleased too.

CHAPTER 42
Bafflegab

Bureaucrats don't make it easy. Every time I sat down to read a Metro agenda, I had to put on hip waders. I knew I would be up to my ying yang in nitrogen-rich organic products composed of a mixture of cellulose, inorganic salts, like phosphates, expelled from a digestive tract. It's not that the swivel servants who write these reports are deliberately trying to snow you. (At least, not most of the time.) It's just that so many of them can't write. They were promoted for their technical skills, not their ability to communicate.

In Grade 10, I learned a valuable lesson. I was a pubescent hoodlum. My interest in my friends and social life far exceeded any academic ambitions. I failed my Grade 10 year. Then fortune intervened. My parents just happened to move, and I repeated Grade 10 in another school. I didn't know a soul, so while others fooled around in the halls between classes, I read the next chapter in the history book. I discovered if you did some preparation people actually thought you were smart, even if you weren't. I won the grade history prize that year. From that time on, I vowed never to go into a situation unprepared. In all my 32 years in politics, I never attended a meeting without having first read the agenda.

It was my obsession. I poured over the agenda for committee or council meeting, tabbed pages, made notes in the margins and actually wrote motions out in advance. I discovered if you were the one who made the motion you controlled the debate. You could count on the fact that most of your colleagues hadn't read most of the items on the agenda. There were even a few who didn't open the agenda until they arrived at the meeting.

You could easily tell who hadn't done any reading by the questions they asked.

"Controller Shiner, you'll find that answer on page four."

"That's on page 11 near the bottom of the page."

"You'll find that at the top of page seven."

It was the easiest way to silence someone who shot from the lip. Much of the debate at committee and council meetings revolved around what somebody had said, rather than what was in a report. Many didn't even know the contents of the report they were debating. Over the years, if you read a lot of reports you accumulate a lot of information. If you are there long enough, you become the "corporate memory" of the organization.

When I was first elected, Sid Cole, the North York traffic commissioner, sat me down in his office: "Listen kid. I want you to understand something. Politicians come and go. I'll be here a lot longer than you will. If you learn to play ball we'll get along."

He was wrong. I was there a lot longer than Sid was.

Herein lies my frustration. Many of the staff reports read like they were written as drunken Shakespearian soliloquies. They were filled with technical jargon, unwieldy phraseology, exceedingly ornate language, unnecessary repetition and bureaucratic mumbo jumbo. It seemed every plan put forward was "strategic." Oh how I hated that word. I begged Dale Richmond, our CEO, to do something about the style of reports that were finding their way to council. He promised he would, but nothing happened. My hip waders were getting heavier and heavier.

About a year into my first term at Metro Hall, my frustration got the better of me. I took two mind-numbing paragraphs out of staff reports that were 240 and 250 words long and re-wrote them, editing them down to 63 and 95 words respectively. They were re-written without sacrificing one iota of content. I fired them off to Dale and their authors with a new plea for mercy.

Mercy never happened. The waves of mumbo jumbo rolled on.

At that point, I announced the creation of the new Unofficial Metropolitan Toronto Obfuscation Award to be presented to writers of exceptionally bad staff reports. I advised the CEO's office and told him that because I had no desire to publicly embarrass anyone, the awards were to be confidential, with the recipients to remain anonymous.

The truth was I never really had the heart to present one. It would have been pretty cruel of me to do that. I simply wanted the CEO to follow up on his promised improvement program. Did the quality of staff reports improve? My sense was yes. I do know before a report was tabled at a committee someone was reading it with an eye to the way it was written. I noticed that generally, reports became easier to read, but I couldn't yet hang up my hip waders.

CHAPTER 43

Could Bureau Business be Better?

I spent hundreds of hours listening to complaints, not as a councillor but as a member of the Metro Licensing Commission. We were a tribunal that regulated some 55,000 businesses. Every business that required a licence, from body shops to strippers, taxis to tow trucks – you name it, we licensed it.

Complaints against almost every sleazy business in town at one point ended up with a hearing before the licensing commission.

In 1990, there seemed to be an unusually large number of complaints against home renovators. Some of the stories were truly heartbreaking. Many of them were from seniors who had been ripped off for thousands of dollars spent on botched jobs by contractors intent on squeezing every buck out of them that they could. What did many of these complaints seem to have in common? Time and time again at a hearing a witness would say: "I contacted the Better Business Bureau and they told us the contractor was a member in good standing and had no complaints registered against him."

It was a frustrating task because all the commission could do was suspend or revoke a licence. It had no power to order repayment or restitution. Often times, a contractor who lost his licence simply re-opened the business under another name with a spouse or cousin fronting for them and they would be on their merry way ripping off seniors again.

There was obviously a need for some kind of co-ordination among agencies that purported to act on behalf of consumers.

One day, the Better Business Bureau directory was delivered to my home. As I flipped through it, I happened to notice the name of a home renovation business we had just stripped of its licence in a hearing a month before. As I continued flipping through the directory, a number of other names of home renovation companies looked familiar.

The next day, I passed the book over to Carroll Ruddell-Foster, our CEO and asked her to have staff cross reference the home-renovation companies listed as members against the commission's files. I was astonished to learn that 40 companies listed in the BBB directory as members were unlicensed. They were operating illegally. As it turned out, a number of them were home renovators whose licences had been revoked by the commission after licensing hearings. While the BBB told us they had no complaints, we had files bursting at the seams with complaints about the same businesses.

Enter Paul Tuz.

PAUL TUZ

If you met Paul Tuz, you had to be impressed. He was a tall, stately and very distinguished man that dripped authenticity. He spoke English with the faint hint of an Austrian accent. Paul not only headed the Better Business Bureau in Toronto, he did double duty as the ambassador (oops... sorry, honourary counsel general) for Mali and Togo. If you want to find them on a map, they are just south of Algeria. He looked ambassadorial. This gave him a fancy diplomatic license plate and a ticket to all high-level cocktail parties. Very impressive. When you think Better Business Bureau, you just have to think "authority," "honesty" and "integrity."

What could be straighter or more upright than better business?

I asked our staff to set up a meeting with Mr. Tuz at his offices to talk about how we could co-ordinate our efforts to protect consumers. At that meeting, I suggested to him that, for home renovators, the bureau require a valid Metro licence as a pre-condition to membership. He didn't seem particularly interested in that. I offered to notify him when a home renovation company had their licence pulled by Metro so that he could de-list the company. He wasn't sure about that. I came away from the meeting with the feeling that the Better Business Bureau wasn't much interested in co-operation and had even less interest in protecting consumers.

The more I learned about the BBB, the more concerned I became.

Ontario had its first NDP government and Peter Kormos was now Ontario's minister of corporate and consumer affairs. I had known Peter for years. He was always an advocate for consumers, so I wrote to him and asked him to investigate the Better Business Bureau of Toronto. It was as much of a scam as some of the businesses it claimed to be evaluating.

The Better Business Bureau, which collects more than $1.5 million annually in membership fees, is nothing more than a business whose primary function is to sell memberships.... The major criteria for membership seems to be the ability to pay the fees, and few, if any, of its members are ever suspended from membership for anything other than non-payment of fees.... The price of membership buys its members instant respectability, the right to be listed and the right to display the BBB logo, all for only $220 (1990 rate).

It's the same old story. The reason the BBB was established in 1912 was because of the threat of government regulation. "Self-regulation" was touted as the answer. It has never really worked. Because the organization depends on membership dues, it has a basic conflict of interest. ABC News, in a documentary, exposed the American BBB for selling ratings for membership fees. Of course, Mr. Tuz was not interested in suspending 40 unlicensed home renovators; the bureau would lose 40 membership fees.

I asked Mr. Kormos to investigate the bureau with a view to protecting consumers. Nothing happened. I then met with his successor, Marilyn Churley. I was sure Marilyn would do something. Alas, not. She wrote to me in September of 1991: "Because the Better Business Bureau is not engaged in the sale of goods or services to consumers, there is no authority under the Business Practices Act or any other piece of consumer legislation administered by my ministry for an investigation into the activities of the Better Business Bureau."

In 1993, the Toronto Star did an expose. Tuz was fired by the BBB board, which paid him a severance of just over $1 million. It was also discovered that in two years he had charged the bureau some $45,000 in expenses incurred in his diplomatic post. The credibility of the Toronto BBB board was further blown when they hired Tuz back shortly after paying him severance. The Toronto BBB, by the way, was stripped of the right to use the BBB name in 2001. Even so, their staff continued to solicit memberships. The only thing that really resulted from my altercation with Mr. Tuz was the Toronto bureau stopped publishing its directory.

For the record, BBBs are profit-making franchises that exist to sell advertising and memberships. While they purport to be, they are not consumer protection agencies. They are selling legitimacy to marginal businesses. If you go on their website today, you will be hard pressed to find any member business rated at less than A+. Bureau business couldn't be better.

CHAPTER 44

Perfect Harmony: The Blue Box, or How Coca-Cola Conned Ontario

Cities in New York State have cleaner streets than those in Ontario. Why? It's because New York State has a deposit return system for beverage containers. When my daughter, Candice, lived in Brooklyn she would place her empty pop cans into a plastic grocery bag and hang it on the rail fence in front of her brownstone. It would be picked up every day. That's because pop cans were a major source of income for homeless street people, and that's why the streets of Brooklyn were cleaner than those in Toronto. Most people in New York State take their empty beverage containers to the supermarket to drop into a vending machine. The machine then dispenses a credit slip, which they can use to purchase groceries or redeem for cash. In 1990, 11 jurisdictions in North America imposed deposits on beverage containers.

In Ontario, a battle was raging for the hearts and minds of the members of the provincial government.

Environment groups were pressing for deposits on beverage containers. The beverage industry was touting the blue box as the answer. Jim Bradley, the environment minister, was being assaulted from both sides. I knew Jim before he was elected. We were both elementary school teachers active in our teachers' federation. He was a nice guy, but a wimp. I knew he would cave to the pop companies.

May 1, 1990 was Environment Day. Gloria and I picked a project that was dedicated to bottle deposit advocacy. We were angry. Ontario environmental regulations required retailers to stock soft drink shelves with at least 30% refillable bottles. Two weeks earlier, soft drink companies asked for a reduction to 20%. They argued that their financial contributions to the blue box program had warranted such a reduction.

We threw three darts at a map of Metro to select random locations. The closest main intersection to where the darts landed became our target area. The targets were Weston Road and Eglinton, North York Civic Centre and Kingston Road and Midland. Gloria, her friend Sheila and I drove to each location and clicked on a stopwatch. We picked up as many pop cans as we could in 25 minutes and put them into green plastic garbage bags. We were careful not to take any cans from litterbins, only those on the ground or mashed into curbs, roadways and sidewalks. We collected 377 cans in 75 minutes.

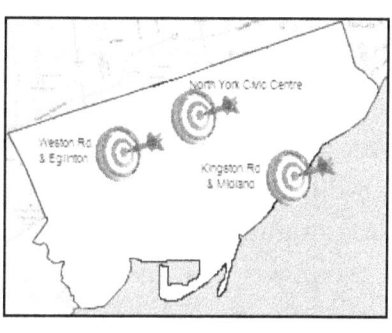

Originally, soft drinks and even milk were sold in washable, refillable glass containers. Pop and milk companies provided local industrial jobs. Remember when every city and large regional town in Ontario had its Coca-Cola bottling plant? That's because it was more expensive to ship water than concentrated syrup. When I was in Grade 9, I got my first summer job, night shift at the 7UP bottling plant. There I either loaded bottles into a washer or stacked them into boxes as they came off the line. Bottling plants were labour intensive. Those jobs are gone.

In the '90s, the Ontario government was wrestling with environmental legislation. Pop and milk companies were moving towards disposable containers. They were constructing large, centrally located mechanised plants to fill cans and cartons. Yet, Ontario was the home of the most efficient product management system in the world. The beer industry, which sold its products through the Brewers' Retail, had a deposit return bottle system that recovered 98% of all beer bottles and 81% of all cans. It had been in place for 60 years. You had to look long and hard to find a discarded beer bottle by the roadside in Ontario. The North American trend was towards legislating deposit returns on beverage containers for environmental reasons.

The ministry of the environment was established in 1971 and it appeared the province was moving towards a deposit-return system. The Environmental Protection Act scheduled the phase-out of non-refillable containers by 1982, and it looked like Ontario was headed for mandatory deposits. Industry lobbyists moved into high gear and managed to convince the province that they would voluntarily produce 75% of their product in refillable bottles; they never did, and over time the environment ministry gradually whittled away at regulations that required refillable bottles until they disappeared completely.

Industry was hustling the blue box system as the saviour of the environment, and they were prepared to throw millions into its establishment. (Of course, they would save hundreds of millions). The Soft Drink Industry set up OMMRI (Ontario Multi-Materials Recycling Inc.), a company devoted to pushing curbside collection. Joan King, a councillor from the east end of North York, represented Metro on OMMRI. Like Jim Bradley, she was a "Liberal" and, as it turned out, an even bigger wimp than he was. Joan became a cheerleader for the pop industry and their blue box.

OMMRI drew up the blueprint for the blue box system. Here's how it worked. The province and industry would finance

50% of the start-up costs for municipalities that established the blue box system. After three years, the blue box system would be self-financing, largely through the sale of products collected. The underpinning of the blue box was the aluminium pop can. It was the waste that was highest value, and the proceeds from its recovery would more than offset the cost of establishing the blue box system. Belief in the blue box system became as popular as a belief in Santa Claus. It made everyone feel good, but it was about as truthful. By 1986, industry contributed $41 million to curbside recycling. Provincial and municipal governments had contributed $2.33 billion. Municipalities ended up carrying the can for the soft drink industry.

Our environment day project continued. We carried our pop can collection to a press conference at Toronto City Hall in gift boxes wrapped in glossy silver paper with red bows. This, we said, was Jim Bradley's legacy, his gift to the people of Ontario as we dumped the 377 mashed pop cans onto a table. We pointed out that despite Toronto's active blue box program, only 2% of pop cans end up in the blue box. From the pop cans we picked up from the streets on Environment Day, we were able to calculate that with a 5-cent deposit on a pop can a student could earn an average of $18.05 an hour picking up pop cans and significantly more if the cans in litter bins were included as well.

From that we were able to secure a Metro Council resolution in support of deposits on beverage containers. Subsequently, AMO (Association of Municipalities of Ontario) became a strong advocate of deposits on beverage containers. It wasn't hard. The markets for blue box materials just weren't there. Much of what was being collected in blue boxes was being quietly carted off to landfill sites.

That year, as vice-president of AMO, I wrote a letter to the editor of OMRRI's newsletter, the Recycler, which was now being distributed to all councillors in Ontario. I expected they would never print it, but they did: "Your decision to include us in your mailings suggests that you have now come to the realization that elected officials are now beginning to see the awful truth behind the blue box program.

"Many thousands of people will be dutifully sorting their cans, bottles and newsprint only to have it being dumped, (albeit separately) into landfill sites. The truth is that recycling is a fool's paradise, cleverly crafted by the soft drink industry to stave off the inevitable; that is mandatory deposits on all bottles and cans. Those responsible for producing today's excess packaging are those who must ultimately accept responsibility for its disposal. OMMRI has managed to transfer the major cost of their enterprise onto the backs of municipalities."

It was costing Toronto municipalities $195 per ton to pick up blue box materials and another $30 per ton to haul it away, all at municipal taxpayer expense. Most of what was being collected was languishing in warehouses or being dumped in landfill sites. The Metro Works committee was upset enough to endorse a mail-a-pop can to Premier David Peterson's campaign.

I was wrong. The beverage industry lobby was too powerful, too well funded with too much to lose. Deposit legislation was not inevitable. It never happened in Ontario.

In May of 1991, Coca-Cola took another kick at the environment by announcing its decision to move from aluminum to steel cans. But the profit from the recovery of aluminium was to finance the material recovery from the blue box. Recycled aluminium was worth $1,500 per ton compared to $70 per ton for recycled steel.

My staff, Ben, Irene and I, each purchased one share of Coca-Cola and as shareholders took our travelling can collection to the Coca-Cola annual meeting. President Neville Kirchman spent two uncomfortable hours defending his company's decision to change from aluminium to steel cans.

"We're not in business to subsidize all other products that go into the blue box," he said.

The switch to steel cans would cost municipalities in Ontario $90 million in lost scrap revenues over the next five years and save Coca Cola $150 million over the same period. He conveniently forgot to mention the Coca-Cola lobbyists promise that aluminium's recovery would offset the cost of curbside recycling when they were promoting the municipal blue box. The only happy note about the meeting was at the end, when each of us was rewarded with a case of Coke to take home.

One final note: In 1994, the soft drink industry further sabotaged the municipal curbside collection system by succeeding in persuading the province to accept the PET bottle in the blue box. Every $1 of revenue generated from the sale of plastics from PET (polyethylene terephthalate) bottles adds $8 in additional municipal waste processing costs to the municipal tax bill. That's because PET bottles take up so much space in blue boxes, trucks and transfer stations. To make matters even worse, soft drink companies are now increasingly moving from steel cans, which at least have some recovery value, to PET bottles that have almost none.

When Coca-Cola sings, "We'd like to teach the world to sing in perfect harmony," they certainly know what they're talking about. They sure taught Ontario and its municipalities a thing or two.

CHAPTER 45

Taking the Elderly for a Ride

As I get older, I can better appreciate the difficulties that come with aging. Gloria has told me she never wants to finish her days in a nursing home. Neither do I. So why are there so many new nursing homes? It's not only because more of us are aging. It's also because our governments haven't yet figured out how to provide all of the services required for people to remain in their own homes.

In the 1950s, developers were carving subdivisions out of North York cow pastures. In the midst of all this, Canada's second shopping centre was built at the northwest corner of Lawrence Avenue West and Bathurst Street. It anchored a neighbourhood the developers dubbed "Lawrence Manor." Lawrence Plaza opened in 1953. It was considered so unique that it merited a visit from the Queen when she came to Canada. I can just imagine her majesty chomping on a bagel and lox at the United Bakers Restaurant.

The centre core of any shopping plaza in the '50s was a supermarket. Even Yorkdale had one until they figured out they could make more money using the space to hustle high fashions.

You can imagine the neighbourhood angst in the '80s when the Dominion Store in Lawrence Plaza closed. The population of Lawrence Manor was aging. Many residents were no longer able to drive and the Dominion Store was the only supermarket for kilometres around. The most persistent plea I received as a councillor was for a supermarket in the neighbourhood – something that was well beyond my control.

Around 1990, I learned that Bernac Leaseholds had purchased Eaton's warehouse. Eaton's warehouse was a huge concrete structure perched over the west side of the Allan Road on the north side of Lawrence. This is where they sold surplus or slightly damaged goods gathered from all of their stores. Bernac was planning to cut the middle out of the building, add two other floors and construct a three-tier shopping centre. Lawrence Square was to be anchored by a Kmart store, a Canadian Tire outlet and a huge Fotinos supermarket. The Fotinos store was a welcome addition to the neighbourhood, but the problem was how do you bring seniors who do not drive and the supermarket together?

When I first was appointed to the Toronto Transit Commission, I had a lot to learn about public transit. I vowed to consume a section of their 16-centimetre thick policy manual every week until I was reasonably familiar with the nitty-gritty details of the system's policies. It was full of exciting things, like "No passenger may expectorate on TTC property" (don't spit on the floor!). One week, I stumbled across policy 2.3.1. "Special Subsidies for TTC Scheduled Services." It allowed for corporate sponsorship of TTC bus routes. It was designed as a way for corporations to fund low-volume routes that would not otherwise be feasible. The policy had been on the books for some 10 years, but nobody had ever made use of it. Presto! Here was a policy that might be used to bring Lawrence Square's supermarket and seniors together.

Staff in my office worked with TTC staff to design a bus route that would connect all local community facilities. Note that it begins and ends with a supermarket. The community bus was to be a stretch Wheel-Trans bus. It operated on a fixed route with fixed stops, but unlike a regular TTC bus, you could access it anywhere along the route by hailing it from the street.

It would accommodate a Wheel-Trans passenger, but you didn't have to be a Wheel-Trans passenger to use it. At that time, a Wheel-Trans passenger had to book a ride four days in advance. There was no pre-booking required for a community bus ride. The fare was a regular TTC ticket or token and you could transfer from it to any other TTC route, including the Spadina subway line at the Lawrence West station. I had to find a corporate sponsor. The policy required that a sponsor would have to agree to pay any operating losses on the route.

I approached Joe Burnett, chair of Burnac Corporation, the company that was building Lawrence Square. Joe is an interesting person. He is a billionaire and holds the distinction of being the defendant in Canada's longest running tax evasion trial. It lasted for nine years. They had to build a courthouse in Orillia especially for this trial. He is also a noted philanthropist. Joe didn't hesitate for a moment. He signed an agreement to cover any operating losses for the bus for a period of five years. We couldn't have done it without him. Toronto's first community bus route was born.

It proved to be more successful than the TTC had ever imagined. A one-way Wheel-Trans ride cost the TTC an astounding $33 in 1990. The community bus took the pressure off the Wheel-Trans system in the Lawrence Manor neighbourhood. Here, the cost of an average ride dropped to $12 per trip. That means for every trip that could be diverted from the Wheel-Trans system to the community bus, the commission would save an average of $21. That sent the TTC planning department rushing to the drawing board. They began to identify neighbourhoods with a high concentration of Wheel-Trans riders. In June of 1991, the TTC launched a network of five new community bus routes: Parkdale, Roncesvalles, Spadina/University, Bathurst North, Yonge/Sherbourne. Later, they added Etobicoke and Dundas West.

Natural changes began to occur as the system matured. The TTC had tightened its eligibility criteria for Wheel-Trans.

Computerised scheduling and an enhanced reservation system began to drive the cost of a Wheel-Trans ride down. It is now under $25. The TTC began a program of retrofitting the subway system with elevators at a capital cost of about $6 million per station to make subway system accessible. Community bus ridership dropped from 100,000 in the '90s to around 60,000 in 2013.

At one point, the drop in ridership threatened the viability of the Lawrence Manor community bus. I conducted a use-it-or-lose-it campaign. I recall a public meeting at the Baycrest Geriatric Centre where we discovered that not only did many of the elderly not know about the service, many who did were afraid to use it. We realized that we had to take new riders through an orientation program where someone actually walked them through their first bus ride and taught them how to use the system.

The success of any system can be measured by the number of its imitators. The idea spread rapidly to Ajax in 1992, Richmond Hill, 1993, Newmarket, 1994, Oshawa, 1995. Now Sault Ste. Marie, London, Welland, Hamilton, Ottawa and a number of cities in Florida have community bus systems.

To think that it all started here in Toronto makes me enormously proud of the TTC.

CHAPTER 46

The Battle of Downsview

It was my baby, and like any parent, I would fight to the death to protect it from evil people intent on destroying it. All right, I may be a bit overdramatic, but that's the way I felt at the time. I'm talking about the Downsview subway station. It was 1994. Mike Colle was the chair of the TTC and I was vice-chair. The TTC, with the blessing of the provincial government, had approved the extension of the Spadina subway one stop northward, and Downsview was to be the new northern terminus of the line. It happened to be in my ward, and I was determined the station would be built with community input.

The design process was kicked off at a town hall meeting where I invited residents to meet the architects, Adamson and Associates, and share their ideas for the station. Downsview had grown up around the aircraft industry. The southeast corner of Sheppard Avenue West and the Allen Road was the site of Canadian Airways Field (1926), where the station was being built. To the west was de Havilland Airport (1926), immediately south of that was the Toronto Flying Club (1931) and further south at Dufferin Street, just below Bridgeland Avenue, was Barker's Field (1928). Its hangar became Katz's Deli. In the centre of all of this was the de Havilland Aircraft Company Ltd. plant, which ground out more than 500 Mosquitos, one of the fastest airplanes to fly during the Second World War. The plant also delivered more than 1,000 Tiger Moth training aircraft to the war effort. After the war, the plant produced a number of famous Canadian aircraft, among them the Otter, Beaver and

Caribou. Today, Bombardier builds the Dash 8 series of aircraft at the same Downsview plant.

The design of the station emerged from community consultations. There was a broad consensus that it should celebrate the importance of the aircraft industry to Downsview. The station was to have high, curved ceilings like an aircraft hangar. There were no pillars; an oversized mezzanine and the overhang on the bus bays were to resemble the wings of an aircraft. The key feature of the station would be a series of skylights that would bring natural light to the interior of the station, even down to the subway platforms.

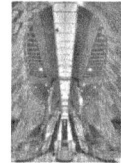   

The architect took a trip to Boston where one of their stations was built around skylights and natural light. Downsview was to be one of the most beautiful stations in Toronto. Now stepping to centre stage, we have Al Leach, the chief general manager of the TTC, the villain of this melodrama (sans moustache). Al had spent 23 years in various Ontario Ministry of Transport positions prior to his appointment as chief general manager. He was a staunch Conservative and in 1977, he succeeded in getting himself appointed as managing director of GO, Ontario's regional transit system. It was clearly a political appointment. In 1987, he came to the TTC.

Al didn't particularly like Mike Colle or me. We clashed on a number of issues, not the least of which was his battle to curb the TTC's electric bus (i.e., trolley) system. Mike Colle led the fight to keep the trolleys; I stood with him. Leach told the commission there were more than enough buses to meet service. The trolleys were not needed. We lost. The commission voted to remove the last two remaining trolleys, the Bay and Annette Street routes. Leach was also determined to get rid of the skylights in the Downsview station. I pleaded that the skylights were the rationale around which the station was designed. The commission said no to Al, the skylights were to stay.

I can picture Al picking up the phone and dialling one of his pals in the Ministry of Transport. "Send me a memo saying that you were 'value engineering' the design of the station and I have to get rid of the skylights."

I was livid when I saw the letter. Ontario had elected the Rae government in 1990 – it's first NDP government. Gilles Pouliot was the minister of transportation. I had known Gilles for a long time. He agreed to meet with me over the issue. The architect and I trooped up to Queen's Park with a model of the station. We met with Gilles and his deputy minister. He had obviously been briefed by the deputy. He was not particularly sympathetic. The thought that Leach had been able to reach into Queens' Park and yank the chain of the minister was too much for me.

I stomped out of the meeting with the architect in tow and barged into Bob Rae's office. I glared into the eyes of his staff and said: "If I don't get the skylights for the Downsview station I am going to do everything in my power to screw up your government's transit plan for Toronto. You had better have a talk with your minister of transportation."

We cut the ribbon on the Downsview Station at 10:20 a.m. on Friday, March 29, 1996. The ceremony was illuminated by sunlight streaming through the skylights, yet the battle of Downsview wasn't quite over yet.

Al Leach resigned his position at the TTC to run as the Conservative candidate for St. George-St. David riding in the 2005 provincial election. His retirement from the TTC was not greeted with regret. His management style didn't enamour him to a lot of people. Steve Monroe, Toronto's leading citizen transit activist, characterized him as "autocratic and arrogant."

"At commission meetings he would speak to members of the public and members of the commission in ways that really were intolerable for someone in his position," Monroe said.

I asserted that he was better cut out to be a politician than a transit manager.

Al was tough, persistent and he wasn't about to let any politicians jerk him around. He wasn't able to make the distinction between management and politics, and maybe it's fitting that he should run for political office. He was more cut out to be a politician than a general manager. We wanted to put a new stamp on the TTC. The system had run into difficult times and needed to be overhauled.

Al was on the executive of the American Public Transit Association (APTA), which gives out numerous awards each year. He engineered an APTA award for himself in order to enhance his political aspirations. In 1994, APTA named him "North American Transit Manager of the Year." It was great for his campaign literature.

Several months after he left the TTC, David Gunn, the new chief general manager, released a report on the condition of the fleet. It was appalling. I wrote to APTA and suggested they ought to rescind the award.

"After he retired, we discovered that the bus fleet was falling apart," I wrote. "Al is campaigning on the need for a leaner, meaner government. He's the guy who built the biggest, most bloated bureaucracy ever at the TTC. We got rid of 285 administrative positions."

I suggested if they couldn't see their way clear to rescinding the 1994 award, they should name him "Transit Boob of the Year" in 1995.

Gunn's report told us the bus fleet was in crisis and there were not enough vehicles to meet service. The proposal was to spend

$28.3 million to purchase 100 new buses. One could conclude that Leach was either an incompetent manager and was unaware of the condition of the fleet, or he had lied to the commission. When Gunn's report was tabled, I was charitable and asserted the latter. That's what got me into trouble. Tories on the commission were outraged and I quickly backed down from "lied" to "misled," but alas, it was not enough.

Leach, who was by then the minister of municipal affairs and housing in the Harris government, filed a statement of claim through his lawyers, Mark Freiman and Anthony Alexander, at the law firm of McCarthy Tetrault. He was claiming $2 million in damages for libel. The irony of this was Mark Freiman had canvassed a poll for me in each of the last two elections. I engaged Peter Jacobsen, a libel and slander specialist, who did most of that kind of work for the Globe and Mail.

All of this prompted Allan Tonks to issue a memo to all Metro councillors.

"Now is not the time to go out of our way to publicly belittle or objectify members of the Legislature. Whether it is deserved or not, let's recognize what is at stake here and ask ourselves whether the 'fun' is worth the possible price... we might have to pay."

My response: "It's kind of a kindergarten memo. Sort of, be nice to the Lion who is about to bite off your head. If anyone is suggesting that bending down to kiss the posterior of members of the provincial cabinet is going to mitigate the cuts they are about to make, they are truly writing from a kindergarten perspective.... We have nasty people doing nasty things to us and we are told not to publicly object to it, because they might get even nastier."

The Tonks strategy was to pucker up and attack from the rear. It wasn't going to work.

Both Metro and the TTC have insurance policies that will cover the cost of a first libel or slander defence if the councillor is exonerated. I was advised the suit would likely not succeed. The courts do not look kindly at politicians suing politicians. It's sort of expected that these kinds of conflicts will occur in the rough and tumble of politics.

Here's where the cronyism and the old boy's network kicks in. Ozzie Doyle, the Metro solicitor, a long-term colleague of Al Leach and a known Tory, opined that since the remarks were made as a TTC commissioner I was not covered by the Metro insurance policy. The TTC solicitor, a man who was hired by Leach and who worked under him for many years, opined that I was not covered by the TTC insurance policy because I made the remarks as a Metro councillor outside the commission meeting. The Tories on the commission rallied to ensure that my expenses would not be paid. The punishment for me was not to lose the lawsuit, but rather to have to bear its costs.

My office kicked into high gear. Ben, Irene and Isaac, my fundraising chair, treated it like they were raising money for an election campaign. We held a fundraising banquet that brought in enough money to cover all of my legal expenses. Now Al had lost his hammer. A Toronto Star editorial summed it up: This lawsuit is unseemly. Why can't Moscoe swallow his pride and apologize? And why can't Leach develop a thicker skin – that will serve him in good stead in the Legislature – and drop the lawsuit? Shake hands boys.

We did. I issued an apology. Al dropped the lawsuit. So now, the battle of Downsview was over. I am not sure.

It is TTC policy to name stations after the streets they cross. By policy, this station should have been named Sheppard West Station. That policy will prove to be problematic as the system expands and more subway lines are built. There already was a Sheppard Station on the Yonge line. I wanted the community to choose the name of the station. We mailed out ballots to everyone within a one-mile radius of the station. Residents declared they preferred the name Downsview by a two-to-one margin to the second choice, Wilson Heights. Sheppard West was a distant third choice. The TTC received more than 2,500 ballots.

Now, the line is being extended northward and five new stations are being added. The next station on the line was to serve Downsview Park, a national urban park that came about as the result of a 1999 election promise. The park wanted to grab the name Downsview for their station. I resisted for three years and was able to convince the commission that it ought not to be changed.

They could call their station Park Station or Park Downsview Station if they wished. It would be no more confusing to have two stations with the word Downsview in it than it would to have two Sheppard Stations. How much more confusing is it to change the name of a station after it has been in use for many years? Alas, it was only after I retired that they were they able to persuade the commission to change the name. Perhaps this will be the last skirmish in the Battle of Downsview.

CHAPTER 47

Desert Deadbeat

The thing the Jewish Community cares most passionately about is Israel. Stephen Harper's strong pro-Israel policy had wrested at least three federal ridings away from the Liberals. It is easy for him to do because it supports one of the few electoral democracies in the Middle East and at the same time plays to the Christian right.

My left-wing ideology grew out of the labour Zionist movement and, like most Jews, I share the same passion for Israel and its survival. My ward had the most concentrated Jewish population of any political jurisdiction in Toronto, if not in all of Canada. While municipal government has nothing whatsoever to do with Middle Eastern politics, occasionally the two intersect.

In 1991, the Saudis came to the Canadian National Exhibition to showcase their culture. They had put together a travelling exhibition that was housed in a giant tent. The deal was they would cover the cost of free admissions for everyone who came to the Ex on opening day. They put down a deposit of $20,000 and were to pay the balance of $170,000 after the show. I was on the board of the CNE. In 1992, while reviewing the budget of the previous fair, I noted a deficit of $170,000. I checked with Bill Moore, the general manager. He confirmed the shortfall was due to the Saudis not paying their bill despite repeated attempts to collect for almost a year.

I dashed off a letter to King Faud: "It seems strange that you would spend so much money and make such a great effort to court the goodwill of Canadians and destroyed all of that by walking away without clearing up your debt. Is this the image of your country you want us to remember?"

I had heard the Saudis were so arrogant that this was the way they normally did business. Calling the affair "desert stall," I released my letter to the media knowing that embarrassing them might be the only way to get them to pay their bill.

KING FAUD

"If a taxpayer in Metro defaults in payments we take his house. We don't have a place big enough for King Faud's house," I quipped. "The free day may not have been so free at all. It could be the Metro taxpayers that end up paying the bill."

Metro Chairman Allan Tonks fumed. He called the embassy to apologize for the story appearing in the newspaper. He blamed the "loose tongue" of one of his councillors and my impatience for the incident. He admitted to having written the mayor of Riyadh some months before requesting assistance in collecting the bill. (Good luck with that!) At that time, Tonks had been told they were in the "final stages of paying." (Sure they were.)

"This represents the individual agenda for a grandstand play by one member of council," said Tonks.

He was right. What did I care? There wasn't a soul in my ward that had any sympathy for the King of Saudi Arabia. If I hadn't exposed that we had been stiffed, we might still be waiting for the desert winds to blow the money our way.

Yes, they finally paid after all the fuss.

CHAPTER 48
Jakobek

For the record, I never liked Tom Jakobek. I considered him the most despicable municipal politician I have ever known. I know there were many others who felt the same way. I am sure that likewise, I was no fan of his. You can imagine our delight when Madam Justice Bellamy in her Toronto Computer Leasing Inquiry into the MFP Financial Services scandal exposed him publicly for what he was and what we knew him to be: (her words) "a congenital liar and a corrupt politician," the kind that gave us all a bad name.

Tom was mean and unforgiving. He was a bully. If a civil servant or a colleague got in his way, you knew he would do everything in his power to get even. That's why he was feared and pandered to by many of the bureaucrats and his colleagues at City Hall. We all had complicated reasons for being in politics. I never felt there was anyone more "in it for themselves" than Tom Jakobek.

Mel Lastman and I were always sparring, but it wasn't the same kind of relationship. Many of the Lastman-Moscoe dust-ups were for show. While I often disagreed with Mel on policy issues and we would duke it out publicly, we would usually shake on it after it was over. In politics, you have to learn to forgive and forget. If you carry a grudge you end up eating yourself up alive. You need your enemy on one issue to become your ally on the next. Disagree with Mel Lastman as I might, I never seriously questioned his motivation and I acknowledge there were many good things he did. With Jakobek, I just couldn't find any.

My first head-to-head encounter with Jakobek was in 1983 over street vending. The Metro government did not permit vending on Metro roads. The City of Toronto did. Yet there was almost as much illegal vending on Metro roads as there was legal vending on City of Toronto streets. There was a confusing mess of bylaws, regulations and enforcement. In 1985 alone, some 800 charges were laid against vendors. A City of Toronto health department blitz that year inspected 272 hot dog carts and found 97 health violations. Tourist attractions like Harbourfront and the SkyDome were magnets for vendors. Case in point: The Eaton Centre. Vending was illegal on Metro roads, yet there were hundreds of vendors fighting each other for space on Yonge Street next to the Eaton Centre. Everything from hot dogs to T-shirts was being peddled, and the crowded sidewalks and jostling for position were becoming a hazard for pedestrians. There were too many vendors, too few spots and too many government bodies issuing permits. It was a mess.

In July of that year, as chair of Metro legislation and licensing, I organized a seminar for everyone involved at all levels, including police, bylaw enforcement, roads and traffic departments and health department officials of all seven municipal governments in Toronto to try and develop a means of sorting out the disorder.

Before we continue, let me try to clarify the difference between a licence and a permit. Metro issued licenses to operate food carts. A Metro licence only assured that the cart and the vendor met health and bylaw regulations. Having a licence only gave you the right to own a cart, not a spot from which to vend. A licensed vendor could rent space on private property; say a shopping mall, service station or parking lot, so long as it met the zoning regulations. Most vendors, however, wanted to be on a public street. To locate on a public street you needed a "location permit" from the municipality. Local municipalities, like Toronto, permitted vendors on the street under tight regulations. Metro, however, did not permit vending on Metro roads, which were the most desirable streets for vending. In 1990, there were 1,465 licences issued by Metro, but only 178 had permits for approved spots on public streets. Most of the approved vending spots were located within the City of Toronto and most were downtown. This put pressure on the other municipalities, and vending was quickly spreading into North York, Scarborough, East York, York and Etobicoke.

Tom Jakobek was chair of the City of Toronto city services committee, the committee that gave out permits. I was chair of Metro legislation and licensing committee, the committee that oversaw licensing. There were no Metro permits because until that time we did not allow vending on our roads.

I was not against vending. Vending was part of the city's and my family's immigrant experience. It was a first job for many new Canadians and an entry-level business. A successful vendor would often save enough money to open a store and move into the mainstream business community. When my grandfather immigrated to Canada after the First World War, he started by operating a pushcart on Toronto streets. When I was in high school, I sold football ribbons outside Varsity Stadium. I remember being furious when the City of Toronto banned street vending south of Bloor Street. I had a great deal of empathy for the vendors. When the Bloor/Yonge Business Association came before our vending subcommittee during the public hearings on vending spots and argued their area was "too upscale" to allow vending, we told them to get lost.

It became apparent to me that to bring some kind of order out of this chaos, Metro had to open its roads to vending. The dispute between Jakobek and myself revolved around how spots were to be allocated. In the City of Toronto, where Jakobek was the chair of the committee that controlled the distribution of vending permits, the system was based on a so-called "first come, first served" principle. In other words, the vendor scouted out a potential spot, applied for a permit and if staff agreed and it met with technical requirements, it could be approved. It then went before Jakobek's committee for a public hearing and final approval. In truth, it was often who you knew – wink wink nudge nudge – that determined which vendor would get a prime spot, or get a spot at all. It was a system that was wide open to corruption.

I put forward a lottery system as a method of distributing spots. Vending was to be considered entry level. It should not be allowed to become a permanent business occupying public land. A problem with the Toronto system was how could you tell a vendor who had occupied a sidewalk space for 25 years that it wasn't really his? How much more painful would it be if the city needed the space for public purposes and tossed out the vendor? Should you permit his "poor destitute" wife and children to occupy the space when he died? Jakobek, who was also a member of Metro Council, wanted Metro to adopt the City of Toronto system. I suppose, for whatever reason, he wanted control of those permits as well.

We fought it out and I won. Metro adopted a lottery system.

We tried to make the lottery as fair as possible. The vendors were asked to scout out locations for spots. After all, who better knew the business than those who were already in it? After holding public hearings, we approved 100 locations. These were placed on a huge map. The lottery took place at Exhibition Place. Registered vendors were given a number and when their number was called, the vendor went up to the map and claimed a spot. Those who were drawn early got the best spots, but they could hold them for only five years. After five years, all permits terminated, the lottery was re-run and the vendors were shuffled.

As chair of the vending subcommittee, I attended the first lottery as an observer. A photo of my daughter, Candice, and me at the event appeared in the Toronto Star. Candice designed T-shirts and she and her sister, Vicki, had both entered the lottery. Did I have a conflict of interest? I was pretty sure I didn't. Any public discussion of the lottery had occurred prior to their entry. It was indeed a lottery so there was no way I could have influenced its outcome. In any case, neither won a vending spot. I learned a valuable lesson that month when Basil Mangano, a "private citizen," filed a conflict of interest charge against me. The case was heard by Justice James Farley.

Who in the world was Basil Mangano? All I knew was that he owned a bar on Yonge Street. Was he just an ordinary citizen who, suddenly infused by public spirit, was determined to see that justice was done? Did he wake up one morning, see the picture of Candice and me in the Star and become so outraged that he rushed out to hire a lawyer to right a wrong?

Well not exactly. He was, I learned, a friend of one Councillor Tom Jakobek from his high school days at Monarch Park Collegiate. I might, to be charitable, believe this was a co-incidence except for the fact that some years later he admitted to my daughter Vicki, who sometimes had a coffee in his bar, that he was strongly motivated by someone at City Hall who always gets even.

Justice Farley recognized it as being frivolous and tossed the charge out.

Was it politically motivated? As the judge noted, what ordinary citizen issues a press release after laying a charge? The judge levied costs against Basil Mangano. They amounted to about $9,000. Because the city was self-insured, the City of Toronto, taxpayers, had to pick the balance of some $28,000 of my legal bill.

There were two other successful vending lotteries before amalgamation. When the City of Toronto and Metro merged, we were faced with two very different vending structures. Should we adopt the lottery or Toronto's first come, first served system?

When facing the daunting task of merging two disparate systems, the typical bureaucrat response would have been to do nothing, and that is exactly what was done. All of the existing spots were frozen into place and nothing has been changed to this day. As the system ages, it has begun to crumble. Vending spots are bought, sold and leased, all of this illegal under the bylaw. The system has ossified into what it is today.

For me, from that time forward, I never hesitated to go on the record as declaring an interest in anything that might be considered by anyone, no matter how remote or insignificant, to be a conflict.

At least, Tom Jakobek, or as some called him Councillor Jackboot, is no longer at City Hall, but then again, neither am I.

CHAPTER 49

Better to be Disabled in Toronto than in Paris

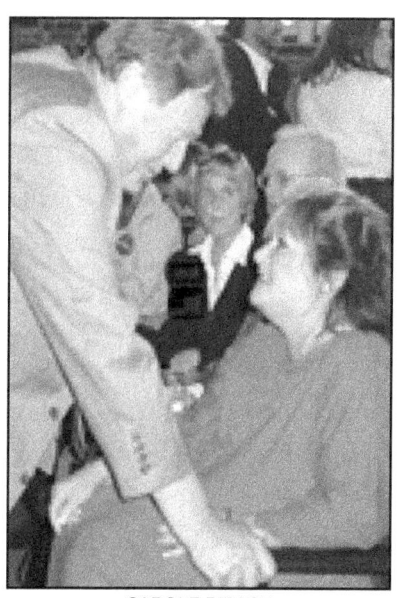

CAROLE RIBACK

Carole Riback was one tough lady. She had to be. Carole grew up in Montreal, the daughter of a Montreal lawyer. She graduated from Cornell and landed a job with the International Red Cross in Geneva, Switzerland. Part of her job was to organize international conferences for the United Nations. Then an injury and deteriorating spine put her into a wheelchair. Carole became a paraplegic, yet despite her declining health she managed to earn a master's degree from the University of Toronto and began working on her doctorate in counselling psychology. Carole was an activist at the forefront of the fight for disabled rights in Toronto. I loved her dearly. Shortly after she was appointed to the TTC's advisory committee on accessible transportation, her colleagues recognized her talents by electing her chair.

Carole was in constant disagreement with David Gunn, the TTC's general manager, who was loath to spend the money required to make the system fully accessible. The disabled community wanted Toronto buses to be low-floor. Gunn favoured lifts. Lifts met the minimum standard mandated by the Americans with Disabilities Act (1990). Gunn had managed several U.S. transit systems and was prepared to meet only a minimum standard. Installing lifts was far less expensive than buying low-floor buses. The advisory committee on accessible transportation felt lifts were next to useless. I agreed with Carole and her committee. This was the origin of my falling out with David Gunn.

Toronto was in the market for new streetcars and the committee had persuaded us to try to purchase vehicles that were low-floor so the regular system could be accessed by wheelchairs. A few cities were experimenting with accessible streetcars and Bombardier, the only Canadian manufacturer of light rail vehicles, was showcasing its low-floor streetcars at the UITP show in Paris that year. The International Union of Public Transport (UITP) is a worldwide association of urban and regional passenger transport operating authorities and suppliers.

UITP holds a World Congress and Exhibition every two years, and the 1995 show was to be held in Paris, France. The TTC selected Paul Christie, the chair, and I as vice-chair, to be part of the Toronto delegation. Because the World Congress was featuring accessibility as a theme, Carole Riback was asked to attend as chair of our advisory committee. Carole's medical condition required an attendant to travel with her. She was the only one of our party that was fluent in French.

You would think a country that had been through two world wars would provide a reasonable level of service for people with disabilities. Not so. While Toronto had the TTC's public Wheel-Trans system, Paris had nothing. The only disabled transport was provided by a private company that had some 75 vehicles to service a city of 11 million people. They charged a full fare that was higher than taxi rates. Their fleet consisted of vans with pullout ramps. The wheelchair was pushed into the vehicle from a rear door and clamped to the floor of the truck. The city itself didn't have ramped curbs at intersections so wheelchairs could climb sidewalks. These have been standard in Toronto for years.

The adventure began the moment we landed at Charles de Gaulle Airport. Because we were public transit advocates, we felt duty bound to use the public transit system to our hotel. Big mistake! Charles de Gaulle has a TGV (high speed train) station right at the airport. It took us more than half an hour to make our way to the TGV station, and it quickly became apparent that most Parisians had not yet discovered the benefits of public transit from the airport. You could have rolled a bowling ball down the platform without hitting anyone. It was all but deserted.

I have never understood the public demand for a transit line in Toronto to Pearson International Airport. When the Union-Pearson Express opened in June of 2015, ridership was well below the wildly optimistic passenger projections of its promoters. Even though they have cut the fare for a one-way airport trip from $27 to $12, to this day, the provincial operating subsidy for the line has totalled $39.3 million dollars or a whopping cost of $56.26 per ride. It will never be well used and, in any case, the money wasted on it would have been better used for rapid transit in areas that really need it.

When we arrived in Paris, we had to travel by city bus to make our next connection. Wouldn't you know, there wasn't a single city bus in Paris that was accessible. Picture us dragging a wheelchair onto a bus along with our luggage and the extra luggage Carole had to bring to carry her medical supplies.

Our next trial took place at the Gare du Nord station, where we decided to grab a couple of taxis to get to our hotel. Taxis cue up inside a carriageway alongside the station. I opened the front passenger door:

"Will you please move your things off the seat? I have to put Carole into the front seat," I said to the driver.

"She can't sit there. Passengers cannot sit in the front seat."

"She's disabled; she is unable to sit in the back seat."

"She can't, it's not allowed. Take the next cab."

"I know the rules," I said. "You have to take the first passenger in line. I'm taking your cab and I am not moving till you let us in."

I took out a note pad and began to write down the number of his cab. Other cabs behind had loaded and began to honk their horns. At that point, he hurled a string of curses at me and squealed out of the station empty.

The UITP had over 3,000 attendees that year. Even though the theme of the conference was accessible transit, Carole was the only person at the show in a wheelchair. Her presence was in great demand. Bombardier had installed a full size, two-car mock-up of their low-floor streetcar at the show. The plan was to leave the show after two days and take a day trip to Brussels to see the Bombardier system in operation. We would then return for the rest of the conference.

Before we left the show, Freddy Thielemans, the burgomaster (mayor) of Brussels, approached us and asked Carole if he could take some pictures of her entering the Bombardier vehicles. She agreed. We were to travel to Brussels by TGV the next morning. Before I left, I telephoned the railway company: "Is the train to Brussels disabled accessible?"

"Most definitely", they informed me.

When we arrived at the station, we learned what they meant by accessible. Four porters met us on the platform and attempted to lift Carole in her wheelchair onto the train. When they discovered the door was too narrow, they shrugged, turned and left. I had to lift Carole out of her chair and carry her to her seat while Paul folded the wheelchair and carried it and the baggage onto the train.

A porter met us when we arrived in Brussels. The plan was to take a freight elevator at the end of the platform down to the basement and access the station from there. The freight elevator was broken. We had to lower Carole and the wheelchair down from the platform to the track level, carry her across the tracks and lift her onto the next platform in order to access the station. At least this time, the porter stayed to help.

The most difficult thing to swallow was that when we arrived to look at Bombardier's low-floor streetcars, we discovered while the streetcars themselves were low-floor, the city hadn't bothered to build platforms by which they could be accessed. Carole again had to be lifted onto the vehicles and carried off. Carole was livid. The next day, when we arrived back at the conference, she sought out the burgomaster of Brussels:

"If you use one of those pictures, I'll sue the ass off you."

That evening, we headed out for dinner. I remembered a delightful restaurant we had dined in on our last trip to Paris. Try as we might, we just couldn't get a taxi that would stop for us.

"Don't worry," I said. "I've checked the map. It's only a few short blocks away."

Well, they may have looked short on a map but they weren't. After we had trudged about a kilometre, the clouds opened up and it began to rain. Not a gentle storm, but a torrential downpour. Gloria (my wife) tried to keep Carole dry, but the one small umbrella we had was useless. We all arrived at the restaurant soaked through to the skin. I remember having to wring out my shirt in the washroom basin. It was a miserable meal.

The next day at the trade show, the City of Paris was hosting a press conference to unveil its first disabled accessible bus. They asked Carole to attend. I suppose they needed some background colour. They got more colour than they anticipated.

The problem you have in making a bus low-floor is the wheels. In order to lower the floor, you have to put the wheels inside the cabin and in order to do that you have to encase them in some kind of a box. TTC buses are accessible from the front door. Only the small back portion of a TTC bus behind the rear door is elevated. The Parisian bus had obviously been designed without any consultation and not much thought. It was a design disaster. They had sited the low-floor portion of the bus at the rear end. It was entered from a separate door and the passenger ended up sitting in a well at the rear of the bus. It was like being trapped in a closet. Nobody had thought about the person in the wheelchair being unable to see out the windows, nor could the driver see the customer.

The horde of media and photographers rushed to interview Carole to ask her what she thought of the new bus. She told them in quite colourful language. If I remember correctly, she drew an analogy with the old "back of the bus" policy in Selma, Alabama.

The City of Paris was so embarrassed by the incident that they scrambled to make amends by putting a limousine and a city chauffeur at our disposal for the balance of the trip.

I have concluded that despite many of its failings the TTC can be proud of its efforts to make public transit in Toronto accessible to all of its citizens. We owe a lot of what we are to the persistence and courage of people like Carole Riback.

CHAPTER 50

Tow Tale No. 1: It's Sometimes Hard to Separate the Good Guys from the Bad Guys

You would think towing under police contract would be as pristine as a newborn babe. Think again.

I had the sudden realization that not all was kosher when I returned from a meeting to find my car dangling at the end of a tow truck. There was a ticket on the windshield, punishment enough, but why did I have to witness my car be dragged away when I was there to drive it away myself? Was it the police officer's objective to clear the street or generate revenue? Why did I have to follow the tow truck in a taxi and pay a ransom to get it back? There seemed to be no coherent policy here.

I wasn't alone. When my complaint hit the media, there followed more than 24 telephone calls from others who had suffered the same fate. Clare Westcott, police commission chair, disagreed:

"The police are just trying to keep traffic going.... No one is out there to make money or get people."

There seemed to be some kind of a disconnect here. My towing incident happened in November of 1986. The telephone calls just kept coming. After three months of complaints, I decided I had to take the matter to the police commission. In March of 1987, I appeared before Westcott and the commission meeting to try and sort it out.

Police Chief Jack Marks told the commission that Metro police contracts with towing companies stated that motorists who get to their vehicles as they are being hoisted are supposed to get their cars unhitched for a $20 drop charge. The Metro licensing commission sets the tow rate. So who is policing police towing? We all agreed there should be a flat tow rate and someone had to police the rules. The police commission also agreed to consider a campaign to advise drivers of their rights when their cars are towed.

"I think it's a great idea," said Westcott.

How were towing contracts let? Toronto was divided into districts and firms were required to bid for the right to do police tows in each district. In order to bid, a tow company had to meet a number of standards, most of them designed to protect the public. For example, to win a police tow contract a bidder had to maintain a lot within the district. It had to meet minimum size requirements, be easily accessible and staffed 24 hours a day. Services associated with the tow that could be charged were clearly laid down. All things being equal, the key bid figure was the price for a tow. If a company met all other requirements in the competitive tender, the contract went to the lowest bidder. The downtown core was the most sought-after contract. That's where the bulk of police tows originated. It was a huge area and Byers Towing had won the police contract for the past 25 years.

It's like honey attracts flies. Politicians who become associated with an issue attract complaints. I was contacted by Steve Sanderson, a towing company owner. Steve had been bidding on the police contract for the North York district for several years. The contract had somehow always gone to Yorktown Towing. Steve was a straight shooter. He patiently laid out the evidence. Yorktown did not meet the police standard. They had sold off a portion of their lot and their pound was now below minimum size. Steve showed me a copy of his bid for the North York contract. It was the lowest bid. He then showed me the report that went to the police commission. Someone had changed his bid figure in the report to make it higher than Yorktown's. He then produced a number of Yorktown tow bills for police tows that were higher than allowed by the contract.

STEVE SANDERSON

I set up a meeting with Chief Marks, and Steve and I trooped down to police headquarters with the evidence in hand. I never got to see Marks. We were shuffled over to one of his deputies, who patiently listened while Steve laid out his evidence. I said to the deputy:

"I want someone to review the bidding process and I am asking you to have internal affairs investigate this particular bid."

His face turned red, he rose to his feet and said:

"Nobody tells me how to do my job."

I'm sure he was restraining himself because he didn't add, "You little shit!"

He didn't have to. We got the message. Then again, so did he.

At the next commission meeting, the police commission announced sweeping changes in police towing. The new rules limited charges to fees for the tows, dolly use where necessary and storage fees. Storage fees were now at an hourly rate, rather than a bulk day rate, and safety lights could not be charged. Commissioners also said they would remind police officers that drivers who arrive on the scene before the tow had the right to demand the truck drop their vehicle for $20. And they called for advertisements to be placed in newspapers to explain the public's right to a drop charge.

The commission also split the central district into two towing areas. Buyers got only one of them. One-year contracts were also approved for six districts and Commissioner Westcott hinted that to increase competition, other districts would be further split.

Steve Sanderson never got the contract for North York District. He did one better than that. He got the contract for the collision reporting centres – all of them. (More about that later).

The secretary of the commission, the person responsible for administering bids for contracts? He took an early retirement.

CHAPTER 51

Tow Tale No. 2: Scum-Sucking Bottom Dwellers

Now ask me how I really feel about the towing industry. When you chair the licensing committee at Metro, you meet them all. Don't get me wrong. There are actually some loving, sensitive, empathetic passionate people driving tow trucks. I once met one. The truth is, it's a tough industry that lurks on the fringes of society.

Some people toss around shibboleths about wanting "less government" and "de-regulation"; that is until they have been towed from an accident scene. In 1997, we were faced with a raft of complaints from angry motorists who had been towed and ripped off. At that time, it was said an accident tow truck driver in Toronto could make a decent living if he had two tows a week. That's because his main source of income was not the fee for the tow, but rather the kickback he got from the body shop in exchange for the business; sometimes as high as 20% of the cost of the repair job. That is why the tow truck driver would bust his gut to steer you to his "friend" who owned a body shop that "did excellent work at reasonable prices."

Think about it. It is 6:30 p.m. on a snowy Friday afternoon. You are driving along Highway 401 west of Keele Street and have just been sideswiped by a misdirected vehicle. You are in a state of semi shock and have two crying children in the back seat. You are suddenly surrounded by four tow trucks that have rushed to the scene. The OPP officer who arrives directs the tow to the first tow truck and shouts "Get this vehicle out of here." How vulnerable are you?

The driver tows you to the Hereiam Collision Repair Shop. It is closed for the night, so he leaves the car on the lot and you take a taxi home. Next morning, after you have discussed the situation with your partner and contacted your insurance company, it is agreed the car should go to the body shop that usually does your work. You send a tow truck to retrieve the vehicle and the body shop refuses to release it because you signed something the tow truck driver handed to you. After some negotiations, they agree to release your car if you pay a fee of $850. The insurance company pays.

About a decade earlier in Toronto, the police decided it was a waste of time and police resources to investigate every little fender bender that happened on the streets. They set up what was called a "collision reporting centre." If your car was smashed and the damage appeared to be less than $1,000 (later raised to $2,000) and there was no personal injury, you were to exchange information with the other driver and head off to a collision reporting centre, usually at the end of a tow hook. As you sat in the cab of the tow truck, the friendly driver told you he would wait around at the centre until the police report was completed and then tow you to the repair shop.

At the centre, the damage was photographed, a police officer listened to both parties and wrote the police report and you could talk directly to your insurance company. It either had a representative in the back room or could be reached by way of a direct telephone line. It was sort of a one-stop shopping centre for smash-ups, all very efficient.

Friday, January 17, 1997 was the public hearing. The Metro licensing commission had before it the report of a task force investigating towing practices in Metro. Councillor Blake Kinahan had originally headed up the task force, but he had dithered for more than a year and a half without any results. I was asked to take over the lead and had promised to table a report within six months. This was the opportunity for the public to address the sweeping changes recommended to prevent accident chasers from preying on shaky motorists at crash scenes. It was not a love-in.

The tow operators were not happy. The report recommended several rule changes that might force them to actually have to earn their living from towing vehicles, rather than from illegal kickbacks. They were out in force and they flexed their muscles. Tow trucks ringed Metro Hall for more than an hour, blocking all approaches. When the drivers went up to the meeting, they hooked their trucks to the bumper of the truck behind so they couldn't be towed.

More than a hundred drivers crowded into the committee room where security guards stood by to keep order. When deputations began, the angry drivers booed, jeered and shouted out their displeasure. The insurance industry presented hundreds of tow bills in the $300 to $500 range, many issued by some of the same drivers in the room.

When the chair, Charles Archibald, demanded tow truck driver Rick Tilling be thrown out of the room for disrupting the meeting, Tilling leaped up yelling he would take on all comers. The meeting descended into a minor riot while security guards attempted to keep order and his colleagues tried to hustle Tilling out into the hall. The meeting was recessed to allow the police we called in to maintain order. The recess lasted for two hours, but everyone hung in.

What was being proposed that was so upsetting? Among the some 25 recommendations, the key ones were:

- Accident tow rates would be capped at $125 on streets and $150 on expressways;

- Kickbacks among towing firms, towing companies and insurance companies were prohibited;

- Tow truck drivers must drop the vehicle at the collision reporting centre. The centre would arrange the tow out;

- The tow bill was standardized, with the rates pre-printed on them;

- No one in a collision reporting centre could recommend a body shop, including the insurance company agents. Customers would be presented with a list of all certified body shops.

- Every repair shop, body shop and tow truck operator must be properly certified and licensed.

When the commission re-convened, there were three uniformed police officers in the room.

At the end of the deputations, I was the first to speak. I waved a tow bill for $384.

"Do you think this is a fair charge to levy on a motorist who's been in an accident on highway 401? I have no sympathy for drivers who stick people with a huge bill for towing short distances and then get the customer to sign a lien against their own car."

At that point, Danny Sanderson, a tow company owner who was spokesman for drivers and had been a member of the task force, shouted, "Let's get out of here. This is fixed."

DANNY SANDERSON

Several drivers rushed the table where I sat claiming I was in bed with the insurance companies and was on the take. One of them yelled, "The biggest crooks in the city are on the commission."

I didn't resent the drivers' anger, but I had some difficulty with some of the anti-Semitic remarks. In any case, they left an impression on me. I installed a remote starter in my car.

The new bylaw was endorsed by the Licensing Commission. It then had to be reviewed by the Metro Social Issues Committee before it was sent to Metro Council for final approval.

Danny Sanderson, by the way, was the brother of the Steve Sanderson we met earlier. Steve owned and operated the collision reporting centres for the Metro police. After our bylaw went into place, Danny organized several demonstrations against the North Collision Reporting Centre on Toryork Drive in North York, where drivers pelted the building with eggs. There was no brotherly love here.

CHAPTER 52

Tow Tale No. 3: Cockroaches are Hard to Eradicate

Here is a scenario that was repeated almost 800 times a week in Toronto. You are attending an event and are searching for a parking spot. There's a strip mall nearby and all of the businesses are closed. A sign says, "immediate" customer parking only. The word "immediate" gives you pause for thought, but you park there anyway. The lot is empty, so what harm are you doing? When you return, you get a sinking feeling in the pit of your stomach; your car is gone. You have been towed.

After a closer reading of the sign and a telephone call to the police, you locate the pound and set off by taxi to retrieve your vehicle. At the pound, the gorilla behind the barrier hands you a bill for $250. That includes the cost of the tow and a day's storage. Luckily, they accept credit cards. When they lead you to your vehicle, there is another surprise waiting for you – a ticket on your windshield for $40. The ticket, by the way, is phoney, designed to look like a police-issued citation, but you don't notice that so you pay it over the telephone with your credit card. You have just experienced a Toronto Car Trap.

In the 1990s, this sleaze-ball scam of towing from private property had become so lucrative that tow operators were offering plaza owners a $5-per-car commission for the right to tow from their lots.

One notorious car trap was a plaza in the shadow of the North York Civic Centre, located on the east side of Yonge Street next to the Madison Centre; one of the few remaining strip plazas in downtown North York.

One complainant took me for a walk. We watched as an unsuspecting driver pulled into the car trap, parked his car and walked into the Madison Centre next door. It was less than a minute before a cockroach dressed in a security guard's uniform popped out of a parked car at the end of the lot, whipped a yellow ticket on to the windshield and waved towards one of the tow trucks lined up across the street on Spring Garden Avenue. It was less than three minutes before the vehicle was dangling from the end of a hook travelling north on Yonge Street. We watched as two more vehicles were yanked out of the lot. They were headed towards the Co-Up impound lot in the Finch and Keele Area.

I was chair of licensing and a member of the Metro licensing commission. I felt a strong compulsion to eradicate these vermin. The next day, I armed myself with my licensing commission ID, a copy of the Metro Licensing Bylaw, a wooden stool and a thermos of coffee and headed for the Co-Up pound. There is a clause in the bylaw that allows any licensing commissioner to inspect a licensed business during their hours of operation. Since Co-Up was opened 24 hours, I knew I was in for a long night.

After showing my credentials and the bylaw to the tattooed hulk behind the counter, I parked myself on a stool off to one side. He made a few frantic phone calls. He was not too pleased, but tolerated my presence stoically.

The first customer came through the door. I flashed my ID and gave him my card.

"From where were you towed?" I asked.

"Yonge Street near Sheppard Avenue," she replied.

This was an important question. Here's where it becomes confusing. There was a policy vacuum. Etobicoke, Scarborough and East York all had "towing from private property" bylaws. Under these bylaws, the tows had to be ordered by a police officer or a parking control officer. In other words, there had to be a legal City of Toronto ticket on the windshield. In addition to that, there was a waiting period after ticketing (depending on where the tow originated) of 15 to 30 minutes before a tow could be ordered. The motorist in these municipalities was, however, obliged to pay the tow fee and the impound fee to get a car released.

In York, North York and the old City of Toronto, there weren't any "towing from private property" bylaws. This kind of towing was under "common law." These were instant snatch zones. The tow could be initiated without a real ticket or any waiting period, but the pound had no right to demand a fee to get the car released. In effect, they were stealing the car. The scammers all used some kind of phoney, look-alike parking ticket, which most people paid because they assumed they were real.

I turned to the attendant.

"You can't legally collect a fee for this tow," I said, "Give her the keys."

I spent the next four hours releasing cars from the Co-Up pound.

Parking on private property was a zoo and a very confusing zoo at that. All the animals seemed to be in one cage. Not only were these vultures preying on cars, they were preying on people's ignorance. Most victims paid the tickets (usually to a box number in Brampton or by telephone with their credit card) because they assumed they were real.

Car scooping had become a major industry in Toronto. In any given week, there were 600 to 850 cars snatched from private property. That amounts to about 40,000 a year. In addition to the towing, storage and tagging fees, the tow invoices demanded an "administration fee." Some 15 tow companies were raking in anywhere from $5 million to $6.25 million a year in administration fees alone.

I took the matter to Metro Council and initiated almost a year of debate, discussion and public hearings. In the latter part of

1996, council brought in tough new rules for towing from private property that applied to all parts of Metro. They slapped a $75 cap on tows from private property. Every car required a legal ticket on its windshield before it could be towed and there had to be at least half an hour between the time of the ticket and the tow. Extra charges, like dollies, were prohibited and the fee that could be charged for storage was $5 per hour to a maximum of $20 in any one day.

There, we did it. The scam had been closed down. Well not exactly.

If you put a barrier between cheese and a rat, it will quickly gnaw his way through it. It wasn't long before the scammers had found a way around the new restrictions. It's not easy to eradicate a cockroach. Read on.

CHAPTER 53

Tow Tale No. 4: Scams Evolve

Vermin are adaptable and the tow companies adapted quickly. Some of them established pounds just outside the Metro boundaries; places like Vaughan, Mississauga, Richmond Hill and Markham that weren't covered by the bylaw. Yes, because they were licensed to tow in Toronto they had to observe the $75 cap for the tow price, but if they dragged the car outside the bylaw area, the storage limits did not apply. The pounds were under different municipal jurisdictions. They were still handing out $250 invoices. Anyone who bothered to ask was told the extra $175 was for storage.

When victims called the police to sort out the mess, the police didn't know what to do so they began referring complaints to my office. It's one thing to have your car snatched from a downtown lot, but to have to retrieve it from a pound in Mississauga is beyond tolerance. I partnered with Councillor Lois Griffin and took the matter to council.

"The general public is confused, angry and unaware of the complexities of the bylaws and... unable to take action that is necessary to stop these illegal activities," I said.

The notice of motion called for Metro's legal department, Police Services Board and Licensing Commission to "forthwith" set up a special prosecution task force to nab towing firms that take autos to pounds outside Metro. The task force would "bring charges on behalf of members of the public in order to stop these bandits in their tracks." I played a tape of a telephone message from a Metro citizen who had to retrieve his car from a pound in Markham. Council approved the motion.

Station Street is a street that runs west from York Street at the west end of Union Station. It looks like any other city street. The station loading docks are along the south side, and parking metres line the curb on the north side. It's not a real street; it is a private road. Drivers who overstay the meter get a ticket on their windshield, but it is not a real ticket; it's a phoney designed to look as much as possible like a real city-issued ticket.

Those private parking enforcement companies that didn't establish pounds outside Metro refined the art of scam ticketing. They issued thousands of them. Knock-off tickets were printed on the same yellow paper as the real police tags. They had bar codes and serial numbers and they even listed the same tick-off infractions that are on a real ticket, but only the "Park vehicle on private property without consent," was ever checked off.

The back of the ticket gave detailed payment instructions. Most of them directed the money to be mailed to a post office box and set a time limit after which, if not paid, the fee would go up. Some threaten a bad credit rating and even wage garnishment for unpaid tickets. If you telephoned the number on the ticket, you never got a real person but rather a tape that instructed you how to pay the ticket. Some tapes went even further: "Welcome to the parking help line. At the sound of the tone, please provide the information requested…"

The message then went on to elicit personal information, including your name, address and telephone number. Most of these companies do not have access to the province's vehicle registry. Without your personal information, they can't identify you and can never collect the ticket. Those drivers who identify themselves are added to the company hit list. They then are harassed by collection agencies; have to fend off attempts to screw up their credit ratings and, in some cases, are taken to small claims court.

Joseph Staszewski, one of the owners of Private Property Owners of Ontario Ltd. (POOL), proudly credits himself with having invented the private ticket. He has an interest in other parking enforcement companies as well. Many of these scum bucket companies are linked and some do their collections from the same offices. Municipal Parking Management Ltd. uses a parking meter as its logo. GTTA Parking Control puts something that looks like the former City of Toronto logo on the ticket and others use logos that look somewhat like the Toronto Police crest.

Impark (Imperial Parking Corporation) is a Vancouver-based corporation administering 3,400 parking lots in Canada and the United States. Impark administers Station Street along with a large number of Toronto lots. Despite their corporate façade, their practices are just as deplorable as the other companies. There is one difference. Impark lobbyists were able to convince the Province of Ontario to violate your privacy.

AL PALLADINI

Al Palladini was elected in the 1995 Tory sweep and became Mike Harris's minister of transportation. He was a car dealer from Vaughan whose business slogan was "Al Paladini is a pal of mine." He certainly was no pal when he signed an agreement to give Impark access to your private licence plate data, something Impark couldn't convince most provinces to do. This enabled them to collect their phoney parking tickets. Previously, that data had been limited to public law enforcement agencies. The province sold the data to Impark for $14 a plate.

In Ontario, everything was for sale. David Turnbull, the minister of transport who succeeded Paladini, subsequently expanded access to the licence plate registry to a host of other companies, including every two-bit collection agency and bailiff who could afford to pay. Turnbull added 10 parking control companies in Toronto, two of which have since gone out of business along with one that had its licence revoked by the Metro Licensing Commission. The floodgates were now open.

In 2004, after a lengthy debate, Toronto Council by a vote of 24 to 13 enacted a bylaw that made it illegal to put anything but a City of Toronto ticket on a windshield. Money was never the issue for the city. Gary Ellis, superintendent of parking enforcement, told council that police get 500 complaints each month from irate motorists. The most insidious aspect of the private tickets was that there was no appeal process. When you got a city-issued ticket, you had the right to "due process"; you could go to court and fight it. With the private tickets, all you got was the right to be hounded by a collection agency.

Many of the institutions fell into line. Sunnybrook and Women's College Hospitals immediately switched to issuing legal tickets. York University simply ignored the new bylaw. Impark's general manager, Solomon Ayeneababa, said his company would sue.

"The city cannot tell a business how to do its business, especially on private property," he said. "We'll continue to do our business the way we want to."

He saved his kindest comments for me.

"Moscoe is just being an idiot and a jackass and he is going to pay for it."

The City of Toronto's prosecution task force sprang into action.

The entire mess became entangled in a game of courtroom Ping Pong from that time forward. So far, only one company, Impark, has managed to weasel their way around the bylaw. In 2007, the court of appeal ruled Impark had the right to ticket cars on its private lots. Impark successfully argued they erected signs at entrances to their lots specifying motorists crossing the boundary were agreeing to pay the charge for parking and they were within their rights to try and collect it. They were not tickets being issued, they were invoices that were attempting to collect the money drivers owed them. The city had argued, unsuccessfully, that it was impossible to read the signs from a moving vehicle, especially with the pressure of traffic lined up behind, thus there was no contract. Impark was the only company that managed to win in court. The city beat all of the others.

One of the worst offenders is a company named Parking Control Unit, registered in Brampton. Their ticket attempts to scare people into paying. It demands a payment of up to $350, but reduces it to $25 if you pay in less than four days, $35 before 10 days and $75 before one month. The city has charged them 75 times for breaking the private parking ticket ban. They have been convicted five times, but those convictions were overturned on appeal and the city was asked to go back and take another look.

In November of 2009, the courts again sided with the city.

It took more than 10 years to sort out the towing industry. Most of the scammers are either out of business or have switched to towing legally. The hardcore scam artists will always be there. Like measles, the disease hangs in even though the epidemics have been largely eradicated. We are not off the hook yet. Next time someone tells you they want "less government regulation," let's hope they get to learn what it feels like to be tagged and  towed from private property or scooped by a bandit tow truck from an accident scene.

CHAPTER 54

Whacking Yourself Over the Head to Feel Better is a Dangerous Game

Irving Chapley was not the brightest pebble on the beach. He was a big, beefy loudmouth who by some stroke of luck got elected as alderman for North York's Ward 7. My father, who drove taxi for 25 years, was fond of saying he was just a dumb cab driver who got lucky. Irving made his money in the insurance business, but it was his Progressive Conservative Party connections that got him elected.

IRVING CHAPLEY

DAVID ROTENBERG

FRANK DI GIORGIO

The Wilson Heights Progressive Conservative Association hated me. It was their avowed desire to get rid of me, and they had tried by running candidates against me in past elections without success. Chapley was on their executive and both he and David

Rotenberg, the Wilson Heights MPP, were beating the bushes looking for candidates to run against me in the 1988 election.

I represented North York-Spadina on Metro Council. The ward was made up of two North York Council wards. Ward 7, in the north, was represented by Chapley. Ward 4, in the south, was held by Frank Di Giorgio. Both were Conservatives.

Under the Municipal Elections Act, a candidate can only raise funds for a campaign if they are registered. Registrations are accepted up to one year before an election. I had registered as early as possible. It was common knowledge that Chapley and Rotenberg were hunting for someone to run against me.

Stan Gordon was an earnest young man. He was a member of the Wilson Heights NDP Riding Association. I knew he was helping to plan the election campaign of his wife, who was going to be running for school board. I approached Stan.

"Do me a favour Stan. Irv Chapley and David Rotenberg are searching for a candidate to run against me in the next municipal election," I said. "Register against me. You don't have to actually run, but if it becomes publicly known that I have a credible opponent they'll stop looking."

Stan was a good choice. Before he switched parties, he had been president of Campus Conservatives at York University. Everyone knew him as a Conservative. Stan agreed to help. He registered in North York-Spadina against me and the heat was off.

The end of the yearlong registration period was approuching. By this time, Chapley had a registered opponent. He now knew he had to face an election as well. There had been so much animosity between Chapley and myself that Lastman decided to try and broker a peace treaty. He convened a meeting with us in his office and after a long discussion we came to an agreement that if Chapley didn't mess around in my election campaign I wouldn't interfere in his. We shook hands on it.

Nomination day is about 55 days before Election Day. Candidates who have previously registered must file nomination papers by nomination day. On nomination day, nominations close and no other candidates may enter the race. Once you have been nominated, you have 24 hours to withdraw. The clerk can then begin to prepare the ballots.

As nomination day approached, I was getting nervous. Because Stan hadn't filed nomination papers, the rumour mill again began to grind. Once again, it was widely rumoured the PCs had resumed their search for a candidate to run against me. We had to take remedial action.

This was in the early days of desktop publishing. To bolster the perception that Stan was a real candidate, we mocked up a Stan Gordon leaflet that viciously attacked Howard Moscoe. It was an excellent leaflet. Who better than I knew how to attack me? We printed about 30 copies and dropped them into the mailboxes of all known members of the Wilson Heights PC executive, including Chapley and a few extra on his street at his neighbour's doors.

We even mocked up a sign that I was prepared to print in my basement sign shop if necessary.

"Stan, let's take it one step further," I said. "Why don't you file nomination papers? Here is a blank set. Go up to Chapley's street and knock on doors. You need 10 signatures. Get 12 or 13 just to be sure. You don't actually have to run. You can pull out at the last minute."

Stan drove up to Hopewell Avenue. The third door he knocked on was Chapley's house. He was greeted with enthusiasm.

"It's great to finally meet you," Chapley said. "Of course, we'll sign your nomination papers. Norma, come here, you can sign too."

Chapley took him out to the garage, lifted the garage door and showed him a garage full of sign stakes.

"I want to make a donation to your campaign. Take as many stakes as you want."

We sent a truck up that night to pick up a load of stakes.

The next morning, Stan walked into the clerk's office and filed his nomination. Later that morning, the deputy clerk stepped into my office to advise me that Stan had filed nomination papers. He gave me a copy. I glanced at them, gasped at Chapley and his wife's signature and stormed into Chapley's office waving the papers.

"You son of a bitch," I said, "We had an agreement that we would not interfere in each other's election. We shook hands on it in the mayor's office. Now you've gone and nominated someone to run against me. I can beat Stan Gordon. I am going to spend all of my time this election making sure that you get defeated."

I then flung another mocked-up leaflet on his desk and stormed out of the office. The North York Mirror, a weekly newspaper, had just done a report card on North York councillors. I received an A+, and Chapley got a D-.

The leaflet featured a comparison of how the citizens of our mutual ward were represented at the Metro and local levels.

Stan's phone began to ring. He ignored it for a while. The calls became more frequent. It was Chapley.

"Hi Stan, maybe you should think again about running against Moscoe. He's been there a long time and will be hard to beat. Why don't you put your effort into your wife's campaign? Perhaps you should withdraw."

"I can't withdraw," said Stan. "I've already put about $3,000 into my campaign."

"Let me think about it," said Irv.

Chapley didn't waste much time at all thinking. He gave Stan $3,000. Stan used the money to fund his wife's trustee campaign and the stakes given to him to support her signs.

After nominations closed, Stan withdrew from the councillor campaign.

I was acclaimed.

CHAPTER 55
Up Close and Personal

If you don't love the job for the sheer joy of it, you ought not to be in politics. One of the most powerful assets that a politician has is a sense of humour. In this job, it is what, to use a biblical quotation, "separates the sheep from the goats."

After the dust of the 1988 municipal election had settled, my office received a number of the customary congratulatory letters. They are sort of like getting greeting cards. They simply mean someone's secretary had your name on a list. They are kind of warm and fuzzy to get, but really don't mean all that much.

My secretary, Irene, handed me one of these marked "PERSONAL AND CONFIDENTIAL." It was from Premier David Peterson. It offered me congratulations on my acclamation as a member of the new Metro Council and reminded me that: "It will be particularly important to maintain and strengthen the provincial-municipal relationship during this period."

Alas, it was a form letter.

I replied: "PERSONAL AND CONFIDENTIAL

"Thank you for your form letter dated December 16, 1988 marked Personal and Confidential. I wish to take this opportunity to thank you for congratulating me. Since you have expressed a desire to work closely with me, I would ask that you call my office and provide your private telephone number. I will need to contact you frequently to discuss our mutual 'provincial-municipal relationship.'"

About two weeks later, Irene buzzed me. There is a constituent on the line. His name is Mr. Peterson. It was the premier. I was so flustered that I wrote the number down incorrectly.

A week later, I fired off another letter to the premier. I enclosed a bubble gum card with his picture on it that I had cut and pasted together and wrote: "I can't begin to tell you how delighted I am

MR. PETERSON

to have you as a friend. As a token of our new friendship, I want to share with you one of my prized possessions. It is my most valued bubble gum card."

I went on to say: "I am so delighted that you have provided your private number that I want to share with you the private telephone numbers of some of my other personal friends so that you can also discuss matters of importance with them."

Whereupon I listed numbers for NDP Leader Bob Rae, the Queen, the Pope, the Dali Lama, Mother Theresa and several other world figures.

The response: "I am not interested in the other phone numbers. I am only interested in yours and now that I have it I am happy!"

Not to be outdone, I couldn't resist a follow-up. Andy Brant was the Tory leader. I had known him since his days as a municipal politician from AMO. The next step in this exchange was a letter from Andy to the premier: "I understand that you have the personal telephone numbers of the

ANDY BRANT

Pope, Mother Theresa and other VIPs... for many years now I have been trying to get Howard Moscoe's personal number. If you could share just this one number I would be most grateful."

Not long after that, I received a form letter from the Ontario Liberal Party seeking a donation.

I wrote to the premier indignantly: "I can't begin to tell you how much I value our newfound friendship. That's why I was shattered to receive your latest letter. No sooner do I become your friend then you ask me for money. What kind of a friendship is this?"

It was a short, but intense, relationship.

CHAPTER 56
Politics Brings out the Stupid in Some People

I breathed a sigh of relief. Nominations had closed and lo and behold I was acclaimed. There were three Metro councillors acclaimed that year, 1988. The election of '88 was going to be a yawn. It wasn't.

It was 3:40 a.m. on Sunday, November 7, and the jarring sound of a ringing telephone had me groping in the dark for the receiver. It was Anthony Perruzza's campaign manager. Perruzza was running in a field of five candidates for the Ward 5 North York seat. The election was a week away and Anthony was locked in a two-way fight with Bruno Rea, a Liberal Party affiliated candidate who had won the endorsement of the Toronto Star newspaper.

Anthony and I had been friends ever since the time Maria Rizzo had plucked him off an NDP-sponsored cruise of Toronto harbour. Maria recognized his potential as a politician, and we had mentored his election victory as a trustee for the Catholic School Board.

Rea was a credible candidate. He was 29 and held a Ph.D. in political philosophy from Oxford University. He worked as a policy advisor for the Ontario Ministry of Labour and had written an editorial piece for the Globe and Mail opposing capital punishment.

I had been rousted out of bed in the early hours of the morning because security guards at York University reported to the Perruzza campaign that they had apprehended Rea, his father,

Palmino Rea, and campaign manager, Vince Quattrociocchi, at the edge of a woodlot on the campus dumping Perruzza election signs from the back of their truck. They also discovered an additional pile of Perruzza signs deeper in the forest, along with a number of Maria Augimeri signs. Maria was another NDP candidate in the neighbouring ward.

Security officers became suspicious when they saw a truck with its headlights off driving to a remote area of the campus. They recovered more than 160 Perruzza signs and charged the trio with trespassing.

How stupid can an Oxford University Ph.D. be? It's one thing for an exuberant campaign worker to kick down an occasional election sign. That sometimes happens, although I always instruct my campaign workers, "No matter what, don't touch their election signs." It's another thing to be caught red-handed dumping a truckload of signs in a remote location at night.

After a hasty briefing at Anthony's campaign office, I rushed to York University where I met with security officers Robert Hughes and his partner Ed Canter, who toured me around the dumpsite. This is far juicier than a simple trespassing charge, I thought. This could be North York's municipal Watergate.

With that in mind, I raced over to 31 Division district police headquarters.

"This merits more than a simple trespassing charge." I told the duty sergeant. "I am asking that you have senior staff review the seriousness of this matter and lay the appropriate charges."

Later that morning, the police charged the trio with possession of property obtained by crime and with violation of the Canada Elections Act by removing a candidate's advertisement.

I then returned to the office and dashed off a press release, which we faxed everywhere. It began: "Candidate caught red handed dumping opponent's election signs. Police lay criminal charges."

I spent the rest of the morning telephoning the city desk of every newspaper, radio station and TV outlet in the GTA. It became a hot story. The media flocked to Downsview in droves. The Toronto Star headline topped them all: "North York election signs seized by police – Council candidate faces stolen goods charge."

The Ward 5 election results in Downsview for North York Councillor:

Candidate	Total votes	% of total votes
Anthony Perruzza	5,207	50.65
Frank Crudo	1,967	19.13
Bruno Rea	1,557	15.14
John Butcher	951	9.25
Charles Olito	599	5.83

Was Bruno Rea convicted? I don't remember, but it didn't matter. That one dumb political move in the last week of the campaign cost him the election along with his political career. As Richard Nixon said: "Well, I screwed it up real good, didn't I?"

CHAPTER 57

We Stand on Guard for Something

There is nothing like a debate on the national anthem to stir patriotic rhetoric and unrestricted blather. On June 21, 1990, Metro Council voted 12 to 9 to ask the Federal Government to rewrite the lyrics of O Canada. It was a motion sponsored by me and Councillor Maureen Prinsloo.

To put the matter into context, it was at a time when women were beginning to question being relegated to a secondary status by the structure of our language. We were all becoming more conscious of nuances that downgraded women.

Prior to this, we had engaged in a language debate about the term "manhole," which appeared frequently in municipal works reports and many of our technical drawings. Quite surprisingly, it was Councillor Brian Harrison, a Conservative and also an engineer, who proposed the compromise. We would henceforth use the term "maintenance hole." That way, we could resolve the gender specificity dilemma without having to change all of the drawings, which for the most part were labelled "MH."

The offensive part of the national anthem revolved around the line: "True patriot love, in all thy **sons** command,"

It was a national anthem whose wording excluded the majority of the people in the country. The proposed wording would have been: "True patriot love, in all **of us** command,"

Councillor Richard Gilbert, who had immigrated to Canada from England, contributed the second change.

"Our home and **native** land" ought to be changed to "Our home and cherished land."

Gilbert said large numbers of Canadians were not born in Canada and the majority of those people in Toronto were in that category. The national anthem should be revised to be inclusive; that they had come here by choice and also wanted to be included.

Before you consider these changes a radical move, you should be aware that Canada's national anthem was not like the Ten Commandments, carved in stone. There had already been several written versions and at least 17 specific wording changes to the English version of O Canada since it was written in 1876. The last change had been made in 1980, only 10 years earlier. On January 1, 1980, it was officially proclaimed into law as Canada's national anthem. Metro Council's proposed amendment was simply an attempt to draw it into the 20th century.

We knew we were on the right track when the Toronto Sun excoriated Maureen Prinsloo and me in an editorial calling us: "Two nit picking nitwits that deserve a kick in the pants."

Most English-speaking Canadians aren't aware that the French version of O Canada bears little resemblance to the English version. If the national anthem is going to belong to everyone, it has to be a song most Canadians feel comfortable with. The music for the French version was composed by Calixa Lavallee to accompany the words of a hymn written by Judge Aldophe-Basile Routhier for the St. Jean-Baptiste Day celebrations in Quebec City in 1880. It is essentially a religious song.

As a non-Christian, I have a high level of discomfort with its use as a national anthem. Its lyrics talk about: "The authentic faith" and about how Canadians "know how to carry the cross."

Given the sensitivity of French/English relations in this country, few people have had the courage to make an issue of it. That is why my attempt to have the clerk stop printing the French version on each council agenda failed miserably.

There is nothing like a national anthem debate to bring the eccentrics crawling out of obscurity. One woman threatened to sue. She claimed she had obtained a copyright when the exiting copyright had run out in 1979. She wanted $350,000 to adopt the changes.

Another woman wrote to object to our proposed changes. She claimed to be one of "six generations of full-blooded Canadiens" (sic) and blamed "newcomers for stirring up anthem angst." (Why don't you go back to where you came from?).

A man from Nova Scotia wrote to complain that he wanted God written out to make atheists happy. He had a point, but at this juncture, I was barely holding my own against the Philistines on the changes we already proposed.

By this time, Maureen and I realized we had probably bitten off more than we could chew. Alas! You just can't tamper with a nation's psyche. The country will just have to wait for madness to strike Parliament to get any further revisions.

By the way, here is the first English version, written in 1906.

O Canada! Our fathers' land of old
Thy brow is crown'd with leaves of red and gold.
Beneath the shade of the Holy Cross
Thy children own their birth
No stains thy glorious annals gloss
Since valour shield thy hearth.
Almighty God! On thee we call
Defend our rights, forfend this nation's thrall,
Defend our rights, forfend this nation's thrall

CHAPTER 58
Sometimes the Little Guy Wins

Francesco Grosso died on September 14, 2015. He was a Toronto icon, the last street popcorn vendor. When I was a child, every neighbourhood had its popcorn vendor. I remember clutching the six cents my uncle had given me as I anxiously waited for the popcorn vendor to pour butter over the paper bag brimming with hot popcorn. If I was lucky, I had a dime for one of his red candy apples.

Franco's popcorn cart had been parked in front of the main doors of the Royal Ontario Museum (ROM) on University Avenue in Toronto for 33 years. He was part of the museum, so much so that the ROM featured him in one of their advertising posters. He was a colourful character who everyone loved. He was so much a part of the street scene that he and his cart were commissioned as an extra for scenes in several movies that were filmed in Toronto.

For some reason, in May and June of 1996, the city's bylaw enforcement officers started a blitz on vendors vending on private property. Franco was hit with a flurry of $125 tickets. George Demos asked me to intervene on Franco's behalf. George had an ice cream truck location in front of the museum. The ice cream vendors had also been treated like criminals. Under our vending bylaws, an ice cream truck could not remain at a single location for more than three hours. They were constantly being chased and ticketed by bylaw officers. There were about 45 ice cream trucks in Metro at the time. Most of the ice cream vendors were

Greek immigrants struggling to make a living for their families. Their business was seasonal. If they didn't make it in the summer, they couldn't make it at all. They wanted stable locations.

FRANCESCO GROSSO

They approached me as the new chair of the Metro licensing committee and found a sympathetic ear. My mother's father had started life as an immigrant working the streets with a pushcart collecting scrap for sale. My father's dad plied the same trade, but had the luxury of a horse and wagon, which he stabled behind his house on Markham Street. When he enrolled at school, my dad listed his father's occupation as "antique collector." Working through Metro licensing, we managed to come to an arrangement that found curbside locations for most of the trucks. I became sort of the patron saint of the ice cream vendors. I could never pass a truck without being offered an ice cream. Too bad that I'm diabetic!

Private property vending was not under the jurisdiction of Metro. It was a local City of Toronto matter. I was a Metro councillor and Franco was being charged under the city zoning bylaw. I knew how little sympathy the vendors would get from both Tom Jakobek, chair of the City of Toronto vending committee, and the downtown councillors, who viewed all vendors as "the enemy." That's because one of their most powerful constituencies, the

Business Improvement Area Boards (BIAs) representing the retail merchants, hated street vendors. The BIAs had considerable influence on local politics. They worked on an ongoing basis with their local councillors, and their businesses contributed heavily to their election campaigns. It looked to me like it was the local BIAs, aided by the downtown councillors, that had initiated this blitz against the street vendors in the first place.

It was surprising how little empathy we got from Mayor Barbara Hall. Bylaw enforcement staff told us point blank at a meeting in her office: "He (Franco) has nothing to do with the museum. He shouldn't be vending on their property."

"He's been vending there for 33 years," I said. "Why are you harassing him now?"

"There have been complaints."

"From the museum?"

Silence

"How do we resolve this?"

"He can make an application to the committee of adjustment under the zoning bylaw."

Franco was mystified.

"I can't understand why this is happening to me," he said. "The museum never complains. They've known me for a long time. For me, they're like family."

We were battling a lost cause. In the first place, a person cannot apply to rezone someone else's property. Secondly, a zoning application would cost thousands of dollars and would take months. The only way to deal with the city was to embarrass them. We went public.

This resulted in a Toronto Star story on June 24, 1997, headlined: "Tickets swamp popcorn man. Museum 'landmark' faces extinction."

It also prompted the Star's editorial board to give the bylaw enforcement officers a Dart "for going overboard in harrassing and charging a long-time vendor outside the Royal Ontario Museum. Franco Grosso has occupied the same spot for 33 years.... We can't turn a blind eye to the infraction, they say. Does this mean bylaw police have been blind for 33 years? So why change the see-no-evil practice now?"

The city bylaw officers looked like thugs. The criticism was brutal.

The museum was terrific. The director's office set up a meeting for us with Jack Vecchio, head of museum security.

"Frank has been in front of the ROM so long that he's a virtual landmark," he said. "I am unaware of any complaints by museum patrons against him and we welcome his presence. It would be a disappointment if he was forced out of business."

I offered a suggestion.

"Would the museum consider hiring him for $1 a year?"

That way, he would then become an employee and his cart would be an accessory use to the museum. He would then be legal under the zoning bylaw.

"I'll check with our solicitors," he said.

That was the answer. On June 24, 1997, a year after the city harassment had begun, the museum hired Franco as an independent contractor for $1 a year to sell popcorn and novelties.

Franco's zoning problem was solved. He was now legal. However, the matter of his outstanding $125 tickets would not be dealt with until November.

The stress was too much for Franco. On September 27, he suffered a stroke. Fortunately, bolstered by George Demos, the ice cream truck association president, and a new cane, he had recovered enough to appear in court at old city hall on November 27. Justice of the Peace Marcel Bedard presided. There were three charges. Franco pleaded guilty to the first charge and not guilty to the others. The city bylaw officer grimly presented the evidence.

"He was peddling popcorn, your worship, not crack-cocaine," I quipped.

I proceeded to tell the court about the $1 contract with the museum. Bedard pointed to the first ticket: "This ticket is stamped with the wrong date. A good agent would have noticed that."

He laughed.

"I plead guilty to being a bad agent," I replied.

"The charge is quashed," he said.

"I haven't worked since September," Franco told the court. "My balance is still not very good, but I would like to get out into the fresh air again."

"In view of the arrangement with the museum," said the judge, "the other charges will be withdrawn."

Toronto quietly celebrated Franco's victory.

When Franco died in 2015, an entire generation and a bit of Toronto died with him. It is people like Franco who give this city a heart and soul.

CHAPTER 59

Federal Election Campaign 1993

It's not very often that municipal politicians have a hand in steering the outcome of a federal election campaign. The 1993 campaign was an exception. In Toronto, it revolved around Pearson International Airport. Despite the high prices Canadians pay for airfares, aviation is, in a sense, a quasi-public utility funded by the Federal government. The airlines themselves are private companies, but they depend on a federal airport and navigation system that requires public support. The federal government established a long-term plan to divest itself of the responsibility for airports by creating airport authorities. These were community-based boards designed to manage and modernize major airports. The Ottawa Airport Authority, for example, was established under the National Airports Policy and given a 60-year lease by Transport Canada. In the 20 years it has been in operation, it has spent more than $507 million on infrastructure improvements.

Airport authority boards were composed of members nominated by municipalities, business groups and other stakeholders. The one stipulation was the nominees could be neither elected officials nor government employees. There were only a couple of airports in Canada that were actually profitable. Toronto (Pearson) was the most profitable airport in the country.

A rumour was afloat that instead of establishing an airport authority, the Progressive Conservative government of the day was negotiating a deal to privatize two terminals at Pearson. The government was about to sign a secret deal with a consortium that included developer Donald Mathews, a former PC Party president and friend of Brian Mulroney, the prime minister who had negotiated the deal, but had since retired; lobbyist Fred Doucet, a former Mulroney chief of staff; Bill Neville, a long-time Tory advisor; and Otto Jelinek, a former revenue minister. A federal election was weeks away when the Ottawa Citizen broke the story that the cabinet had approved the deal despite the fact that Ottawa bureaucrats had reported it would cost taxpayers millions of dollars in lost revenue. The deal had not yet been finalized, but the parties were moving ahead with indecent haste to ink the documents.

When confronted on the issue, Kim Campbell, the Tory leader who had succeeded Brian Mulroney as prime minister, asserted that the deal would go forward. She parroted the lobbyists who had been hired to grease the wheels. It was an "infrastructure project creating 14,000 new jobs." The best Liberal leader Jean Chretien would promise: He would "examine the deal." That was not surprising given that Charles Bronfman, one of his major backers, was part of the consortium. It was pure, unadulterated, old-fashioned pork barrel politics.

After that week's TTC meeting, Mike Colle and I began to discuss the airport deal. "Are we going to let them get away with it?" I said.

"No," he replied, "let's draft a notice of motion to seek an injunction."

Our notice of motion called for a special meeting of council to condemn the deal. We called for an airport authority for Toronto, the same deal as all other major airports in Canada.

"The airport ought to be owned by the taxpayers of Metropolitan Toronto and Region and not end up in the pockets of Tory fundraisers," I told a press conference. "The federal government has shown abject contempt. Metro must act now to prevent Mr. Mulroney and his friends from hijacking the airport."

Mike added: "Ottawa has got us in the coffin and is stripping us of the jewellery before they put us in the hole."

I worked late into the night painting signs. At 9:00 the next morning, we threw a picket line in front of Terminal 1 with the national press in tow. We managed to catapult the privatization of Pearson onto the front page of every newspaper in the country. Mike Colle and I were joined by Metro Councillors Olivia Chow, Raymond Cho, Anne Johnston, Toronto Councillor Steve Ellis and MPs John Nunziata and Dennis Mills, plus a number of ordinary taxpayers who had heard about the picket line on the radio and came out to join the demonstration.

Metro Council endorsed our resolution, but on the advice of our solicitors they stopped short of an injunction, which might have put us into a high-risk liability situation if we failed to get one. Council called on the feds to delay the deal. As Councillor Blake Kinahan pointed out: "If we are going to win this, it will be in the court of public opinion."

He was right.

The next day, October 6, the Tories rushed Public Security Minister Doug Lewis down to Metro Hall to do damage control at a hastily called news conference. Big mistake! Several of us got wind of the conference and muscled our way in. They could hardly keep us out of a news conference on our own turf. He was shouted down by Mike Colle: "What are you trying to hide?"

Lewis pressed ahead with his defence of privatization. He made it clear the deal would go ahead; however. when pressed by reporters he couldn't provide any details of the agreement or even say when it would be signed. When reporters squeezed an acknowledgement out of him that the deal was structured to avoid paying the $10 million land transfer tax, he said: "Absolutely, the private sector does it all the time."

We howled in disbelief. Lewis scooped up his papers and beat a hasty retreat.

My comment: "They'd be wise to back away.... There's a bad smell that is hanging over the airport and it's spreading across Canada."

That week, the Tory vote dropped 4%, from 26% to 22%, in the opinion polls. Kim Campbell and her party were hammered. They lost 154 seats and were reduced to a rump of two seats in the House. It was the worst defeat of a governing party ever.

Despite the Tory defeat, the odour of the Pearson airport deal remained. What to do?

Jean Chretien, the new Liberal prime minister, promised during the campaign to review the deal. He had to do something. In an effort to diffuse the issue, he asked the consortium to voluntarily delay the signing for 30 days. They had no more choice but to agree to the delay than Chretien had to ask for it. The prime minister appointed Bob Nixon, former Ontario Liberal leader, to do a quick and dirty review of the deal and to report in two weeks directly to the PM. It was not to be public. The tacit implication was "Don't screw up the deal."

Where this was headed was quite clear. Liberal lobbyists replaced Tory lobbyists. John Nunziata, who had made a speech in caucus about killing the deal, was privately rebuked. The Toronto airport authority, which had been appointed six months before, remained in limbo waiting for recognition, and Bob Nixon set about his instant, just-add-water-and-stir, investigation.

Mike Colle and I asked and were granted a meeting with Bob Nixon. The first thing he said to me was: "Who's your friend?"

"This is Mike Colle," I said. "He's chairman of the TTC and his only fault is that he's a Liberal."

"You just can't rip up contracts," said Nixon.

Mike left the meeting shaking his head: "I don't think he understands the whole goddamn thing or what the uproar was about. If he doesn't cancel the deal, there'll be questions forever."

For a guy who had been conducting an investigation for 15 days, Nixon didn't seem to have much information. As John Nunziata, a lawyer, suggested, they would be hard pressed to sue the people of Canada for a deal that was cut in the heat of an election. As it turned out, Bob Nixon was extremely astute. He recommended that Chretien pull the plug and he did on December 4.

This was really a victory by the little guy and the media over big-money lobbyists. The media kept the deal in the public eye and the voters turfed the Tory government.

CHAPTER 60
Poof, You're Gone

The demise of Metropolitan Toronto may have started with the Mike Harris Tory sweep of 1995 when he drove Bob Rae's NDP government into the ground. But Metro's demise was as much the fault of Metro as it was of Mike Harris.

Dick Chapman put his finger on the problem in a November 1995 Toronto Sun column when he wrote: "There is a serious, I would contend, fatal communications gap between Metro politicians and the Harris cabinet but even worse, between the Metro council and its own public."

Everyone knew the Harris agenda. He was elected to bring about the "common sense revolution" and, as revolting as it may have been to many, it was a platform that shouted cut government spending, throw the undeserving bums off the welfare rolls and hack away at the size of government.

Chopping the Metro level of government was an easy hit because nobody was quite sure what it did. Sure, there were daily news stories about the TTC and police sirens regularly electrified media coverage, but these things were there before and would go on forever. Nobody really cared who pulled the strings. Three quarters of the services were already amalgamated. While it was their Metro councillor who got them to work and sent out police and ambulance and made the whole thing pull together, people still felt closer to their local councillor, who ploughed their street and shovelled their sidewalk and did things that they could smell, feel and touch.

In a 1997 plebiscite, the local councils asked the public: "Should the six municipalities that made up Metro be amalgamated into a single government?"

Well, that's not quite how it was asked. The North York plebiscite actual wording was: "Are you in favour of eliminating the City of North York and all the other existing municipalities in Metropolitan Toronto and amalgamating them into a megacity?"

Despite the bias built into the question, the results were overwhelming: 76% of voters opposed amalgamation. The Toronto Star headline blared out, "Mega No to Megacity."

It didn't matter. The Harris government could ignore the results of the plebiscite. They were just doing what they promised to do. Coupled with that, Metro was led by Alan Tonks, who had a talent for saying in a thousand words what could have been spit out in a two-second media clip. By the time he finished speaking, everyone had changed the channel.

While the six mayors ranted and raved and preached doom and gloom, Allan Tonks, Mr. Nice Guy, developed his own secret war strategy.

He warned Metro councillors and department heads:

"Stop slagging each other and especially the provincial government at a time when Metro's future is at stake."

His strategy was so successful that amalgamation took place on January 1, 1998.

Did amalgamation live up to the Harris "common sense" promise? The Tories predicted it would save $645 million in the first year and $300 million a year later. A subsequent KPMG study showed it actually only saved $135 million,

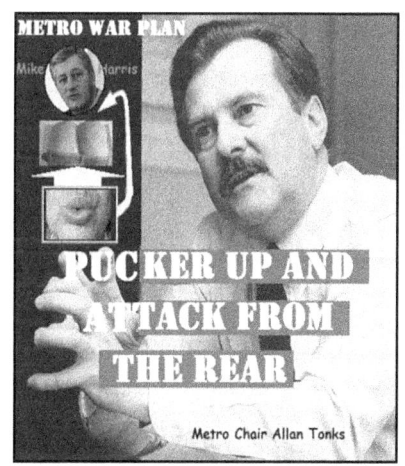
Metro Chair Allan Tonks

which was offset by transition costs of $275 million. Toronto's budget went from $5 billion in 1997 to $8.1 billion in 2008. That's a 62% increase in 11 years. The 2017 budget came in at $11.8 billion.

Given these facts, should amalgamation be reversed? Nobody has yet figured out how to successfully unscramble an egg.

PART III

CHAPTER 61
Bizzaro – No. 1

ON REVIEWING THE STRIPPING BYLAW

It is within the context of a whole range of bylaws. Let it be understood that while I don't look for titillating things to do, we do have the right to put conditions on bylaws and find possible ways of bringing some change into this industry. This is a legitimate area to explore, and I am not doing it because I can get a bunch of media guys to buy me a beer.

Most municipalities in Ontario license adult entertainment clubs, but Toronto is one of the few municipalities that requires an "adult entertainer" to have a licence. As a licensing commissioner, I had numerous complaints from women about the abysmal working conditions in the industry. I undertook a review of the bylaw by touring the clubs. The media were keenly interested in joining my tour. Of course, once you hit the first club word quickly spread to all of the clubs. By the time we arrived at the House of Lancaster on the Queensway, the TV sets that I am told normally show pornography were screening equestrian jumping, and all of the entertainers were sporting the required modest apparel – that is, G strings.

SPA FOR POOCHES

I held the item at Metro Council. The Management Committee had approved $1.6 million to build a facility for the police K-9 unit. The eight dogs were now housed in a Metro Parks building that was too cramped and had the neighbours complaining about the barking.

"It's a luxury hotel for dogs," I suggested. "For $1.6 million you could buy each dog a bungalow in Scarborough."

It cost Metro $100 per square foot to build a senior citizens' home. The kennel was budgeted at $150 per square foot. Council referred the item back.

TOUGH TISSUE, BIG ISSUE

On October 29, 1996, the North York Mirror wrote:

"Alderman Howard Moscoe is having a rough go of it lately, in city lavatories at least. Moscoe called for a more tender tender, when it comes to renewing the $61,753 contract for toilet paper in City Hall washrooms. Moscoe took a swipe at tissue quality, comparing it to a minor grade of sandpaper. 'In the Soviet Union they use orange wrappers for this purpose,' he said. 'They're luckier than we are.' His political colleagues assured him that George Hardy, Commissioner of City Hall Services, would look at softer tissue next year. Earlier in the brief debate, Alderman Mike Foster drew laughter when he declared a conflict of interest and excused himself to go to the bathroom."

ON BAD BOY ADS

Mel Lastman's problem is that he's a one-man band. He does what he wants when he wants, and he hasn't realized that some members of council are sensitive about that. He's a good advocate, and I used to think that he was a good salesman until I heard that they replaced him with a trained monkey in the Bad Boy commercials, and sales went up by 25 per cent.

INSANE

Magistrate: You have 15 traffic tickets here Mr. Moscoe. How do you plead? Guilty or not guilty?

Moscoe: I plead temporary insanity.

Magistrate: What do you mean?

Moscoe: I must have been insane to allow my daughter to put her car into my name for insurance purposes.

Everyone: LOUD LAUGHTER

Magistrate: Dismissed.

PARDON MY FRENCH

On the bottom of TTC bus windows are signs that tell you to pull the handle to release the windows in an emergency. My granddaughter Rebecca complained to me about the French translation. "My French teacher says that it is spelled incorrectly." Handle is spelled "Poingnee" when it should be "poignee." "Poingnee" isn't even a word. By federal law the French spelling had to be changed. There wasn't an option. Not only was it misspelled on the new buses, it was mispelled on the old ones, too. The TTC found 773 buses with the wrong message, each with multiple windows. It was enormously expensive to correct. Fortunately, it was not a TTC cost. The cost was borne by Orion, the manufacturer.

STICK 'EM UP

How would you react to having to pay a $300,000 ransom? The contract for elevator maintenance at Metro Hall was up. As required by policy, the $3.6 million contract was put out to tender. Of the three bids, Schindler Elevator Corporation was the highest by $300,000. The company had built the elevators, and it had the 10-year maintenance contract that was now expiring. But Schindler was refusing to give up the secret codes required to operate the elevators. Metro was being held hostage. I proposed to council that we offer a $10,000 reward to anyone who could hack the codes. Our lawyers went nuts on me; they're so damned conservative.

"You can't do that. If someone steals money from you, you can't break into their house to take it back."

"Nuts I can't. These are the codes for our elevators in our building. It's time to change the locks."

My phone was ringing off the hook with calls from hackers. "Don't worry," I said. "We're going to take back Schindler's Lifts."

THE BROKEN GAVEL AWARD GOES TO

When I attended Etobicoke's annual weekend auction of unwanted municipal property in October of 1989, I scanned the room looking for the Metro licence. Every auction requires a licence. There was none showing. When I asked around, nobody seemed to know anything.

If a homeowner in Etobicoke had tried to build a porch without a permit, the City of Etobicoke would be all over them with hob nailed boots. They were lucky, it was Saturday and I couldn't find a Metro bylaw enforcement officer. I would have closed the place down. As it turns out North York had used the same auctioneer the previous week, the same scenario. It won't happen again.

THE DEVIL MADE ME DO IT

It's like peering at a cream pie over a diet menu. Sometimes you just can't resist. We were discussing the TTC budget and Councillor Frances Nunziata was doing her usual rant about the TTC. She was complaining about the lousy TTC service in her ward and how buses and streetcars bunch up on city streets.

"Why don't you walk the streets, Councillor Moscoe and see exactly what's happening on the streets?" she whined.

It was an opening wide enough to drive a streetcar through. I just couldn't resist.

"Well councillor," I quipped. "I'll leave walking the streets to you."

Oops. Nunziata demanded an apology; said I was a "chauvinist pig." I quickly withdrew the remark, and after the lunch break I rose to tender an apology.

"On occasion my mouth gets ahead of my brain. I made a remark that I regret and would like to apologize to Councillor Nunziata and anyone else that might have been offended."

Would I do it again? An opportunity like that comes only once in a lifetime.

LASTMAN SHRINE

When I heard that Mel Lastman's Bridle Path mansion was up for sale, I couldn't resist proposing that the city buy it for the $1.9 million asking price and turn it over to the John Howard Society for a half-way house for released criminal offenders. After the lease expired, say in 20 years when the mortgage had been paid off, we could turn it over to the City to create a museum: a shrine to North York's longest serving mayor.

"Toronto has a museum to honour William Lyon McKenzie," I argued, "so why not a museum for Mel Lastman? I will personally donate his toupee as the first offering."

My wife had purchased his toupee at a charity auction a year earlier and was looking for an appropriate home for it.

"The nice people on the Bridle Path wouldn't mind a half-way house for a neighbour," I suggested. "It would be an improvement over what they have now."

Lastman called it a "waste of taxpayer's money." He had opposed the establishment of halfway houses in North York. I can't imagine why he would decline the offer. The John Howard Society said they wouldn't object.

LORD MAYOR OF TORONTO

DENNIS FLYNN
LORD MAYOR OR CHAIRMAN

Dennis Flynn was a man with an imposing stature but a wimpy title. Metropolitan Toronto had come into its own as a level of government, the largest municipal government in the country. Yet its head was simply a chairman. Chairmen were a dime a dozen. So I put forward a proposal that we change the title to "Lord Mayor." After all, the only other lord mayor I knew was Lord Mayor of London, and wasn't he the most important mayor in the UK? I wasn't prepared for the debate it got. Both Toronto Councillor June Rolands and Etobicoke Mayor Bruce Sinclair supported the idea. They both agreed that the term "chairman" didn't adequately reflect the position's importance. As people began to warm up to the idea, Flynn got more and more annoyed, but he lost it when members of council began calling him "the Lard Mayor of Metro" and "His Heftiness." That's when Flynn blew up.

"Any attempt at levity – I went along with for a little while – is overdone (and)... now it reflects on my personal character."

His outburst put the kibosh to the whole idea. People were so embarrassed that the vote to kill the idea was 32-2. That's too bad. I really wasn't trying to demean the Chairman.

"Dennis Flynn looks like a Lord Mayor. He has the stature of a Lord Mayor," I said.

The only complaint I received about the whole affair was from a councillor in Niagara-on-the-Lake. He accused me of trying to steal the title. Niagara-on-the-Lake has the only lord mayor in Canada. Pity!

HIGH ON CONSULTANTS

Between 1986 and 1989, Metro Toronto's consulting bill doubled from $28 million to $66 million. That's $7,534 an hour, every hour, every day.

"We're consultant junkies. We're shooting up on consultants and we can't stop," I told the management subcommittee.

The problem was that every department was an entity unto itself. Nobody seemed to have the "big picture." I knew that much of the work we did was technical and short term, but if several departments were doing the same thing and buying the same expertise. it may be less expensive to hire new staff. A lot of the consulting reports, like environmental assessments, were required by law. One problem was that consulting studies under $20,000 did not require council approval, and were approved administratively. It wasn't beyond some senior bureaucrats to split a $40,000 contract into two jobs; nudge nudge, wink wink.

"It's amazing that politicians will spend two hours debating a $300 expenditure and let a $66 million consulting bill go through without discussion," I explained to the subcommittee. "If I hadn't held this item it would have been routinely approved. It's the big expenditures where the real savings are to be found."

There are a whole lot of studies done that are piled up and gathering dust on shelves. On controversial projects some managers love to hire consultants. That way the consultants get the blame if the politicos don't like the answers. So what did the management subcommittee do? It asked staff to bring it a report on consulting studies. You can be sure that management hired a consultant to write it.

GET YOUR DAMNED HOUSE OFF MY STREET

I don't like gated communities. One of the earliest in Toronto was Wychwood Park. They managed to keep the Jews and other minorities out for at least 75 years. That's why I reacted so negatively when I saw one springing up in my ward. Balmoral was an enclave of about 200 luxury million-dollar-plus homes being constructed by Bramalea Ltd. to the east of Downsview Airport. I freaked out when I saw that the marketers had erected a gatehouse across Joel Swirsky Boulevard, inviting prospective buyers to make an appointment to view the models.

"I want them to get the damn thing off the road," I told the Toronto Star reporter. "They've tried to turn a public road into a private road running into their exclusive little enclave. I find it very offensive."

Apparently North York had passed a bylaw in 1967 to allow this, and Bramalea was negotiating with the city solicitor behind the scenes to make it happen. It didn't. The publicity killed their marketing plans. The gatehouse disappeared.

CHAPTER 62
Bizzaro – No. 2

FEEL THE LOVE

After direct election in 1988 when Metro came into its own as a separately elected government, there was a huge residue of resentment back at the local municipalities. Local councillors, in many cases, were miffed that they had to be the ones left behind, and the media were focusing all of their attention on the superstar, the new Metro government. Some, not officially of course, declared war on the Metro colleagues with whom they had to share a ward and with whom they had to "compete" for the affections of their constituents. North York councillors were particularly resentful. They issued instructions to North York staff to have no relations whatsoever with their Metro counterparts. I remember, for example, Wanda Lycik, the North York treasurer (she later became the amalgamated City of Toronto treasurer when Lastman promoted her) refusing to take a telephone call from me or even respond to a letter.

DOODLES

I love to doodle. What with a larger council and longer meetings, there was a lot of "butt time" at Metro. As the speeches droned on I would amuse myself by scribbling.

Here are some scribbles that capture the mood of the times.

MERRY CHRISTMAS

In November of 1995, Metro taxpayers got an unexpected Christmas gift. It was all of the provincial highways within the municipalities' boundaries, including Highways 2, 2A, 27 and the Queen Elizabeth Way (QEW) – 20 kilometres of roadway. It was a great way to kick off your holidays; sort of like dumping a couple of tons of snow on your driveway Christmas morning. The QEW was the biggest prize of all.

Doug Floyd, Metro's transportation commissioner, told us the province had allowed major highways inside Metro to decay because it was planning to give them to us. He estimated the repair bill was $50 million, and it would add about $1 million in annual maintenance costs to our budget. To add insult to injury, the province also cut road subsidies by $4.7 million for 1996.

What would you do if somebody gave you their Visa bill to pay as a Christmas gift? As chair of the transportation committee, I had to do something. I drafted a five-point emergency response strategy, which even I will admit was a trifle outlandish.

1. Kick it all off by staging a handover ceremony. It would take place on a Monday morning from 7:30 am to 9:30 am in the centre lanes of the QEW just outside the Mississauga boundary. Invite Transportation Minister Al Palladini to address the multitudes of Mississauga commuters jammed into the collector lanes. A large brass band would drown out the cacophony of horns from celebrating commuters. Fold, rather than cut, a ribbon. (No sharp instruments please!)

2. Each road would have its own handover ceremony. We would do a series of staggered celebrations. Highways 2 and 2A would require detours to be set up.

3. Erect large signs on the Metro boundary on each of these roads. And over a period of time, increase the number of signs.

4. Discontinue road maintenance in the express lanes of the QEW. Do the minimum necessary to keep the collector lanes safe on the premise that the collector lanes are for local traffic and the express lanes carry commuters.

5. Discontinue snow plowing of the express lanes. Close them completely in the winter and direct commuters to the GO stations.

Councillor Brian Ashton added an additional proposal: Re-name the QEW the Dalton McGuinty Freeway and Highway 27, the Bob Rae Parkway.

Jack Layton got into the spirit of the debate by suggesting we label each pothole with the name of a cabinet minister until they ponied up with the maintenance money. Alas, while the debate was spirited, most of my colleagues had about as much gumption as a guppy on Valium. They were too wimpy to meet an outrageous download with Newton's third law. In the end, they were discussing ways to save money, like turning out the lights on expressways. They asked for a report from Police Chief Boothby on the additional costs for policing these highways. Sad, Isn't it?

BONEHEADS ALL

While Mel Lastman and his bumbling band of boneheads failed in their attempt to remove me as chair of the TTC, another band of low-lives actually successfully did that, but it led to their downfall.

Undercover TTC officers arrested 15 people and laid 50 charges. It was the result of a four-month investigation of forged tickets. What was their mistake? They left my name off the ticket. For as far back as I can remember, the name of the chair of the commission has been imprinted on TTC tickets.

That'll teach them to leave me out.

The arrests sent thousands of customers scrambling to search for my name. The TTC estimates 400,000 counterfiet tickets were in circulation and they were all invalid. Most of the vendors who were arrested knew the deal they were getting was too good to be true.

I proposed an additional security measure. Put my picture on the ticket. Nobody would forge that.

"EXTREMIST LESBIAN"

In the 2000 election, I ran in partnership with Kathleen Wynne. This was her second run as a public school trustee and my ward was the western half of hers. I was willing to overlook her Liberal connections because she was both intelligent and progressive.

Her literature was delivered stuffed into mine and we shared campaign office space. The "Concerned Citizens of North York" had dubbed her an "extremist Lesbian," so I knew we could safely endorse her.

CHAPTER 63
Bizzaro – No. 3

I THOUGHT I WAS ME

Sometimes I'm not me when I'm on TV. City TV did an interview with me on cab driver training. Their question of the day was who is the chair of the Metro Licensing Commission? Their answer.... Howard Moscoe. That would come as news to Bob Sanders, who was actually the chair.

I telephoned right away.

"It's about your question of the day," I said.

"Sorry, but we already have a winner."

"Let me talk to the news desk.... I have a tip."

They put me through to the news desk.

"You've got the wrong answer to your Question of the Day," I said.

"No. No." he said, "the answer is Howard Moscoe."

"But I am Howard Moscoe."

"OH!"

THE BARE FACTS

Betty and Bill Sutherland were a husband and wife team elected to North York Council. Bill was on the Board of Control, and Betty was the alderman representing Ward 14, which is in the northeast part of the then borough.

Betty was determined to close down the Valley Village Restaurant and Tavern in the Peanut Plaza. It was one of those naughty places where nubile dancers took off their clothes for money. A strip club.

It was a public hearing in the North York Council chamber.

Betty addressed the council: "The place is too close for comfort in an area with a large concentration of young people. It's near schools, a church and an arena and it is threatening to bring about the complete degradation of a shopping centre in a respectable residential area."

The public were lined up to speak. Among them were a number of strippers from the club, who had come to plead for their jobs. One of them noticed Bill.

"Hey girls, there's Bill," she blurted waving wildly. "You haven't been in for lunch this week."

Bill Sutherland liked to imbibe. He normally had a ruddy complexion. I've never seen him redder. More than bare bottoms had been exposed.

CAUGHT WITH HIS HAND IN THE COOKIE JAR

Poor Chris Stockwell. His credibility came crashing down one night in October of 1995 when he quietly slipped an application into the Metro clerk's office to apply for his severance pay. He did nothing wrong, he was entitled to a severance of some $11,000 because the rules allowed him to get it. The concept of severance for politicians is a valid one. It is based on the premise that if one interrupts a career path in order to go into public service, the public had some obligation to help get you back on your feet again when your job is abruptly terminated.

Many former politicians would be otherwise destitute without it. Metro severance was fair. You got one month for every year spent on council to a maximum of six months. It's just that Chris wasn't out of office. He had been elected as a Tory MPP during the "common sense revolution." He was moving from one elected position to another and a higher paying one at that.

What caused his credibility to crash and burn was Chris had always railed against severance, denigrated it and voted against it as a councillor. He had made a career out of knocking excess government spending.

I told the Toronto Star: "He didn't even have time to say oink when he moved from one trough to the other."

Chris told the Star: "Every one of those suckers are getting it... Why shouldn't I take it – because I voted against it? What do you think I am, stupid?"

A day later, his story had changed:

"My rationale for filing was to show what a fraud this thing is. I didn't do it for the money. I wouldn't accept the money. I want to make the point that it's wrong."

Sure, Chris and they all believed you too? Poor Chris. There's a point in time when your past comes back to haunt you. Those who live by the sword die by the sword.

GOTCHA

Newspaper columnists are hyped-up journalists. Unlike reporters, who are expected to report the news dispassionately, columnists are expected to have opinions. Often they reflect the bias of their paper but not always. To put it mildly, the Toronto Sun doesn't like me, but some of their columnists, such as Ted Welch or John Downing, treated me fairly. The meanest, nastiest columnist I have ever encountered is Sue-Ann Levy. She hated me with a passion; she out right-winged the Sun by a long shot. Every time she interviewed me, she would twist what I said into something ugly. It got to the point where I simply wouldn't talk to her. "Sue-Ann," I said. "I'd be happy to exchange pleasantries with you, but don't ever ask me any questions. I just won't respond to them."

One day we shared a panel on an open-line radio show. Sue-Ann was ranting on about allegations of patronage. Apparently Joe Pantalone was accused of using his influence to get a cousin a job with the City.

"You have to be careful Sue-Ann," I said. "These are allegations. It's not fair to run around repeating allegations. For example, it is widely alleged that you got your job because your uncle, Jeff Lyons, the lobbyist, is a friend of Paul Godfrey." (Godfrey was the publisher of the Toronto Sun.)

My words were met with stone cold silence. There was no response because it was true.

STICKS AND STONES

Am I sensitive about my weight? Perhaps just a tad. Christina Blizzard was a columnist for the Toronto Sun. We traded words for a long time. She wrote a column about me being in the hospital in which she referred to me as "tubby" and "roly-poly." When I bumped into her at the next council meeting I thanked her for her well wishes, but pointed out that I wasn't "tubby." I preferred to think of myself as someone with "a large girth," or an "imposing stature," or I might even be "rotund." We settled on "Howard is only short for his weight." In her next column she complained about me referring to her as "Christina Buzzard."

BLIZZARD   BUZZARD

"I wouldn't dream of making fun of his name. I wouldn't stoop to calling him Councillor Miscue or even Moscoe the Circus."

Please accept my sincerest apologies Christina. I had no intention of making fun of your name at all. I was referring to your style of journalism.

DO YOUR JOB

It is bad form for a councillor to interfere in another councillor's ward. So, when I received a call from a very upset woman about a bloody gun battle on her street I told her she should contact her councillor, Norm Gardner. Norm was on the Metro board of police commissioners. If anyone could help, it would be him.

She broke into tears.

"It was awful," she said. "There was blood all over the street. The house next door is a crack house. It's rented out to a gang and we've begged Norm to do something about it, but he says he can't. The police have no jurisdiction over the landlord. Will you come to a meeting with the neighbours in my house tonight?"

I've known Norm Gardner since we were teenagers hanging out at the YMHA at Spadina and Bloor. (Now the Miles Nadel Jewish Community Centre) Norm was never the brightest star in the galaxy. It seemed his main ambition in life was to shoot someone. He was quoted in the Toronto Star as saying that "store owners should arm themselves against robbers."

Norm was an avid gun collector and supporter of the right to bear arms. I, on the other hand, exercised my right to bear arms by wearing short-sleeved shirts. In 1986, he won a seat on the Metro police commissioners board and ultimately became chair of the police services board.

In March of 1992, he realized his seemingly lifelong ambition by shooting and wounding a man who was attempting to rob his bakery. Apparently, Norm had a secret permit to carry a gun. Fortunately, the robber survived. They managed to pry the bullet out of his back.

I reluctantly agreed to attend the meeting. The neighbourhood was at its wit's end.

"Will you help us to make a submission to the police commission?"

"I have a better Idea," I told them.

The next morning, we all showed up at the local police station, 32 Division, carrying picket signs which read, "Do Your Job." There just happened to be a small mob of Toronto media there to record the event.

The next night, Toronto Police raided the crack house. The gang was never seen again.

SLAMMING THE LID ON MANHOLES

Can a woman crawl out of a manhole? It seems like a silly question. Not in the '80s. That's when society wrestled with the nitty-gritty of the struggle for women's rights. While the bickering about gender specific language was trivialized by many, it wasn't trivial at all.

Language is enormously important. There's a multi-trillion dollar gap between "equal pay for equal work," and "equal pay for work of equal value."

The language of municipal discourse was hotly debated. It was an era when "chairman" became "chair," "alderman" became "councillor," and the "fireman" who rushed to your aid morphed into a "firefighter." So, it's not surprising that many hours in council were devoted to debating gender specific language issues. What is surprising is the twist these debates sometimes took.

Brian Harrison was a tough-talking, hard-nosed politician from Scarborough. You could always count on him to do a rant about saving a buck. If you wanted to find Brian, all you had to do was look right.

I'm not sure how it got started, but the debate centred on the word "manhole" in reports to council. There were lots of jokes and snickers. Maureen Prinsloo joined in: "Women are sensible enough that they don't go down these stupid things."

I contributed my two cents worth: "The snickers sparked by this debate are even more offensive to women than the use of the word 'manhole'.... I don't think that it's a joking matter, frankly."

At that point, Harrison rose to speak: "I move that the word 'manhole' be replaced by the words 'maintenance hole' in all council reports."

It was totally out of character for him and we were all caught by surprise. Brian was an engineer. He said it wouldn't cost us a cent because on plans and drawings they were all designated 'MH.'

The vote was close – 12 to 10 in favour. If it hadn't been moved by Brian, it would never have happened.

CHAPTER 64
Bizzaro – No. 4

POLITICIANS' RIGHTS

Budget Chair David Shiner proposed a $2 million Efficiency Initiative Fund. Here was our exchange in council:

Moscoe: "I want to ask the chief administrative officer about the efficiency slush fund."

Shiner: "Councillor, if you refer to that I'll ask you to sit down."

Moscoe: "Why, is that unparliamentary language?"

Shiner: "You're calling things that council is doing as if they are slush funds and we are spending inappropriately."

Moscoe: "Yes, I'm entitled to my opinion, Mr. Chairman, am I not?"

Shiner: "Sorry, I would ask that you not call it that and I would appreciate your using…"

Moscoe: "Okay, I'm sorry. I'll call it the David Shiner slush fund. This fund…"

Shiner: "Sorry, now I will ask you to withdraw that."

Moscoe: "Okay, I'll withdraw it."

Shiner: "And I will ask you to be proper in this council or I'll ask you to sit down. We all work in a proper manner. Please don't grandstand for us."

Moscoe: "Well, Mr. Chairman, I'm an elected official. I have an absolute right to grandstand."

HAPPY BIRTHDAY

We celebrated two first birthdays on Valentine's Day 1979. February 14, 1978 was the day North York received the charter that turned the Borough of North York into the City of North York. It was also the day my dog, Muppet, was born.

There was a giant celebration planned at the civic centre. It was all decked out in bunting and hearts. What an opportunity for an ambitious politician to get some attention. Members of the board of control were salivating at the possibility of seeing their name in print. That's how they got elected. Controllers were elected across the city. It was largely a name recognition game. Electors picked four from a long list of candidates. That's why they were always dreaming up ways to get their name into print.

Controller Esther Shiner was controller No. 1. She was a master at stealing the show.

This time, she wore a sweatshirt she had made for the occasion. It was festooned with the bold caption "Happy Birthday North York, No.1" on a huge heart. It was a sure-fire "take my picture" attention getter.

My daughter, Candice, 12, was excited about the party. She cut out a cardboard heart with the caption "CITY DOG" and tied it around Muppet's neck. Esther was furious. Muppet stole all the publicity. Upstaged by a dog!

SHABBAT SHALOM

They may not know it, but Toronto motorists all quietly observe Jewish Sabbath if they drive on Bathurst Street. Orthodox Jews are prohibited from doing "work" on the Sabbath. The rabbis in ancient times defined the meaning of "work" and the rules have been debated for a couple of thousand years. They will likely be debated for the next 2,000 years as well. One of the rules is that you cannot ignite an electrical spark (i.e. light a fire). That is why in Jewish institutions like hospitals one elevator is designated a "Sabbath elevator," one that is programmed to stop at every floor from Friday at sundown to sundown on Saturday. That way, nobody has to push a button to go up or down.

The Orthodox Jewish community is largely clustered on either side of Bathurst Street. That is because, not being allowed to drive on the Sabbath, they have to live within walking distance of a synagogue. In March of 2002, 18 traffic signals on Bathurst Street between Eglinton and Steels Avenues were activated to flash automatically at pre-set intervals from sundown on Friday to sundown on Saturday. They were marked with the Hebrew letter "shin" to indicate they were now Sabbath signals. Did it aggravate motorists who were unknowingly observing the Jewish Sabbath? Not at all. The loss in time was offset by the lighter traffic on Bathurst Street.

There are no Orthodox drivers on the road on the Sabbath. Shabbat shalom.

LIVING OFF THE AVAILS

The City of Toronto began the licensing of bicycles on May 20, 1935. They ended bicycle licensing on February 4, 1957.

On December 15, 2009, Igor Kenk was sentenced to 30 months in jail for allegedly stealing some 3,000 bicycles in Toronto. The Toronto Police reportedly supervised the return of 582 to their owners. So, what happened to the other 2,418? The Toronto Police Services Board has been partying on the proceeds from the sale of stolen bicycles.

Who says crime doesn't pay?

The Toronto Police Services Board has been living off the avails of stolen bicycles for years. Each year, bicycles not returned to their owners are auctioned off. The proceeds are deposited into a "slush fund" the board uses to pay for things that are sort of on the "edge" of prudence. It's been happening for years. In 1994, stolen bikes contributed $76,000 to the fund and another $300,000 came from cash from lost wallets or money unclaimed by robbery victims.

Police board policy says, "Money from the fund must be spent on youth-related programs, community events and public awareness campaigns." The special fund is used to pay for tickets to testimonial and retirement dinners, Caribana floats, sending police commissioners to conferences, refreshments at board meetings, the police pipe band, celebrations and luncheons. I think at least half of it should be spent on trying to unite owners with stolen property.

The commissioners don't seem to see or care that they might have a conflict of interest.

FLUSH WITH PRIDE

I was flush with pride. The staff presented me with a key that unlocks employee washrooms in subway stations across the entire system, a sort of executive washroom privilege.

"I've made it. I've finally gotten enough acceptance from senior management to get a key to the washroom."

Alas my pride was quickly deflated when I discovered that they were as dirty as the public washrooms.

SEXUAL REVOLUTION

In 1988 my eldest daughter, Cheryl, at the age of 23, was the youngest trustee elected to the North York Board of Education. The '80s were at the height of the sexual revolution. Cheryl successfully championed the installation of condom vending machines in high school washrooms. The debate raged. Would easy access to condoms promote promiscuity or offer protection to teens that were becoming increasingly sexually active? Just how sophisticated were our teenage children? The issue was settled for me when I caught the tail end of the comments of a girl exiting a high school washroom. "Yech," she said. "This gum tastes like rubber."

CHAPTER 65
Bizzaro – No. 5

LAST MEETING, LASTMAN, LAST OFFICIAL SNUB

It was a day full of emotion, the last meeting of the Council of the City of North York. Tuesday, October 6, 1997. Mel Lastman was visibly stunned when council presented him with his chain of office in commemoration of his service to the city. The mayor in turn presented a key to the city to the 13 current councillors and around 20 former city politicians. Tears flowed openly among some staff and councillors as Lastman thanked them for their service.

Noticeably absent were the current members of Metro Council all of whom had prior service on North York Council. They had been deliberately snubbed. In all likelihood they would be facing the current members of North York Council in the race for the new amalgamated Toronto seats. The snub was particularly hurtful when the mayor presented a key to the city to former disgraced Councillor Mario Gentile, who had lost his seat when he was jailed for municipal corruption. I think I reflected the feelings of most of my Metro colleagues when I was interviewed.

"This is testimony to the pea-brains sitting around the council chamber from the mayor on down. We were such a threat that they didn't even have the grace to invite us to North York's last meeting."

HOLLYWOOD MISHAP

Clifford Bresnehan and his wife were happy. They hired an architect who drew up the plans, got them approved at the permit department and constructed an enclosed porch for their small Hollywood Avenue bungalow; that is, until a North York building inspector knocked at their door.

"Where is your building permit," he asked.

"Right here," Mrs. Bresnehan replied. "It must have fallen down."

"It's not valid," he replied. "This is an East York permit. You live in North York."

Hollywood Avenue runs east from Yonge Street just north of Eglinton Avenue. It cuts across three municipalities: Toronto, North York and East York. The architect had gone to the wrong building department. Someone at the East York municipal building was asleep at the switch. It was a classic bureaucratic bungle. A complicating factor was that the porch was constructed to conform to the East York bylaw. It didn't conform to North York's regulations and had to go to their committee of adjustment. In the end, it was approved and East York refunded the fees they had collected, but not without a lot of egg on their faces.

Amalgamation gave us one big city, but to this day there remain thousands of bylaws that have not been harmonized.

THE EAGLE NEVER LANDED

It was a done deal. The staff report to the Parks and Property Committee recommended approval of the application from PDM National Helicopters Inc. to operate a business that would give passengers a five-minute helicopter tour of downtown Toronto for $25. The staff report advised that the Bell Jet Ranger produces 75 to 85 decibels at 30 metres on approach and departure. That's only slightly more than a vacuum cleaner. There was heavy opposition from residents of Harbourfront and the Toronto Islands who crowded into the committee room. Someone had brought a vacuum cleaner and turned it on just before the politicians began to speak. The debate was brief. The application never made it to council. It crashed at the committee.

ROBOGOOF

When I say "Robocalls," almost everyone except my spell check knows what I mean. Not so in 1984. The technology was in its infancy and it was mechanical, not digital. I had helped a heating contractor in my ward and when I visited his business, he showed me a new contraption he had purchased. It would telephone the numbers in an exchange in sequence and play a recorded message. Wow, I thought. I was running for Board of Control across the entire city and this would be a great way to talk to a whole lot of people I wouldn't otherwise be able to reach.

"Will you lend it to me for the campaign?" I asked.

"No problem", he replied. "It will be a great way to try out the machine."

Not only did the machine read a 20-second message, but it also had a call back feature. If anyone had questions they wanted to put to the candidate, they could leave their number and I would get back to them. It was as if it was made for a Board of Control race, and I was the only one who had access to it. The concept was so novel we thought people would be fascinated by it.

Ben Rothman, my campaign manager, would go into his shop each night and program a North York exchange. The machine was set to operate from 8:30 a.m. to 9:00 p.m. and on weekends; we programmed it on Friday to operate for the entire weekend with the appropriate shut off times. We debated long and hard about those settings.

"We don't want to turn anyone off," Ben said.

Our calls made their way steadily across the city from west to east until one weekend the turn-off times, for some reason, didn't click in. That weekend, every patient in North York General Hospital received a late-night call. Boy did we ever get feedback.

WHAT'S IN A NAME

PETER LIPRETI

You have got to hand it to Peter LiPreti. He knew how to work his community. He managed to pack 500 people into the North York Council chamber for three hours of public deputations. Speaker after speaker castigated the media for what they deemed negative, exaggerated reports about crime and drug problems in the area.

"We demand respect from the media, we don't ask it we demand it," shouted homeowner Ralph Cinelli to thunderous applause from the audience.

I knew they had a point. I spent a year teaching at Driftwood School in the Jane-Finch Corridor. The area had its problems and they were real, but I didn't fault the media. Their job was to report what was happening – and it was happening. LiPreti then proceeded to put forward a number of motions, including:

- Changing the names of Jane Street and Finch Avenue;
- Having the City of North York assist the community in taking legal action against "libellous" newspapers;
- Withdrawing North York advertising from offensive publications.

None of the motions carried. It didn't seem to matter. LiPreti got what he wanted, the adulation of his community. I was embarrassed to get a laurel from the Toronto Star. I was more used to getting darts. (Back then, the Star would publish brief editorials either supporting, with a laurel, or castigating, with a dart, actions by public figures.)

Here's the text of the Star's laurel: "Metro Councillor Howard Moscoe. For giving sage, albeit graphic advice, to North York Councillor Peter LiPreti, for a 'wacko, hair-brained scheme' to improve the Jane-Finch community's media image. Briefly, last week, LiPreti proposed name changes for Jane Street and Finch Avenue. 'You don't put a lampshade on your head and dance around and complain about the media coverage,' said Moscoe, who contends the real issue is a lack of social services around Jane-Finch."

As it turned out, lampshade aside, LiPreti himself contributed to the negative image of his community when in 2015 he was convicted of three campaign finance offences under the Municipal Elections Act.

KEEPING ABREAST OF THE TIMES

Funny how the littlest thing can blow up into a raging political debate. It was a routine item on a boring parks committee agenda, the uniform parks bylaw. It standardized codes governing dogs, humans and even hot air balloons in Metro parks. If I hadn't held the item, it would have routinely sailed through the political processing machine as hundreds do. It's my penchant for reading the fine print that gets me into trouble.

"The bylaw says people must have appropriate dress, but it doesn't explain what appropriate means. What does it mean?" I asked of the parks commissioner.

That touched off a debate on topless beaches. I tried several amendments to clarify the bylaw, but none of them met with success. In the end, alas, the vote was 7-1 to approve the bylaw.

"Go to the Caribbean, you can see any number of topless beaches," I told the committee. "Not having them in Metro makes sitting on the beach a whole lot less enjoyable. The whole world is going topless. Toronto just hasn't yet caught up."

The bylaw change might have had half a chance, but the committee was swayed by the argument that all of the area municipalities had already adopted the bylaw.

"The status quo discriminates against women. I can go topless on any beach," I quipped.

Ironically, to this day, while Toronto does not have a topless beach, hidden behind the dunes on Centre Island is a nude beach frequented mostly by gay couples. Go figure!

CHAPTER 66
Bizzaro – No. 6

COCKROACH EXPRESS

One of my students dropped his lunch box and a cockroach crawled out. I was a teacher at Queensborough Junior High School in North York. He looked up at me and said: "I'm sorry sir, we just can't get rid of them. Our landlord refuses to spray."

PHIL WYNN

COCKROACH

I was teaching a special reading program and most of my students were recently arrived immigrants from the Caribbean. I telephoned his mom and she told me their building was owned by Phil Wynn. He was one of the most notorious slum landlords in Toronto. The city had thousands of work orders against his properties. Devon lived in a high-rise building on Lawrence Avenue West overlooking the Black Creek Drive Expressway. Many of our students lived there. Wynn wouldn't put a penny into his buildings. He simply milked them for rent. Devon's mom told me they were organizing a tenants' association and would I come to the first meeting.

The meeting was held in the neighbouring community centre. They spent the first hour discussing cockroaches and how they could put pressure on the landlord to spray. They asked me to speak.

"Try this," I told them. "Collect all of the cockroaches you can find and keep them in a jar with a lid. Before you hand in your rent cheque, sprinkle the roaches into the envelope. It doesn't matter if they are alive or dead. If you wish, you can crush them into your cheque."

A loud cheer went up. Rent day was Wednesday. The building was sprayed on Thursday.

Wynn had the chutzpah (nerve) several years later to ask me to give him a reference for a mortgage. He was seeking to buy a building in Hamilton.

Phil Wynn has passed on now. I regret not having attended his funeral. I wanted just once to hear someone say something nice about him.

THE STOP THE GRAVY TRAIN-WRECK PROJECT

It was an almost completely non-partisan civic engagement campaign and rescue mission (and personal enrichment initiative).

The objective of the campaign was to encourage people in Toronto to become actively engaged in an upcoming 2014 municipal election and to make a visible political statement.

Torontonians would be given the opportunity to purchase a lawn sign to erect on their property. Profits from the sale of the signs would be donated to any municipal candidate of their choice running in Toronto.

Electors would be able to order one or more of the lawn signs, which would be delivered to their door.

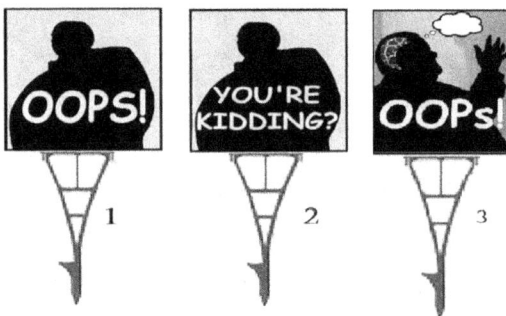

Or, if their preferences ran in the opposite direction, they could order sign No. 4. Signs would include a sign support (spider stake) for easy erection on a lawn. They would sell for $25, which would include delivery.

The project would:

- Give Torontonians an opportunity to make a visible public statement;

- Provide some funding for their favourite municipal candidate;

- Create a part-time employment opportunity for some students;

- Demonstrate that not everyone in Toronto was a bobble head.

Ten dollars of each $25 would be donated to a municipal candidate and $5 would go to the cost of delivery.

While the main purpose of the campaign was civic engagement, I was (and still am) in the business of making and selling election signs and would (reluctantly) make some money for myself.

Alas, the project never came to fruition because there never was a re-election campaign. Would it have worked? I'll never know.

ONE REALLY TOUGH BYLAW

I ran in the 2003 election from a hospital bed. I was just physically unable to canvass any longer, so for the 2006 election we used a campaign bus to work the territory. The Toronto election bylaw prohibits election signs being erected prior to one month before an election. The only exception was a sign on a campaign office. Our bus was parked every night outside our campaign office on Lawrence Avenue W. I am sure it was a complaint from one of my opponents that brought the bylaw inspector to our door.

CAMPAIGN BUS, 2006 MUNICIPAL ELECTION

Inspector (on first visit): "You have to get rid of that bus. It's a sign and election signs are not permitted to be displayed for another month yet."

Ben (my campaign manager): "As you can see we don't have a sign on the campaign office. The bus is our campaign office sign, therefore it is legal."

Inspector (next day): "We've decided that you can use the bus as a campaign office sign if you post a big arrow on each side that points to the campaign office."

Ben: "Okay."

Inspector (two days later): "You have to get rid of the bus. There is a maximum size for a sign. The bus is too big."

Ben: "It is not a single sign. As you can see, there are three candidates sharing the face of the bus. It is several signs and each of them is within the bylaw."

Inspector (three days later): "You've got to get rid of the bus. There is a height limit on a sign. Yours is too high."

Ben: "By how much does it exceed the height limit?"

Inspector: "Two inches."

Ben: "OK. We'll let two inches of air out of the tires. I hope this is your last visit."

AN IRRELEVANT FACTOID

As near as I can figure, my City Hall office was situated on the site of the lobby of the Shea's Hippodrome on Bay Street, where I saw Elvis Presley's first movie, *Love me Tender*. It previewed in Toronto in 1956. The theatre was later torn down to build the current City Hall. Old City Hall, on the other side of Bay Street, was turned into a courthouse.

PART IV

CHAPTER 67

What Was That You Said?

P olitics is one of the most ego-stroking jobs. I read somewhere that former Ontario Premier Bill Davis once said that his worst day as a politician was better than his best day as a lawyer.

Politics is the best job in the world. You can say outrageous things; people write them down and put them in the newspapers. Then the radio and TV stations follow you around asking you to repeat them. Suddenly, you become a personality. You can walk down the street anywhere and people recognize you. I've never considered myself anything but an ordinary person. I shouldn't be, but I'm floored when people say, "I know you!"

In politics, all you really have is your reputation, your public image, how people perceive you. Some councillors have none at all. They toil over their newsletters because in many cases it is the only contact they have with their constituents. I never had to worry about my electors knowing what I did. They read about it in their newspapers and heard about it on their radios every day.

People like "in-your-face" politicians: fighters against injustice. My Jamaican constituents used to compare me to Michael Manley, the feisty prime minister of Jamaica. It's not that I deliberately set out to be that way. It's just that I get angry when I discover something I know is wrong and I can't just sit there and not do anything to fix it. Ask David Miller. I was one of his closest political allies, yet when I saw something I didn't like in a report on an Executive Committee agenda I didn't hesitate to try and amend it. I'm sure I caused him many stressful moments.

I also learned early in the game that words were powerful weapons.

Most of us enter politics to do some good, to better our communities. But if you want to be successful, you first have to learn to use the tools of the trade. Harold Hilliard, an old-timer who covered North York Council for the Toronto Star, taught me how effective a well-placed quote can be. When he interviewed me, he used to make up many of my quotes.

"Would it be fair to say that you said, "Bla, bla, bla, bla, bla?"

"That's exactly what I said," I would reply. "Or 'not precisely, try this.'"

How many times have I heard people in politics say, "All publicity is good publicity, as long as they spell your name right"? I disagree. If the only time electors read or hear about you is when you vote to increase your salary, that's how they perceive you. If it's a minor blip in your public persona, they are willing to forgive and forget.

And then there is humour. Humour is an important tool. It helps to put things into perspective. John Tory once asked me how to deal with Rob Ford. I told him, "Make fun of him... don't take him seriously. It drives him crazy. It's the best way to disarm a bully."

It's also the best way to kill a bad idea. Ridicule it, exaggerate it and mock it. Unfortunately, (or fortunately) that's what gets me quoted. It is something I accept as being the other side of my public persona.

When I retired, I received a nice note from poet John Robert Colombo. John lives in my ward. I manage to knock at his door at least once every seven years. He publishes a dictionary of Canadian Quotations.

"I had forgotten that you were such a quotable guy," he wrote. "I will be sure to include a number of your 'nuggets' in my next Dictionary of Canadian Quotations, out next year. You're more quotable than your nemesis Mel, but not as quotable as Honest Ed, but you're in their league!"

Now I know exactly where I fit into the galaxy of quotable Torontonians. That observation won't make Mel happy; too bad.

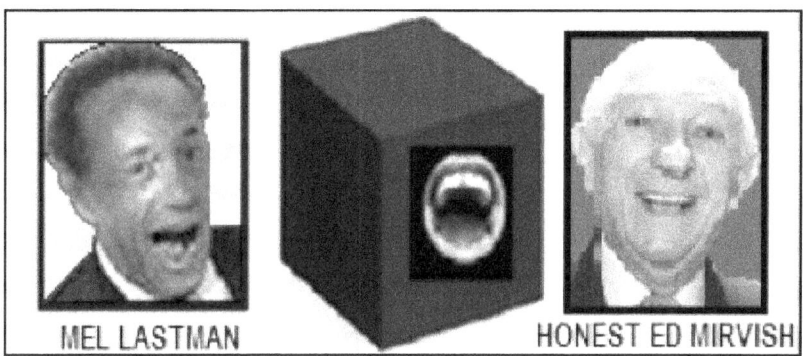

Here are a few quotes that have found their way into public arena:

On the credibility of Tony Rizzo, my opponent in the 2000 election: "The guy's a deadbeat. He wants to manage the finances of the entire City of Toronto, but he can't manage his own personal finances."

On Mississauga Mayor Hazel McCallion: "I've been in politics as long as Hazel McCallion, but the main difference between us is that I have fewer wrinkles."

On the rash of attacks on taxi drivers: "Driving a taxi is far more dangerous than being a police officer in this city."

On Giorgio Mammoliti's proposal to raise a giant flagpole at Weston Road and Finch: "Councillor Mammoliti will have the largest pole erection in North America. I move that council encourage the Emery Business Improvement Association to seek corporate sponsorship from companies like Pfizer Inc., Eli Lilly Canada Inc., makers of Viagra and Cialis." (The amendment carried.)

On Rob Ford's budget cuts: "With all these tax cuts and everything, they are going to have to close the libraries three days a week to pay for it. Rob Ford's supporters won't mind, because they can't read."

On the high cost of scrapping subways: "You know, on Eglinton we dug the tail track for a subway from the Allen Road back to Bathurst Street. It cost $100 million to fill it back in when, in the mid-1990s [then Progressive Conservative Premier] Mike Harris scrapped it. The Eglinton subway is waiting to be built, and we want to build it. So McGuinty, if you break your promises, suffer the consequences."

On speed bumps: "North York has gone speed hump nuts. Councillor Joanne Flint has managed to hump all over North York.... York-Eglinton Councillor Joe Mihevc is the worst humper in the world. Every time I drive south from Eglinton and hit a hump, I think 'Mihevc'.... 'Mihevc'.... 'Mihevc'.... 'Mihevc.'"

On the 25-cent TTC fare hike in 2003: "Mr. McGuinty has forced us into this position, we have no choice. We relied on Mr. McGuinty's 2¢-per-litre promise, and I'm really disappointed to say that he's basically stolen Christmas from the TTC."

On the misuse of disabled parking permits: "Inconsiderate slobs are scooping up free parking... under the rubric of a disabled permit... not only ripping off the city but also... the disabled. I submit to you that the province is fully aware of the widespread abuse of these permits but does not have the political courage to deal with the problem for fear of pushback from some 500,000 permit holders."

On the provincial press conference on Smart Cards: "If they have $250 million to spend on Smart Cards, that's nice, that's warm and fuzzy, but I could buy 400 buses with that money. We're leaving people on the street; people are being shoehorned into subways. We were invited to attend (the press conference), but we respectfully declined. I'm running an election campaign. I haven't got time to be at a press conference as a backdrop for the minister."

On a TTC fare increase: "The bottom line is that we have to keep the transit system running because the health of the city depends on it. I apologize to our riders because we all have to pay a little more."

On a police helicopter in the budget (actually it wasn't even in the budget, but that didn't stop Rob Ford from trying to put one there even though the chief hadn't asked for it): "I think we need five for the divisions and one for spare parts. This could be the beginning of a great air force. But I do hope that someone installs Sidewinder missiles – you can't have an air force without them…. These are big boy toys. This is pure testosterone…. Do we need a helicopter to track down drug dealers in the back alleys of Parkdale? It's tough enough to land a helicopter on a doughnut shop."

On the baby that was born on the Wellesley subway station platform: "I'm tempted to recommend that the baby be named Wellesley, but that would be up to the mother. "

On security on the TTC after the London transit bombing: "I don't want to overstate our vulnerability. We don't have any troops to pull out of Iraq, and I wonder if the terrorists would have to get out a map and find out where Toronto is before they attacked it."

On the federal government giving only $1.6 million for security on the TTC: "It's a spit in the eye. It shows utter and complete disrespect for the citizens of Toronto. It's like handing a bum a dime and saying, 'go buy a cup of coffee.'"

On golf club property tax deferrals: "They protected green spaces for a wealthy few. The guy who is washing the floor in the club house is subsidizing members of the club through his property taxes. Coincidentally, if we had the $20 million [that the golf clubs owe us in back taxes] we could make every recreation program in the City of Toronto free. To raise the money all the golf clubs have to do is increase the price of a martini by half a buck. I resent the fact that ordinary taxpayers are subsidizing the wealthy elite of this city."

On the GTA (Greater Toronto Transit Authority): "Unless the 905 tailpipe-huggers on this board come to grips with the fact that they have been the architects of urban sprawl, they are doomed to be forever shrouded in clouds of smog."

On the retirement of Mel Lastman: "I could always rely on the mayor to disagree with me. I could always rely on the mayor to fight with me. I could always rely on the mayor to snipe at me. And it's a real sense of loss for me to have to do without that. But I guess it's a matter I'll have to take up with my psychiatrist."

On renovating the North York Civic Centre wedding chapel: "It looks more like a place to get buried than a place to get married. (Perhaps some don't see the distinction)."

On my pre-election fundraiser: "Just before SARS I came up with a 12-course Chinese banquet as a fundraiser. Now I have to serve a 13th course: Penicillin."

On Prime Minister Chretien's speech to the Federation of Canadian Municipalities annual meeting: "The Prime Minister proved he is the prime politician and the prime exaggerator in the country. He came to blow his own horn, and he turned a piccolo into a tuba."

On the claim that I sneaked a motion approving a salary increase through Council: "Now some members of Council are caught like deer in the headlights, and they're running for cover saying that they didn't know what they were doing. They don't want to be associated with giving themselves an increase. Everyone knew, and those that claim otherwise are either incompetent or liars."

On retirement: "I haven't lost my enthusiasm for the job; I love the job, but it is just time to move on. I'm batting 1 for 2. My grandson, Max, who is 11, groans every time I crack a joke. On the other hand, my grandson David, 21, has inherited my cornball sense of humour. In politics, a 50% approval rating is not too bad."

CHAPTER 68
Ellis Island

Ellis Island was the gateway to North America for thousands of immigrants fleeing the harsh poverty of Europe. It was located in New York harbour, a short distance from the Statue of Liberty. Here, immigrants were processed, checked for communicable diseases, quarantined and either sent on their way or sent back. The Jews had an added incentive. They were fleeing anti-Semitism and the pogroms of Eastern Europe. *Fiddler on the Roof* poignantly depicts the impetus for the some two million Jewish immigrants who filed through Ellis Island from 1880 to 1920.

Most immigrants to Canada in this period came through Quebec City, but many came through the Port of New York. About 120,000 Jewish immigrants came to Canada between 1909 and 1920. By some twist of fate, my father's family immigrated through Ellis Island in 1920. It was just in time. The U.S. Government, alarmed by the size of Jewish immigration that had grown to almost 50% of the total of all immigration, pinched it off to a trickle through quotas established in 1921.

Ellis Island, off the southern tip of Manhattan, housed a large immigration reception and quarantine building built in 1900 and used to process new arrivals to America until 1954.

The trip through Ellis Island was the first step in my family's "Moscoization." Immigration officers weren't all that careful about the spelling of foreign names. My grandmother's surname was spelled "Moszkawicz" on her passport. Since she was originally from Minsk, in Belarus, I assume that when she immigrated to Lodz in Poland her name was changed from the Russian to the Polish spelling. Somehow, at Ellis Island, Moszkawicz became Moscowitz and later, along the way, it was shortened to Moscoe. I even have relatives who call themselves Moss. The origin of the name has nothing to do with the city of Moscow. It is a derivative of Moses. On her passport, my grandmother's religion is listed as Moses.

Jews were desperately trying to "fit in." When I was born in 1939, one of the most popular Jewish names for boys in Toronto was Howard. There were a couple of reasons. Just like in the '70s, it became fashionable to name your children after soap opera stars. There were some actors around that time whose names were popular. Mel Lastman, for example, is actually Melvin Douglas Lastman. Howard is a very Anglo-Saxon sounding name. Almost every Howard I know in my age group from Toronto is Jewish.

In 1990, I was part of a delegation from Metro who attended the World Congress of Local Governments in New York. This was the inaugural conference to establish the International Council for Local Environmental Initiatives (ICLEI). The conference was held at the United Nations General Assembly building and involved more than 200 local governments from 43 counties. Our delegation included Art Eggleton, Jack Layton, Olivia Chow, June Rowlands, Brian Ashton and several other Metro councillors.

This was the week of the Ontario election and as local politicians who had a direct stake in the results, we were desperate to watch the election night coverage. Satellite TV technology was in its infancy and none of the American stations had any interest in carrying an Ontario provincial election. Someone finally managed to secure a link through the Canadian Consulate and I can recall crowding around a television set in the suite of a New York hotel room gawking as Ontario elected its first NDP government. The mood of the onlookers, or course, varied with their politics, but the excitement was palpable. Those of us who were New Democrats were buoyed by the feeling that anything in the world was possible.

Part of the conference involved attending a reception hosted by the City of New York at the Gracie Mansion. The Gracie Mansion is the official residence of the mayor of New York. At the reception, I had the opportunity to chat with Mayor David Dinkins and we exchanged business cards. I slipped his card into my suit pocked knowing I would, in all probability, throw it out next time I had my suit cleaned.

Later that week, my wife, Gloria, read in the New York Times that on Saturday they were opening a Museum of Immigration on Ellis Island.

"Let's attend the opening," I said to Gloria.

"We'll never get in," she said. "It's by invitation only and you can be sure that invitations have only been given to senators and other high-ranking government officials."

"Let's go down to the ferry docks anyway and see if I can talk our way in."

She was right. There were lines of people waiting to board the ferry and all of them were clutching gilt-edged invitations. I walked up to a police sergeant who appeared to be in charge of crowd control.

"Who's in charge from the city?" I asked.

"Mary-Ellen, over there," he pointed, "the one in the red jacket."

"Are you Mary-Ellen? I'm Councillor Howard Moscoe from Toronto," I said, handing her my card.

"Mayor Dinkins said you would look after us."

Whereupon, I whipped out the mayor's card with a flourish and thrust it under her nose.

It worked. She gave us a program and whisked us to the head of the line at the ferry. We chugged across New York harbour and were ushered to the VIP section. The museum and the reception afterwards were wonderful. It was a very emotional experience for me and, at that point, I vowed Toronto would find a similar way to celebrate our heritage as a city of immigrants.

HIT BY A FORD

Most immigrants came to Canada through Pier 21 in Halifax, the Canadian equivalent of Ellis Island. Those who came to Toronto settled in the Ward, the area around city hall. The earliest waves of immigration were Irish, followed by Jewish and Italian at the turn of the century. They tore out the bottom section of the Ward to construct new City Hall. As a result, the city lost a large chunk of what was, by then, the mid '50s, Chinatown.

In 2005, the city began planning a renovation of Nathan Phillips Square. It was an ambitious effort with a budget of $45 million and a revitalization committee headed by Councillor Peter Milczyn. When the plan for the renovation came before council, I moved: "That particular attention to the history of 'The Ward,' (i.e. the precinct in and around City Hall), and elements be incorporated into the project to illustrate and reflect the history of the Ward and its environs." It carried.

Most of the Ward had been obliterated. All that remained near the site of the new City Hall was Osgoode Hall, Old City Hall and a Hydro building, whose original façade shielded the transformer structure that served the downtown area.

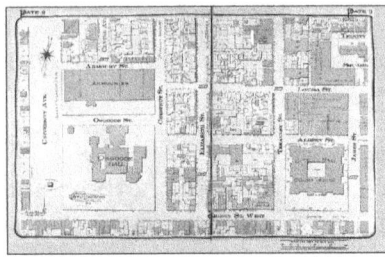 

THE WARD . CITY HALL PRECINCT . 1912   CITY HALL PRECINCT . 2016

Where there is little or no physical infrastructure remaining, the standard practice is to erect plaques. After the inspiration of Ellis Island, I wanted a lot more than plaques. I saw the opportunity of establishing a museum of a similar quality.

Ben Rothman, my executive assistant, came to the rescue. He discovered a hidden floor at City Hall. It was visible from the ground floor rotunda and encircled the entire building. It would make a perfect museum, something akin to the Guggenheim Museum in New York. The exterior walls were glass that faced onto the podium roof. The city had just recently rehabilitated the roof by installing green roof gardens. The space was fully accessible by two elevators that served the council chamber. Most people were unaware of its existence because it had been keyed out of the elevator sequence. It was used to store furniture.

I spent the next two months touring city councillors and senior bureaucrats around the space. I wanted a buy-in from as many officials as possible so the project could avoid snags. I was thrilled when Joe Pennachetti, the city manager, offered his support.

The city had always dreamed of creating a Museum of Toronto. Old City Hall housed the provincial offences courts on a lease that was to end in 2018. It was expected that Old City Hall, which had been declared a national historic site by the Historic Sites and Monuments Board of Canada in 1989, would become the site of the Museum of Toronto. Much of the funding for that museum would have to be raised by public subscription. I was hoping to kick off that effort by establishing the Museum of the Ward, which would be the precursor of the Museum of Toronto.

I visited the Tenement Museum in New York City. It is one of the most financially successful museums in the United States. Admission revenue covered 75% of its costs. It is a restored Lower East Side tenement that offers visitors a hands-on experience. A visit to the Ward Museum would be a similar experience. Visitors would start their visit in a basement theatre where they would be shown a film of the history of immigration to Toronto. They would then go by elevator to the museum floor where they would tour the circular museum.

Architect Viljo Ravel's design for the new City Hall included an elevated walkway. It was intended to act as a path that would shepherd VIPs and visitors over Queen Street to City Hall from the hotel and act as a framing device for the square. The walkway has been intermittently closed due to lack of maintenance for a number of years. It would be partially re-opened to allow visitors to leave the Ward Museum, traverse the green roof, enter the walkway and cross over a bridge built across Bay Street to access the Museum of Toronto.

I lined up a number of Torontonians prominent in the ethnic communities that had originally settled in the Ward as a volunteer museum steering committee. I was sure we could raise the money necessary to construct the museum. I also came in contact with people who had archival material for the museum. For example, Sylvia Searls, in Mayor Miller's office, offered the archives of a black Baptist church left to her by her grandfather. It had been located on Terauley Street in the Ward.

Gail Lord is a prominent Toronto museum designer. Her company, Lord Cultural Resources, has designed museums all over the world. At the time, she was working on the Museum of Human Rights in Winnipeg, which opened in 2014. When the budget for the City Hall Square renovations project came before the executive committee I moved: "That the City Manager be authorized to spend up to $50,000 on elements of the civic square project without the authorization of council." It carried.

We paid Gail Lord $45,000 for her report on the Toronto Museum of Immigration, the Ward Museum. It will probably become one of the best reports to languish in the city archives.

What happened?

We were hit by a Ford.

A traffic accident?

No, a tragic political accident. Squashed by the "Stop the gravy train" express.

CHAPTER 69
Political Hack

Some of my colleagues accuse me of being publicity hungry. They are right and I make no apologies for it. I haven't, however, noticed any of them being shy about seeking the attention of the media. In fact, they all crave it. The bald fact is nobody will interview you if you have nothing to say. When it comes to the next election, it is one thing to do good things as a politician, but unless your voters know about them as far as they are concerned, you haven't done them. In politics, the greatest asset you have (and liability too) is your reputation and that is built one "quote" at a time. Without some kind of public persona, you are reduced to explaining yourself in a 4" x 8" election brochure the content of which nobody will believe because they know you wrote it yourself.

If you get your name in the paper once a year and it's because you supported a salary increase that is how you are remembered. If you are in the public eye three times a week and you also voted for a salary increase, your reputation will override it as a minor blip. I can't begin to tell you how many times people have said to me: "I don't agree with you on (name an issue) but I know that you are out there fighting for me."

Or: "I don't always agree with you, but I know that you are working hard for the community. You have my vote."

Some people perceive me as a fighter for the little guy. Others see me as an irritant. At least they see me.

Marshall McLuhan was right when he said, "The medium is the message," but it is also true in politics that unless the message has some content there will be no media. Standing on your hands in the nude will get you your Andy Warhol 15 minutes of fame, but only once (or so). If you have to do something like that repeatedly to get noticed, that becomes your persona.

In 1990, I was appointed to the Metro licensing commission and chaired the Metro licensing committee. One very large part of the job of the commission was regulating and policing the taxi industry. For years, cabbies had complained that nobody on the commission really understood the taxi industry that it was regulating. In my case, that wasn't true at all.

Joe Moscoe, my uncle, was president of the Independent Taxi Owners' Association. His was the first taxi licensed when Metro was amalgamated in 1952. He owned and drove Metro taxi license #1. My father drove a taxi for 25 years. He drove and owned Co-Op cab licence #238. In 1961, when I graduated from teachers' college, I taught elementary school and drove a cab at night so I could meet my mortgage payments.

I swallowed the criticism and conceded that perhaps they were partially right. After 30 years, my awareness might be a little rusty. So I decided to get some firsthand knowledge of the industry by driving a taxi again. I would donate the money I made to a charity. As I told the media: "I want to learn the industry from the brake pedal up."

If I had to swallow the publicity that might ensue, I could live with it.

So, I enrolled in taxi school. The exam was made up of 80 questions on taxi policy, bylaws and geography. I had been criticized earlier by the industry and staff when I had quipped that it was too easy. Of the class of 45 prospective hacks, only eight passed the test – a failure rate of 82%. Five dropped out and two got thrown out for cheating. I was embarrassed when I scored 99%, tops in the class. I hastily launched into a political back pedal.

"I've revised my opinion," I said. "It was tough, really tough. I worked my buns off last week."

I was knocked down a peg or two when my first fare was Toronto Sun reporter Linda Barnard. She threw a zinger at me. She asked me to take her to a Scarborough address four blocks away and, even with my Perly's Guide Book, I got lost. I've always felt lost in Scarborough. I had grown up in the west end and I knew downtown Buffalo better than the east end of Toronto. I used to get anxiety attacks if I wandered anywhere east of Jarvis Street.

On Friday, I started driving for Royal/A-Quick Taxi wearing my father's old hack hat for good luck. What was the result of the two-week-long effort? I made a couple of suggestions to staff about changes they should consider making in the exam. I came away with a better appreciation of how much tougher it was for cabbies to earn a living than in my dad's day. I made 50 bucks for the Elizabeth Lue Fund, I made Cover Cab of the Month in Taxi News and, to boot, I got an ocean of ink.

One side note; Cameron MacKinnon, executive assistant to Metro Councillor Brian Ashton, when he spotted a streetcar plodding up Bay Street and tilting heavily toward the operator's side, was heard to remark: "Must be Howard's week to drive the TTC."

He shouldn't have said it. It stuck in my mind. I'll tell you later about how I got my licence to drive a TTC bus.

CHAPTER 70

Ultimatum

"You have 48 hours to withdraw the name or I'll go public," I barked into the telephone. I was talking to Councillor Tom Jakobek, who was at the other end of the line in Chicago.

Nineteen thirty-three was a tough year for Jews everywhere. Hitler had been elected to power and Yiddish newspapers were full of stories about the daily persecution of the some half million Jewish Germans. Early in that year, there was a state-sanctioned boycott of Jewish doctors, lawyers and shops followed six days later by the passage of the "Law for the Restoration of the Professional Civil Service," which banned Jews from employment in the civil service. That included professors and schoolteachers, who were considered civil servants in Germany.

Public sentiment in Toronto was highly anti-Semitic. Toronto was largely a white, Anglo Saxon Protestant city. The Jewish community was the largest foreign ethnic minority making up about 7½% of the population and it was highly resented. My father told me it was common to see signs that read "No Jews or Dogs Allowed." The Toronto anti-Semites were inspired by the news coming out of Germany.

A group of Beach residents began to agitate for a regulation that would prohibit "Jews and other obnoxious foreigners" from using the Beach. The Beach provided summertime relief, particularly for low-income people who could not afford cottages on Lake Simcoe or in Muskoka. It was easily reachable by way of the Queen streetcar. They formed the Balmy Beach Swastika Club, Local No.5. Outside the Balmy Beach Canoe Club, they hung a sign adorned with a swastika and the words "Hail Hitler." Club members wore nickel-plated badges adorned with a swastika. One of the leaders and founding members was a young man named Joe McNulty.

The Swastika Club kicked off August by staging a 150-person march along the boardwalk chanting anti-Semitic slogans and songs and attacking Jews on the beaches.

Christie Pits is located on Bloor Street across from where the Christie subway station is located today. It was a neighbourhood where Jews and Italian immigrants were beginning to settle. And that, in itself, raised local tensions.

Christie Pits is an ideal park for baseball. The site, a former gravel pit, had sloping sides where spectators could sit and watch baseball being played on a flat bottom. The diamond was located at the northeast corner of the park, a sort of a natural stadium. On August 14, 1933, the St. Peters team was playing the Harbord Playground team, which was largely Jewish. Despite the anti-Semitic slogans being chanted by the crowd and the waving of the swastika flag, the Harbord team won. Tensions ran high.

That night, someone had painted a swastika and the words "Heil Hitler" on the clubhouse. That swelled the crowd for the next game two days later. There were thousands. During that game, someone opened a blanket with a large swastika painted in the centre of it and the rioting began. It was largely the Jews and the Italians against the "swastika club." Toronto police stood passively by and did nothing until the rioting spread to the streets around and into other parts of the city.

My father had been a prizefighter. He was tough. Sammy Luftspring, who was the Canadian welterweight champion, once told my brother that Alec Moscoe was the only guy he was ever afraid of. My dad had boxed at the Palace Pier and Massey Hall and had done a Depression-era prize fighting tour of the southern United States. The day of the riot, he was in the poolroom at College and Spadina. He grabbed a pool cue and hopped into a truck to join the riot. Word spread across the city that "they were after the Jews," and people came out of their homes with baseball bats and sticks to largely say, "we are not going to sit back and take it like the Jews in Germany."

The Christie Pits riot, the largest ever in Toronto, was a turning point in the city's history. It forced Mayor William Stewart and the council, for fear of rioting, to ban the swastika. The mainstream media largely spun it as a riot caused by the Jews, but however it was spun, it clearly demonstrated that Jews were prepared to fight back.

On May 27, 1998, Councillor Jakobek brought a motion before the Toronto Community Council to name a park in a new subdivision after Joe McNulty. City policy requires that before anything municipal can be named after someone it requires a staff report to the parks committee. That is primarily to give council the opportunity to vet the name. There is one other criterion – you have to be dead to get something named after you.

That is likely to prevent councillors, like they regularly do in Vaughan, from naming streets after themselves.

Sometimes, council makes an exception to the rule and Tom made a good case.

The Toronto Community Council submitted the following communication (May 27, 1998) from Councillor Jakobek: "As members may be aware, the City is currently in the process of rezoning the East of Main area. Part of the rezoning will include a new park (the size yet to be determined). The new park's primary use will be to act as the new playing field for Malvern Collegiate, which is just to the south. Although we would normally wait until the site is dedicated to the city before naming it, we are requesting that this Community Council approve its intention to name the park after Joe McNulty. Joe McNulty is a lifetime resident of the Beach area and former volunteer football coach for Malvern for more than 40 years. He has also been the President, and founding member of the Balmy Beach Club, a paddling coach (for more than 50 years) and a local businessperson. Joe is truly loved by all and is considered a household name. Unfortunately, Mr. McNulty was recently diagnosed with terminal cancer of the liver. Given his condition, representatives of the Canoe club and Malvern Collegiate have asked that we name the new park after Joe McNulty. Please consider this request."

However, Jakobek failed to mention Mr. McNulty's leadership in founding the Swastika Club. The motion carried unanimously and was not held for discussion when Toronto Council adopted the community council report.

Shortly afterwards, I got a telephone call from someone who was writing a book on anti-Semitism in Toronto in that era. He was livid. The Jewish community would have been furious.

So, I put the ultimatum to Tom. If you have the name put on the park, you will have to deal with it in the media. The name, though approved by council, never appeared on the park. It's the first time I've ever known Tom Jakobek to back down.

CHAPTER 71

Brother Jeff

Jeff Lyons was a lawyer, rainmaker and lobbyist. By 1998, he worked primarily, perhaps exclusively, as a lobbyist. Relationships were his stock-in-trade. His style of lobbying was different. He was essentially an influence peddler. Decisions about how to spend public money were made, or looked like they were made, based on who hired Jeff Lyons instead of who offered the best product. Stripped of its folksy embellishments, this was cronyism.

JEFF LYONS

Lyons was a friend of Metro Chairman Paul Godfrey and Mel Lastman. Lyons had been enjoying a long reign as the pre-eminent municipal lobbyist in Toronto. Not coincidentally, he also enjoyed a reputation as an important fundraiser for municipal election campaigns. He had demonstrated over the years that he could bring in the money. Year after year, he would deliver letters to candidates of strategic interest, usually in person. Enclosed with the letters were bundles of cheques he had solicited from donors.

The news that Lyons had applied for the position of Toronto's appointee to the Greater Toronto Airport Authority (GTAA) hit like a shock wave. Airport authorities had been set up by the Mulroney government to rebuild airports across the country. Pearson was a $4.4 billion expansion. Mulroney was careful to make sure municipalities had no way to influence airport decisions. The rules prohibited elected officials from sitting on these boards, and municipalities had no right to direct their appointees. Once appointed, they were free agents.

"I've always been interested in transportation," Lyons told the media.

Sure he was. As chair of the TTC, he had convinced the commission to secretly purchase an airline, Vacation Air, in partnership with a wholesale travel agency owned by "a friend." They used its subsidiary, Gray Coach, which he also chaired, as a way of concealing the purchase. The TTC had owned Gray Coach since 1924. All this was done under the cover of "confidentiality." When I exposed this, it prompted Metro, which was just setting up its level of government, to dump all of the citizen appointees, Jeff included, and replace them with elected officials. Incidentally, Jeff had also engineered the purchase of two bus lines out west.

I told the media: "Appointing Jeff Lyons to the GTTA is like putting Count Dracula in charge of the blood bank."

In the face of all of this, did Jeff Lyons get appointed to the GTTA?

You can be sure he did. He just owned too many councillors.

CHAPTER 72
Gunn Fight

DAVID GUNN

When I recruited David Gunn, I knew we would end up in a Gunn Fight. I had asked him to apply for the job because he had a reputation as one of the best transit managers in North America. The TTC was falling apart and had suffered from shoddy management under the previous chief general manager, who had been a "political" appointment. I also knew, from a conversation I had with Joe Miller, chair of the Washington system, that Gunn had a low tolerance for politicians and a history of ending relationships abruptly. It was worth the chance. Gunn was a hands-on, nuts and bolts manager and was just what the TTC needed at the time. Our buses were falling apart and the subways were suffering from years of neglected maintenance. I knew we would eventually come into conflict, but I thought it would be about policy. I never dreamed that a local development project would be the catalyst.

Councillor David Shiner approached me to resolve a difficulty he was having over a proposed development at the corner of Bayview and Sheppard, which was to be placed over the not yet built Bayview subway station. In order to configure the development to satisfy the community, he had to have it changed in a way that impinged on the design of the station. Councillor John Filion, who represented the area on the opposite side of Bayview, also approached me about the proposed location of an underground hydro vault.

The TTC was going to relocate the hydro vault behind some townhouses. And to do so, they would have to cut down six mature trees. Residents were opposed, but when John Filion went to the TTC they brushed him off.

"We already spent $47,500 on the design of the vault and we're not about to change it," he was told.

It should have been located on some nearby land that was owned by the Dangreen Development Company. TTC staff assumed they would have to pay Dangreen $300,000 for the use of their property so they didn't even ask and picked the townhouse site instead. I intervened and got Dangreen to waive the $300,000 as a gesture of good will.

"As I see it," John Filion said, "Moscoe saved the taxpayers $300,000 and the TTC wasted $47,500 designing a vault in the wrong location all because they acted unilaterally. Howard Moscoe did a terrific job and everybody got what they wanted, but it got Gunn's nose out of joint somehow. I guess he was embarrassed that his staff screwed up, but he should be thanking Moscoe for fixing things."

For Shiner, the building was lowered, a bus loop was re-located and traffic circulation improved.

"In two weeks, we renegotiated a much better proposal," said Councillor David Shiner. "Everyone agreed, including residents in the community, that this is much better."

I had always believed the role of a committee chair was to intervene on behalf of the community and the local councillors. It was no big deal. That's normally what we did. I presume Gunn assumed I was working for the developer. If he had bothered to check around, he would have found I had a reputation for being harder on developers than almost any other city councillor. If he had a problem with the specific changes, he should have shared his thoughts with me, but he didn't.

While I was away at a transit conference in Regina, Gunn circulated a list of grievances to TTC commissioners.

"Either we deal with the situation or I'm getting the hell out of here," he informed transit commissioners.

"As TTC chair, my job, I believe, is more than simply to sign retirement certificates," I said. "I'm sorry he's contemplating resigning. I'm not.... If Mr. Gunn chooses to resign, he will be missed."

Gunn said I was meddling.

Royson James, the Toronto Star City Hall columnist, wrote: "Somebody ought to tell Gunn he is not God; that while he may be the best transit man on the planet, he doesn't have the right to try to bully his political masters.... What the councillor [Howard Moscoe] lacks in finesse he makes up for in integrity. His heart is in the right place. For Gunn to employ brinkmanship to oust Moscoe from a position the councillor has fought hard to achieve is simply distasteful.... From what happened in Toronto this week, one can safely predict this: Gunn's long goodbye has already begun. The TTC will somehow survive. Moscoe will still be there as a vigilant and outspoken advocate. And Gunn will ride off, probably with a golden handshake and a smile on his face as he heads to his cottage on Cape Breton Island. Goodbye, Mr. Gunn. No hard feelings. It's been nice knowing you."

At the commission meeting the following week, the commission voted confidence in me as chair. They also voted confidence in Gunn as chief general manager. Whatever my faults, most of them understood the consequences of a civil servant being allowed to dictate to an elected official. What could happen to me could happen to them. Did the double vote of confidence resolve the matter? Not really.

A week later, Gunn issued another letter about one of my alleged peccadilloes and the tension began to mount again. He would often roll his eyes in disgust at some of the comments made by commissioners at board meetings and his tolerance was obviously strained.

On October 7, 1998, two years before his contract ran out, Gunn announced he was taking an early retirement. He agreed to remain until April 30, when labour negotiations were expected to be completed and until the 1999 budget was put to bed.

In retrospect, allowing him to hang around that long after he announced his retirement was a mistake I came to regret. Now the constraints were off and he lost no opportunity to find a way to seek my demise as chair. If I could be deposed, it seems likely he would have stayed.

He didn't have to wait long. We were in the midst of some difficult labour negotiations with a possible strike deadline approaching. That became the setting for an attempt on my political life.

CHAPTER 73

On the Verge of a Shutdown

It was like two trains on the same track headed towards each other at full speed. The Amalgamated Transit Union, Local 113 train had been chugging southward for the better part of a year attempting to negotiate an agreement. I was on the management train, heading northward with my foot on the brake, a noose round my neck, with the mayor and four councillors tugging at it and David Gunn stoking the furnace. The two trains were destined to meet at midnight, Thursday, April 8, 1999, which was the strike deadline. That's when the 7,800 transit workers were legally able to walk off the job and the TTC was legally able to lock them out. Prospects did not look good.

The previous day, I learned of an emergency meeting called for 3 p.m. that afternoon to "reconsider the position of chair." The petition for the meeting was signed by four of the seven commissioners. It couldn't have come at a worse time. The city was in a quandary about how to fund the unsigned contract. A fare increase would barely raise enough to cover the city's offer of 1%, 1% and 1% over three years, let alone the union ask.

Mike Harris's provincial government had cut ongoing operating funding for the TTC and the mayor had run for election on a three-year tax freeze platform. Not only that, all but one of the TTC commissioners were adamantly opposed to a fare increase. They all agreed the decision to raise fares should be a decision of council even though the commission had the authority to make that decision on its own. The council, however, had final say over the budget, which in turn would dictate the fare increase.

"It was Mel Lastman who put councillors in a straightjacket and they should be the ones who decide how they want to get out of it," I said.

Fare increases always cause us to lose riders, but a strike is worse. People buy cars and abandon public transit. After the 1991 strike, which lasted eight days, it took the TTC eight years to recover the ridership it lost. Fare increases and strikes put the transit system into a downward spiral.

On Tuesday, two days before the deadline, I was interviewed about the negotiations, but because we were under a news blackout, I could say very little.

"How will you pay for a settlement?" said the reporter.

"The important thing is to avoid shutting down the city," I replied. "We'll just have to find the money somewhere. I prefer that it comes out of property taxes."

The mayor went bananas: "I don't know what he was talking about... where he said we'll make a deal and find the money. There's nowhere to find the money. There's no money.... If we give them more, we would have to give everybody else more."

He went on to add: "Moscoe's appointment as chair was the biggest mistake of my life...since I became mayor, it was the only mistake that I made. The union will not want to talk. They'll figure there's more money and there isn't more money."

That was the plan: Get Rid of Moscoe. Send a message to the bargaining table and the union will meekly settle because "there is no more money."

It all looked grim.

CHAPTER 74

Grafitti and Mississauga Buses

Two disagreements helped heighten the tension between David Gunn and myself. The first was a window scratch and the second was a Mississauga bus route.

To put this into context, Gunn was on his way out. His disagreements with the commission had caused him to leave two years before his contract was up. Joe Hall, transportation writer at the Toronto Star, wrote: "With chief general manager David Gunn set to take early retirement at the end of April, an endemic staff dislike of the seven-member commission – always a millimetre below the surface – is pouring out in whispered accusations of incompetence and gamesmanship."

Hall quotes an unnamed transit manager: "Most of the commissioners don't know what they are talking about much of the time. They just come up with ideas they think will get their names in print."

Hall also wrote: "It was this kind of ongoing bickering, which often saw Gunn rolling his eyes in disgust when he was not being overtly hostile to commissioners at their board encounters."

One of Gunn's career accomplishments had been to get rid of graffiti on the New York Transit System. This was no mean feat. Most of the major transit systems in Europe, for example, are plagued by graffiti. I was shocked when I saw subway trains in Rome and Paris totally covered in graffiti.

David Gunn declared war on vandals in New York by establishing a zero-tolerance policy when it came to graffiti. No train or bus could leave the yard in the morning if it had graffiti on it. Those who defaced transit property would feel the full weight of the law. New York graffiti artists had even declared Gunn to be public enemy #1. He is credited with having abolished graffiti on the New York subway system. The New York public loved it.

When he came to Toronto, David brought his zero-tolerance policy to the TTC. The difference was, compared to other cities the TTC didn't really have a serious problem with graffiti. Nonetheless, every TTC employee knew and was aware of the boss's aversion to graffiti. In the lexicon of graffiti crime, the highest order was termed to be "scratchiti," the scratching of window glass.

It was December 5, 1999, at the height of rush hour. Toronto had been hit by a winter storm. The subways were packed as commuters escaped the snowy roads outside. Someone was seen scratching a window on a Bloor subway car. The train was held in a tunnel outside the Old Mill station for 31 minutes until police arrived to make an arrest. By that time, three trains were blocking the tunnel delaying some 7,000 passengers.

I fired off a steaming red rocket to David Gunn: "I fear that in our zeal to control vandalism we've resorted to an unacceptable trade off.... Thousands of people were delayed for 31 minutes at the height of rush hour because somebody scratched a window. It's absolutely ridiculous.... We lose passengers every time a major delay occurs."

I asked Gunn to bring a report on the incident to the next commission meeting so we could review the policy.

The second dispute centred on the route taken by Mississauga Transit buses unloading passengers at the Islington subway station.

Let me preface this discussion with a few remarks. It seems that almost every time a new bus route is established in a residential neighbourhood there are objections from residents along the route. Everyone wants convenient bus service, but nobody seems to want buses on their street. I call it transit NIMBY. I have never been sympathetic to these objectors. The need for efficient public transit, in my mind, always trumps local neighbourhood objections. I faced the issue in my first year of elected office.

There was huge opposition to putting a bus service on Marlee Avenue. If anyone ever tried to remove the Marlee bus today, they would face 100-fold the opposition this bus route faced when it was first proposed. I've never varied from that position.

The Burnhamthorpe bus controversy was different. Burnhamthorpe Road was a local residential street. It had become a major thoroughfare for Mississauga Transit (MT) buses to access the Islington subway station. This was in addition to some 200 TTC buses that regularly traversed Burnhamthorpe Road. Some 300 MT buses used the street as a short cut to the station and that number was growing. There was no other reason for them to be on that street.

I was approached by Judy Shields, one of the spokespersons for the Burnhamthorpe residents. I had known her husband, Allan, from when we were both teachers in Etobicoke where I began my teaching career. For years, the residents pleaded with Mississauga Transit officials to re-route their bus traffic onto Dundas Street, which was a commercial thoroughfare. Dundas Street had High Occupancy Vehicle (HOV) Lanes that could accommodate the buses. There was no need to use Burnhamthorpe as a short cut. Once they crossed the Toronto boundary, Mississauga Transit buses were not allowed to pick up passengers.

Each year as bus volumes increased, it became more difficult to endure the noise, vibrations and pollution of more than 500 heavily loaded buses rumbling past their front doors on a constant basis. Pleas of the residents had been re-buffed by MT officials, who claimed re-routing to Dundas Street would add five minutes to the route, along with $750,000 in annual costs to their operating budget. When they met with Mississauga Mayor Hazel McCallion, her response was cryptic: "Move to Mississauga," she quipped.

They were not amused. In fact, they were hopping mad.

I floated an idea. Why not solve the problem with an open-door policy? If we allowed MT to pick up passengers in Toronto, both transit systems could reduce their fleets and save a lot of money.

"If that's on the table, it's a progressive step" said Angus McDonald, Mississauga Transit commissioner. "Service duplication is the real problem. Quite frankly, we're running into each other on Burnhamthorpe Road."

But the plan would take many months to negotiate.

When they appeared before the TTC, the residents got a more positive response. The commission voted, much to the chagrin of our staff [transit officials are as thick as thieves], to cancel the month-to-month lease of the TTC bus platforms on December 1 if MT refused to re-route their buses.

On Wednesday, November 25, 20 Burnhamthorpe residents and I trooped up to Mississauga to make a deputation to their council. I addressed council: "These people have been shaken, rattled and rolled out of their beds. All they are asking for is to have the opportunity to live peaceful lives in their own homes."

I asked council, as a gesture of good will, to re-route half of the MT buses onto Dundas Street until an open-door policy could be negotiated. I indicated that to help speed the buses up, I would ask Toronto Council to change the HOV lanes on Dundas Street to bus-only lanes.

Rita Alldrit spoke for the Burnhamthorpe residents. She asked them to be good neighbours and have some consideration for their plight. Our remarks were met with hostility, contempt and condescension.

Rita ploughed ahead: "We've stopped being gullible and we've stopped being passive. No business or agency has a right to destroy a neighbourhood.... We will use whatever means we can under the law to protect our homes."

Under pressure from staff to reverse the commission's decision to close the station platforms entirely to MT buses, an emergency meeting of the TTC was held on Thursday, November 26. I can imagine the lines burning up from the flurry of telephone calls between MT and TTC offices. The TTC met, but refused to rescind its decision. Instead, it was modified so only MT buses that did not use Burnhamthorpe Road would be allowed into the station. Despite the staff efforts to convince us otherwise, we hung in.

On Thursday December 1, deadline day, Burnhamthorpe residents hit the streets. They set up picket lines at crosswalks during the morning rush hour and whenever a MT bus was spotted, they took to the pavement.

RESIDENTS BLOCK MISSISSAUGA BUSSES

Gloria Lindsay Luby, the local councillor, and I did a stint in the crosswalk as well.

After two days of delay, the frequency of MT buses began to diminish. It became obvious that MT officials were diverting buses, which is what they should have done in the first place.

One of the picketers, Richard Stevens, commented: "But they're just re-routing them down the East Mall and I'm sure they intend to move them back when we go away."

The residents had made their point. Because of MT's intransigence, for a season or two Mississauga passengers had to plod their way through winter slush to get from their street drop-off point into the Islington station. It could have been resolved by a little good will.

Toronto Star Columnist Royson James wrote: "Moscoe suggested that Mississauga re-route half the buses as a good will gesture and then have both councils negotiate a settlement is more than reasonable.

"The obvious solution is a seamless transit system that allows any transit vehicle to pick up passengers anywhere in the GTA has been studied to death...."

Fare integration and a seamless transit system were scheduled to be implemented in 2016. It didn't quite happen. It all hung on the introduction of the Presto Card, an automated, non-contact digital fare reading system. While the card readers were installed in TTC vehicles and stations, it is now 2017 and they are not fully operational. The system was plagued with equipment failures and cost overruns.

Good news though: They might be working by next year. It would have only taken them 20 years to get there.

After David Gunn left, the TTC named the new transit control centre after him as a tribute to his tenure. It was named the David Gunn Transit Control Centre.

I call it the Gunn Control Centre.

CHAPTER 75

Kindergarten Coup

The stage was set for my political assassination. Mel Lastman and Rod Phillips, his chief of staff, had engineered it perfectly. They had previous experience. They had attempted to dump Gloria Lindsay Luby as vice-chair of the Police Services Board. That failed, but this time they had everything right.

Now four assassins were neatly lined up to have me removed as chair of the TTC. Four commissioners, Rob Davis (vice-chair), Brian Ashton, Chris Korwin-Kuczynski and Blake Kinahan, submitted a petition to the secretary of the commission demanding a special meeting to remove me as chair. It was orchestrated from the mayor's office. The assassins were honing their blades.

I was nominated as chair by Mel Lastman in January 1998. Why was a mystery to me. I can only surmise he was trying to reach out and project an image of wanting to work with all factions on council. When he was questioned about the impending coup, he was quoted as saying: "My appointment of Howard Moscoe as chair of the TTC was the biggest mistake of my life."

Why did Lastman want me removed? We were in head-to-head negotiations with the Amalgamated Transit Union, Local 113, representing some 7,500 employees. A strike deadline was fast approaching and the bargaining team had a mandate from their membership to act on it. In the previous agreement, the union had accepted a very small wage increase. There was an unstated expectation that we would make it up to them in this contract. Things were stalled at the table. In a press interview, I was asked what would happen if the agreement were settled at a level above what the city could afford? My response was "we would have to find the money somewhere."

Lastman had been elected on the premise there would be a tax freeze. If the money didn't come from taxes, it would have to come from either the fare box or the Government of Ontario, and the Harris government had just dumped the bulk of provincial support for public transit. I, on the other hand, had publicly opposed a fare hike. A 10-cent fare hike, while modest, would cost each of our regular riders $60 a year and would hit hardest those least able to afford it. That, in itself, was probably not sufficient provocation to convince Lastman that I must be deposed. He was pushed from behind by David Gunn, chief general manager of the TTC.

From an operational perspective, Gunn was one of the best transit managers in North America. I recruited him. He was recommended by David Gurin, our deputy-planning commissioner. Gurin was a friend of Ben Rothman, my EA (executive assistant), and had worked under Gunn in New York. I telephoned Gunn and asked him to apply. If you wanted an efficient transit system, he was the guy to have and we were lucky enough to snag him after suffering many years of sloppy management. The salary we offered was far below industry standards.

Gunn lived, breathed and slept public transit. He was the guy who got rid of the graffiti on the New York subway system. When we interviewed for his job, he didn't just breeze into town, have his interview and leave as others did. He arrived a week early, bought a fistful of TTC tokens and rode the rails for a week. When he came into the interview, he knew more about the TTC than anyone else in the room.

Gunn was a great manager, but he had one fatal flaw – he couldn't tolerate anyone else playing with his train set, particularly politicians. Yes, he did "make the trains run on time," but it had to be his way or the highway. (Sorry, it's a terrible cliché for a transit discussion.) I knew that when we hired him. Prior to our finalizing his contract, I had a long telephone conversation with the chair of the Washington Metropolitan Area Transit Authority who had clashed with Gunn. I knew Gunn had difficulty separating management from policy. In a democracy, the way it is supposed to work is politicians are elected to make policy, managers manage. The TTC needed someone of his calibre, and I was willing to chance it knowing full well our relationship might result in conflict. It was worth the risk.

As to negotiations, the chair of the TTC is in a no-win situation. Traditionally, the staff did the negotiating. The chair sat on the sidelines and was briefed, as was the commission, from time to time. In this set of negotiations I was provided with very little information. Yet I was the spokesperson for the organization. I bore the ultimate responsibility. I carried the can. If there was a strike, I was wide open to criticism. Where were you? How did you let this happen? If I pushed my way to the table, I was "meddling." I determined at that time I would never allow myself to be put into that position again – that is if I was ever allowed to be in that position again.

Talk about my demise buzzed around City Hall all week. It was as if I had already died. I had three votes, Commissioners Joe Mihevc, David Miller and my own. They (the assassins) had four. It was a done deal. The three of us had a couple of meetings that week to plot strategy, but I knew I was a goner when my friend Joe Mihevc began musing about how we might make him my replacement. One thing that is not in short supply at City Hall is ambition.

Councillor Olivia Chow attended those meetings. She is one of the most effective back-room strategists I have ever known in local politics. Slowly, a strategy began to emerge. The plotters could be tripped up by their own ambition. Olivia ran off to talk to Kinahan.

"Stroke him," I said. "Tell him we don't want the right wing to take over the TTC. Advise him that we know Moscoe is a goner and we thought someone as capable as he was should run the

TTC. Say that from amongst the four of them he would be our choice as chair."

I knew Brian Ashton hated Kinahan. In 1995, Ashton took a run at becoming chair of Metro Council. Kinahan agreed to nominate him against Alan Tonks, but in his nomination speech, Kinahan proceeded to speak in support of Tonks and against Ashton. It was a major embarrassment to Brian, who was humiliated at the inaugural meeting in front of his family and friends. Brian got three votes for Metro chair. He could never tolerate Blake Kinahan as chair of the TTC.

On Thursday, April 8, from about 1:00 p.m., the media ghouls began to gather in committee room two for the kill. They were shoving microphones into everyone's faces collecting pre-game comment. The media almost crowded out the real people that had flocked to City Hall to watch the guillotine fall. Politics is truly a blood sport.

After a short private session, the show began. The public meeting started with public deputations. In the first hour, 10 people lined up to speak, all of them against my removal.

Then Commissioner Chris Korwin-Kuczynski fired the opening shot. He mumbled something about me having revealed privileged information about negotiations and moved the following motion: "That Commissioner Moscoe be removed from the chair; and that vice-chair Davis be made temporary chair until a further meeting is held to discuss the election of a new chair with such a meeting to take place no later than June 30th, 1999."

I couldn't believe my ears. The idiots had been consumed by their own ambition. They couldn't decide amongst themselves who would succeed me as chair. It was a space big enough to manoeuvre a subway train into.

Because Davis, the vice-chair, and I were both named in the motion, I was able to keep control of the meeting by turning the gavel over to David Miller.

I told them the TTC was too important to me and the people of Toronto to continue with a temporary chair, especially since we were in the middle of negotiations and facing a strike deadline. I moved an amendment to replace part two of the motion with: "2. And that Commissioner Kinahan be named chair of the TTC."

When Brian Ashton tried to have the motion ruled out of order, Miller ruled against him. When he challenged the chair, he lost the vote 4-3. Of course, Kinahan voted with us.

My amendment then carried on the same 4-3 vote. The vote held in spite of a series of other attempted amendments, at least until the final vote. When the amended motion, to remove me as chair and replace me with Kinahan, was put, it lost on a vote of 5 to 2, with Commissioners Kinahan and Korwin-Kuczynski in favour and Commissioners Moscoe, Miller, Mihevc, Ashton and Davis against. I guess Ashton and Davis could not stomach the prospect of Kinahan as chair of the TTC.

Ashton later explained his vote: "Making Kinahan TTC chair would have been like getting mowed down by a streetcar only to get up and be mowed down by a bus."

Kinahan was stunned. Korwin-Kuczynski blurted out, "What happened?" and was left scratching his head. It was truly, as Gord Perks, the then chair of the environmental alliance, put it in his deputation, "A kindergarten coup."

The room erupted in wild cheering.

What Happened? *Mowed down by a bus*

Every media outlet carried it as a top story:

Toronto Star: "Moscoe keeps job with deft manoeuvre"

Globe and Mail: "Bid by TTC commissioners to oust Moscoe falls flat"

Royson James, Star columnist: "Mayor's coup bid compounds problems"

Toronto Sun: "Moscoe defeats coup bid, Transit boss stays"

Sue-Ann Levy, Sun columnist: "Axe man Mel swings and misses."

I received editorial support from the Toronto Star: "Thankfully, Moscoe deftly sidestepped the attempted coup and the bumbling executioners were revealed for what they are – sneaking and conniving. The plot was apparently hatched by Mel Lastman…. Frankly, it'll be a long time before the four commissioners involved in this attempted coup retain credibility to speak for the interests of TTC riders."

It was a stunning blow to the mayor's credibility. The standing joke around City Hall was that Rod Phillips, his chief of staff, can pull down a $160,000 a year salary but can't count to four.

Oh by the way, Rod is now the minister of the environment in the Doug Ford government. Isn't that comforting?

ROD PHILLIPS

CHAPTER 76

The 1999 Transit Strike

F lush from my victory over the forces of evil at City Hall, I booked into the Delta Chelsea Hotel and came to join the negotiations. I believed my survival as chair actually helped the negotiations. Vince Casuti, the union president, had appeared at the assassination meeting to make a deputation in my support. He told the commission my remarks had no affect whatsoever on the negotiations. Of course, the kindergarten conspirators wouldn't have believed him anyway.

My remarks to the media may or may not have had an effect on the negotiations, but my survival as chair certainly did. While Gunn had the respect of the union, I had their trust. They knew I wasn't out to screw them. The city waited anxiously to determine if people could ride transit to work on Monday morning and the media were camped out at the hotel waiting for any scrap of news that might leak out of negotiations.

Being the chair automatically put me into a no-win situation. If I interceded in the bargaining, I was "meddling." If I didn't intercede and there was a strike, "I wasn't doing my job." In any case, the talks continued, the strike deadline passed and the pronouncements from both sides sounded like progress was being made.

Vince Casuti told the media, "As long as talks are progressing, TTC workers will stay on the job."

"As long as they're talking, they're not walking and we're not locking," I said. "I anticipate talks will be continuing over the weekend and I would anticipate that you can expect full transit service on Monday."

The first deadline passed. We were miles apart a few weeks ago. ATU Local 113 was asking for a two-year contract with a 10% increase, a signing bonus and reinstatement of some lost benefits. The TTC was offering a three-year contract with 3% spread over three years and the deletion of some current benefits. If taken from the fare box, the union's demand would have resulted in a 35-cent increase in transit fares and a loss of 16 million riders. That would have cost each rider about $175 a year, which was just too high an increase.

That weekend, we upped our offer to 1.5% in the first year and 2% in the second year with a $600 signing bonus, a significant move forward from its previous position. I told the media we hadn't characterized it as "our final offer either." The union was slow to respond.

They seemed unwilling to budge off their original wage demands that I called an "impossible dream."

Vince Casuti admitted: "Right now, we are just down to the money. Everything else is resolved."

Once again, we upped our offer to a three-year wage deal with increases of 2% in each year (6% in all) with some improvements to benefits and the clothing allowance. We called it our "final offer." Under the Ontario Labour Relations Act, an employer has the right to ask that a final offer be put to a vote of union members. It is usually done when the employer believes it is likely the employees will take it as an alternative to a strike. The historical experience is the employer is usually wrong (75% of the time). Given the lack of movement from the Local 113 bargaining team, the TTC had little choice. We asked that a supervised vote to be taken.

That meant a news blackout would be imposed immediately, with neither the union nor the commission able to comment.

Colin Vaughan, the City TV political commentator, joked: "I never thought it would happen, but the one good thing that has come out of this is that they managed to silence Howard Moscoe."

The vote, supervised by the ministry of labour, would take place on Saturday. It was a gamble. If the workers voted not to accept the final offer, the strike would begin at midnight Sunday. That is exactly what happened. The vote was 78% against acceptance.

Most workers interviewed said they turned it down to support their bargaining team, but they were hoping the bargaining would continue. This time, the mayor was right. There was no more money. (Even a broken clock is right twice a day.)

"If the union is prepared to adjust their position, we'll come back to the table," I told the media. "Beyond that, what's the point? We've got nothing more to offer them."

We had until midnight Sunday before the system shut down. I called a rare Saturday commission meeting for 11:00 p.m. at the Delta Chelsea.

Enter stage right. Ontario was on the verge of a provincial election; it was expected to be called in two weeks. At the root of the TTC's troubles was under funding. For years, provincial funding had been to a formula that assured it a source of ongoing revenue. The province paid two-thirds of the operating cost, with the city picking up half of the remaining cost and the balance coming out of the fare box. The Progressive Conservative government of Mike Harris scrapped the formula and withdrew much of the funding for public transit (not to mention he also scrapped funding for three subway lines, partially under construction). By 1999, TTC finances had reached the point where 81% of the operating costs of transit came from the fare box. This reflected the lowest public transit government support anywhere in North America, if not the world; that is why negotiations had been so difficult.

The provinces dislike for public transit could clearly be seen in comments by Tony Clement, Ontario's minister of transportation:

"We're seeing the evidence this morning that if you rely too much on public transit, then everything grinds to a halt. So, I think if you have a proposed mix of car usage and public transit and bicycle usage, that's the best system for any urban municipality. Learn to cope."

There is nothing like the chaos caused by a transit strike to make people appreciate the value to everyone of a well-run transit system. On Monday morning, the city was paralyzed.

Mike Harris rushed in to place a private members bill to order the striking workers back to work. However, it could only be enacted through an emergency session of the Legislature and that required all-party agreement. The Liberals quickly agreed. The NDP, under Howard Hampton, said they would support the legislation if it met two conditions: 1 – That the legislation would specify that the arbitrator could not give the workers less than the TTC's final offer; 2 – That the choice of the arbitrator would be mutually acceptable to both the union and the commission (a normally included provision).

The Tories refused to include either condition. Howard Hampton was risking his four NDP seats in Toronto and with them his party status, but he wouldn't agree to abandon his principles just to keep those seats.

In telephone calls from Howard Hampton, both Vince Casuti and I were invited to meet in Howard's office at Queen's Park to see if we could come to some common understandings. I in turn invited David Gunn and a representative from the mayor's office to accompany me. Gunn said he would get back to me, but never did. The mayor declined, but suggested I bring Rob Davis, my vice-chair. Rob is a staunch Tory and one of the four commissioners who tried to stab me in the back. He tagged along.

Unknown to me, Tony Dean, the deputy minister of labour, had already invited Casuti to meet with him and Gunn that morning. Gunn went off to the labour ministry expecting a meeting. It was there he discovered Casuti elected instead to join me in Hampton's office. Gunn had been sidestepped. He was livid.

It was a tough four-hour session, made even more difficult by the obnoxious Rob Davis, who did everything he could do to prevent a deal from happening. We managed to hammer out an understanding that Vince was prepared to take back to his union executive and I was prepared to take back to the commission: It wasn't yet a settlement, but a framework for one:

- TTC employees would go back to work immediately.
- The TTC would immediately put into effect their final offer.
- The balance would go to binding arbitration.
- The arbitration panel would not be able to weaken the final offer.
- Each of the parties would appoint an arbitrator and the two arbitrators would select a mutually agreed upon arbitration chair.

In the scrum outside Hampton's office, Davis denounced the deal as back-room politics and denounced me for circumventing the commission, but neither the media nor the public were particularly interested in his bile. Both Vince and I were prepared to take the deal back and recommend it. The prospect of the pain ending was what most people cared about.

Hampton pulled it off. He went from "bum" to "hero" in a matter of one day by managing to get the union back to work on terms that the TTC could not refuse.

The Toronto Sun wrote:

"If public transit is operating, then we congratulate NDP Leader Howard Hampton, the guy we labelled a boob here yesterday for blocking a Tory-legislated bid to end the strike on Monday. Yesterday, there being nothing like a political hanging to focus the mind, Hampton, with a huge assist from the TTC's NDP chairman and the union president of the transit workers, pulled a rabbit out of his hat. He helped broker a deal between TTC chairman Howard Moscoe and union president Vince Casuti which was approved by the transit commission last night."

Even Mike Harris credited Hampton with helping settle the strike: "I think that Howard Hampton played an important role in making that happen."

The Tories were no fools. They came to realize that an NDP vote collapse would result in a Liberal victory. They needed the NDP to keep their majority.

It was a victory for everyone. Casuti expected to be ordered back to work, but his greatest fear was the government would select a mediator that would slam the union.

"Arbitration could have gone on for a year or a year and a half. Our members would have had no increase until that arbitrator made a decision which could have been 1-1-1 (1% in each year.)"

At the TTC, the long knives were again unsheathed. Brian Ashton complained bitterly about the union holding the city hostage.

"And it's the union and Howard Moscoe that allowed that to happen," Ashton said. "The union would speak to nobody but Howard Moscoe and the NDP, that's what happened."

Chris Korwin-Kuczynski whined: "Howard Moscoe should have had the commission's permission to attend the meeting."

My response: "If the devil had called me down to his office, I would have gone. I would have done anything to get transit on the road this morning for the people of this city,"

The TTC and the city had no choice but to accept the deal. The strike was over. Transit Commissioner David Miller summed it up:

"If it had been Mel Lastman who cut the deal that Howard did, they'd be showering him with gold coins, he'd have an olive wreath on his head and they'd be parading him down University Avenue."

Joe Mihevc added: "Howard Moscoe is the best thing the TTC has had in a long time. He's put the TTC back on the map and saved this city from an extra two weeks of strike.

So, there you have it. It was all over but the cheering?

No.

The strike was over, but the plotting continued.

CHAPTER 77
Backstabbing Mayor

ALDERMEN'S OFFICE

HOWARD MOSCOE
ALDERMAN WARD 4

CITY OF NORTH YORK, 5100 YONGE ST., NORTH YORK, ONTARIO M2N 5V7 TEL (416) 224-6021

MEMORANDUM

DATE: April 22, 1999
TO: Mel Lastman
Mayor of the City of Toronto
RE: BACKSTABBING AND PETTY PLOTS

Two weeks ago, you orchestrated a "kindergarten conspiracy" to have me ousted as Chair of the TTC. You failed because your four fellow conspirators were so consumed by their own ambition that they ended up pulling the trigger on themselves.

This week, the day after I settled a transit strike, which was costing the TTC almost one million dollars in lost revenue per day, your office is once again attempting to orchestrate my removal. This time you are lobbying councillors to oust me by removing the entire Toronto Transit Commission. Councillor Tom Jakobek and Deputy Mayor Case Ootes, your two henchmen, have been systematically lobbying members of council to this end.

CALL OFF YOUR STOOGES!

Last year we saw the removal of Maureen Prinsloo as Chair of the Police Services Board through an organized conspiracy. Now, there have been two failed attempts on my political life. You may eventually succeed, but by continuing to deal in petty plots and backstabbing, it will only land in your lap, not mine.

The only people who can remove me from my seat on council are the people in my ward, North York-Spadina, who elected me.

Take the high road, Mel and I'll continue to work with you. The people of the City of Toronto deserve better than a backstabbing mayor.

HOWARD MOSCOE
City of Toronto Councillor
North York-Spadina
C: All Members of Council

MEMORANDUM

DATE: April 22, 1999

TO: Councillor Tom Jakobek

RE: BADMOUTHING IS NOT NICE!

Today you accused the Toronto Transit Commission of selling out on its wage settlement with the Amalgamated Transit Union Local 113. The Commission's final offer was a 2% wage increase with the balance of the union demands up to 1% more to go to compulsory arbitration.

The venom in your comments are surprising, since I know that you, as the budget chief didn't even wince when Norm Gardner gave 2.9% to the Police earlier this year. Furthermore, you, yourself, voted to give the Toronto Fire Fighters 3.2%. How do you expect transit workers to want less when you have allowed these two examples to go unchallenged?

By settling the TTC strike within two days, I managed to save 6 million dollars that the TTC would have lost waiting eight days for the Provincial government to send this matter to arbitration.

Your suggestion that my remarks caused the strike is ludicrous. The strike vote by the union membership was 78% in support of their bargaining team. I don't apologize for wanting to see our workers get a fair wage settlement and I believe the 2%, 2% and 2% was a fair offer. This and the arbitration agreement was unanimously endorsed by all of the six Commissioners present.

I have long considered you to be the most despicable politician in Toronto. Your latest rampage simply confirms these thoughts. I don't know whether you should be laughed at, spanked, or your mouth washed out with soap.

Yours in government,

Howard Moscoe
City of Toronto Councillor
North York-Spadina
Ids/TTC/Chair/Jakobek despicable
C: All Members of Council

MEMORANDUM

DATE: April 22, 1999

TO: Deputy Mayor Case Ootes

RE: SLINKING AROUND IN BACK ROOMS IS NOT CONSISTENT WITH EAST YORK MORALITY

I am writing to express my disappointment that you have joined the Mayor's stooge, Tom Jakobek, in attempting to oust me as Chair of the TTC by lobbying Councillors for the mid term removal of the entire Toronto Transit Commission.

Until this time, I've had the greatest respect for you. I naively believed that representatives from East York were too high minded to be slinking about in back rooms hatching petty plots.

I want to continue to work with you in the interests of the people of Toronto. I ask you to stop this unseemly behaviour and spend your time working for your constituents.

Yours in government,

HOWARD MOSCOE
City of Toronto Councillor
North York-Spadina
Ids/TTC/Chair/Ootes slinking

C: All Members of Council

CHAPTER 78

The Chair and the Restless: The Soap Opera Continues

Now that the strike was over, Mel Lastman didn't waste any time in launching his next attempt to orchestrate my removal. It hadn't been two weeks, the day after the strike ended, before his henchmen hit the airwaves with the message that "Howard must go." Never mind that I had negotiated an end to the strike that was costing the TTC $1 million in lost revenue each day. Never mind that the buses and subways were rolling again after two days.

Deputy Mayor Case Ootes gave the first clue as to what was coming.

"Mr. Moscoe's opponents can't be counted on to rid the transit commission of its chairman, city council should see what it can do to get the job done – even if that means booting out all seven commissioners."

Council appointments were coming up in June. At mid-term, council shuffles the deck and re-appoints committees and committee chairs. The TTC is an exception. Its appointments are for the full term.

Budget chief Tom Jackboot joined the blather. He argued that the arbitration agreement I "rigged" with ATU president Vince Casuti and provincial NDP leader Howard Hampton would hamstring the city in impending negotiations with other unions. The base 2% was outrageous.

"It's a total calamity," Mr. Jakobek charged. "It's outrageous that he allowed this to happen. It makes me sick."

Never mind that Jakobek never winced as budget chief when the police services board settled for 2.9% and that Tom himself voted to give firefighters 3.2%.

David Miller defended me: "Howard Moscoe did an incredible job and people who don't like him should respect that."

I wrote to Mel and told him, "Call off your stooges. Take the high road. Mel and I'll continue to work with you. The people of Toronto deserve better...."

It just wasn't in the cards.

At its next meeting, the commission unanimously rejected the proposed fare increase.

In May, the dynamic duo of Ashton and Korwin-Kuczynski tabled a notice of motion at council to dissolve the entire seven-member Toronto Transit Commission and reconstitute it with new appointments. It was clearly another attempt to get rid of me. A kindergarten coup was elevated to a Grade 1 conspiracy.

They had a long way to go before they graduated.

I responded by producing a legal opinion from George Rust-D'Eye, a municipal law specialist with the firm of Weir & Foulds, that essentially said council had no authority to change the commission's term or the term of the chair in mid-stream and any attempt to do so would be unlawful. He concluded that even if they did have the authority to terminate an appointment it would require a two-thirds majority of council. Rust-D'Eye had previously been the Metro solicitor and had the respect of most members of council.

The dynamic duo retorted that they had the opinion of the current city solicitor, Ozzie Doyle, that the motion was legal. They also had a letter from the minister of municipal affairs and housing saying council had the right to change the conditions of appointment of the chair of the TTC. The dynamic duo claimed the TTC was dysfunctional and needed to be replaced. I responded by suggesting they could remedy that by resigning and we would replace them with two new commissioners that could function. The stage was set for yet another dust-up.

At the June meeting of council, after an emotional 2 ½-hour debate, council decided that instead of replacing me or the entire commission, they would appoint two additional members of council to the commission. It was only a postponement of the next assassination attempt. They thought it was a way around the legal opinions. You can be sure that, whomever they chose, a prior condition of appointment would be their vote to dump Howard Moscoe. The head of the appointment committee, Case Oops (my nickname for Case Ootes, which he hated) would ensure that.

Both appointment choices denied vehemently that they were being chosen for the specific purpose of knifing me, but of course, everyone knew otherwise. One was Gloria Lindsay-Luby and the other was Joan King. I was a bit surprised at Gloria. When she had come to me to help her community divert Mississauga Transit vehicles off Burnhamthorpe Road onto Highway 27 where they wouldn't bother anyone, I pulled out all stops to come to her aid. I didn't deserve her knife in the ribs as a reward for helping them. Rita Aldrit from her Burnhamthorpe Ratepayers Association had tried to make that clear to her.

"We would be very disappointed with Lindsay Luby if, in fact, she is going onto the commission to depose Moscoe. What Howard Moscoe said about going out on a limb for us is right. He has worked harder for us than even our local politicians have, and that's not taking anything away from Gloria.... But Howard had no reason to go out on a limb for us, and he responded to our concerns. He responded to us."

I suppose ambition is a powerful motivator. Both Gloria and Joan had extensive transit experience. I suspect they had once ridden a bus. I didn't much worry about that because I am sure in their orientation program our staff would teach them how to put a ticket into a fare box.

Well, at the next council meeting their appointments were confirmed. Gloria was elected with 30 out of the 53 votes. Joan King garnered 32 votes. My firing squad was lined up. All that was left was to hand me the blindfold. On Monday morning, George Rust-D'Eye went into court to seek an injunction to prevent the two of them from being sworn in the next day. I knew I would require Harry Houdini to get out of this one.

The legal bills were mounting and I was determined not to spend a penny of taxpayers' money on the whole sordid affair. That was solved by my supporters. They threw a 10-course Chinese banquet and charged $100 a plate admission. It was called the Howard Moscoe Opened His Mouth Again Defence Fund Banquet.

We were able to raise enough money to cover all of my legal expenses.

George did it. Mr. Justice James Southey of the Superior Court granted a temporary injunction blocking city council's addition of Joan King and Gloria Lindsay Luby to the TTC. Later, Justice Patrick Hartt of divisional court quashed the two appointments ruling the City of Toronto Act requires two-thirds support of council for TTC appointments. Gloria's 30 votes were six short of the required two-thirds; Joan's total of 32, was four short.

That was great news, but it still seemed not to be enough. The conspirators, if they got their act together, would, as before, still have their four votes on the commission. It was enough to pull the plug, even without adding the two commissioners. Blake Kinahan had tabled yet another motion to have me deposed, and this time it was going to work. Chris Korwin-Kuczynski was chomping at the bit to pick up the gavel. We called him "Mr. Limo" because he had used Toronto's car and driver service for councillors 545 times that year. He almost never used public transit. KK had been chosen to be the anointed one.

It didn't happen. At the last minute, word was received that Blake Kinahan would not be at the meeting. He had to be absent for "family reasons." Blake had mysteriously disappeared. With the potential of a tie vote and another loss, the notice of motion was put off to the July meeting of the commission. I felt like a long-standing resident of death row. I was left on the platform with a noose around my neck waiting for the trap door to be sprung. I had achieved yet another reprieve.

Kinahan was the councillor for Etobicoke-Lakeshore. He was a Liberal, had his doctorate from Princeton in astrophysics, a law degree from the University of Toronto Law School and had a coke addiction, (Coca-Cola that is). Ted Welch, the City Hall columnist from the Toronto Sun, referred to him as "Blake the Flake" while some of his colleagues on council called him "Flakie Blakie." Despite his obsession to remove me as chair of the TTC, I liked him. He was progressive, usually voted left on substantive issues and was decent, ethical and personable. He was just a little bit "strange" and in spite of his impeccable academic credentials, perhaps a little too naive to be in politics.

Just when it looked like I was poised to meet my Waterloo, a miracle happened. I let it be known I would be willing to resign if I could negotiate the conditions of my surrender. I wanted a say in who my successor might be and some changes to the TTC bylaw that would put the brakes on the prospect of the chair of the commission being deposed on a momentary whim. The mayor's reponse was: "Tell him to go screw himself."

Then on Wednesday, July 7, during the council meeting, I got word that the mayor wanted to meet with me. His attitude had completely changed and I knew why. We met and negotiated a peace treaty.

The Toronto Sun called it a "hug session." When we met in his office, Mel adjusted his belt. I told him I wasn't going to kiss it.

Hey, the mayor had a long line of people coming in to kiss it – what did he need me for?

When I left, it was all settled. He would call off his hounds. The war was over.

Sue-Ann Levy, in her Toronto Sun column, commented: "Lastman may have met his match in Moscoe and to his credit realized that it was far more practical to declare a truce than continue a war that can't be won...."

She wrote: "'I knew eventually we would iron out our differences,' Moscoe said last week after the peace treaty was signed with the mayor. 'It's a great weight off my mind.'"

Why did Mel suddenly throw in the towel? Simple. Mel could never muster the four votes he needed to dump me. Christine Tebbutt, Blake Kinahan's executive assistant, had tipped off Ben Rothman, my EA, that Kinahan was so stressed by the events of that term he had a nervous breakdown. Mel and I were the only two members of council who had that information. He didn't make peace with me out of the goodness of his heart, nor was it because of the bad publicity surrounding the whole sordid affair. At that point, what did he care about bad publicity? Mel had been around long enough to know that today's news is always displaced by tomorrow's news and people forget. Mel made peace because he realized he had lost. All he could do now was save face.

The final episode of the soap opera played itself out at the next meeting of the commission. The mood had changed entirely. Mel had instructed his attack dogs to back away. The last holdout, Blake Kinahan, recovered enough to come to the meeting and demand that I swear a "truth certificate" over some confidential information my office had inadvertently leaked four years before. I had actually offered to resign, but withdrew my offer after the peace treaty was concluded.

The Toronto Star ran this cartoon:

PATRICK CORRIGAN/TORONTO STAR

A Toronto Star editorial summed it up: "NOBODY KNOWS THE TROUBLE I'VE SEEN: After four attempts in two years to oust him as TTC chair, Councillor Howard Moscoe has taken so many knives in the back that they no longer penetrate. Councillor Blake Kinahan, one of Moscoe's most diligent tormentors, demanded his resignation yet again a few weeks ago, saying he really had the goods on him this time.... After so many failed attempts – usually because Moscoe and his pals outwit his assailants – not even his worst enemies had any enthusiasm for taking Moscoe up on his offer."

When he was rebuffed, Kinahan resigned his seat on the Toronto Transit Commission. David Nickle in the Mirror wrote:

"On the day of his exit, Kinahan seems to have been the last anti-Moscoe holdout in the crowd.... It's probably for the best that Kinahan has left the commission. It puts to bed one of first-term Toronto's most futile political soap operas. Hopefully, future TTC meetings will be about transit."

I went on to finish my full term as chair of the TTC.

CHAPTER 79

Early Signs of an Election in York

One part of Toronto that never quite worked was the City of York. It was a jumble of everything. I spent my high school years growing up in York on the banks of the Humber River. York was the Wild West as far as zoning and bylaws were concerned. Everything was different in York. It had the best politicians that money could buy. Several of them ended up in jail and a few should have but didn't. My father would have rolled over in his grave laughing if he had known that I was on the York Community Council.

After amalgamation, the new City of Toronto had the difficult task of melding the bylaws of seven municipalities into a single set of unified bylaws. They called it "harmonization." That meant re-writing the rules in almost every area of municipal responsibility. There were thousands of bylaws that needed to be harmonized; it would take years to do them all. Prior to the 2000 election staff took on the task of harmonizing the election sign bylaw. It was scheduled to be debated at the June meeting of council six months before the municipal election.

Because I had a keen interest in signs I read every single staff report and probably knew more about the sign bylaw than anyone. There was one caveat, however. I owned a business that made and sold election signs to municipal candidates. I had a conflict of interest and could not participate in the debate. It was like placing a bottle of Crown Royal in front of an alcoholic and telling him he could only look at it.

There it was. Right there in the middle of the proposed new bylaw. A light went on, the answer to a puzzle that had been plaguing me for months. How was I going to get a profile in the new section of the City of York that was being tacked onto my ward for the 2000 election? The bylaws of the cities of North York, Etobicoke and East York prohibited election signs from being erected except within 30 days of the election date. The City of York had no such restriction. In York you could put them up anytime. The staff report was proposing to put the 30-day restriction into the new bylaw for the entire city. That meant that any signs that were erected in the York section of my ward before the bylaw was passed were "legal non-conforming," which meant they were exempt from the new bylaw.

I designed a large arterial sign that read "Howard Moscoe is coming". My wife, Gloria, disputed that. She suggested that adding "to our neighbourhood" would be more accurate. I printed up 125 of them, lined up my volunteers and readied my equipment. We were in a race against the clock.

I knew that the debate would be lengthy and estimated that I had two days before the bylaw became law. That morning I showed up at the council meeting, rose to declare my interest, vacated the council chamber and raced up to Oakwood Avenue where my volunteer sign crew was waiting. The next three days were spent knocking on doors asking permission from people to put my election sign on their lawn. As soon as someone said yes the crew was there to pound the sign into the ground. We managed to cover all of the main streets; Oakwood Avenue, Vaughan Road and Eglinton Avenue and a number of collector roads as well. As it turned out I had a little extra time because when word of what I was doing got back to council they spent another four hours heaping scorn on me or framing motions to try and stop me. (None of them carried.)

The truth is that many councillors were envious that they hadn't thought of it themselves.

GLORIA Lindsay Luby: "Moscoe skipped a TTC news conference on Tuesday claiming fatigue. Instead, I found out he was putting up signs. So there you go. It shows you people's priorities."

TOM Jakobek: "Do not allow him to do what he is doing. It's wrong. It's like insider trading."

DOUG Holyday: "I think its darn fair of him to warn them.... It won't be long before the 'for sale' signs will be going up."

GEORGIO Mammoliti: "I should have thought of this."

There was really nothing they could do. Because the signs were legal non-conforming, nobody could take them down and I had the right to re-erect them if they were destroyed. As long as they were up before the bylaw was passed. My opponents could not erect their signs until 30 days before the election after mine had been up for 5 months.

On Tuesday, at about midnight, my sign crew and I were coming out of a pizzeria on Oakwood Avenue when a car screeched to a stop at the curb. It was Rob Davis. He looked like he was in shock. Rob had previously represented the area on the City of York Council and was running against Joe Mihevc in the neighbouring ward. No calypso dancer alive could slide under my opinion of Rob Davis. I presume that he knew he couldn't win against me in what had previously been his ward because people had come to know him.

"Why are you putting up signs so early?"

"There's an election coming Rob."

"That's not for five months."

"Yes, I know, but the bylaw is changing tomorrow and all of my signs will be legal non-conforming."

You could see the wheels in his head grinding. He wanted desperately to put this newfound revelation to use, but he couldn't. He didn't have his signs printed yet and he couldn't organize it in time.

When he left I phoned Joe Mihevc and got him out of bed to warn him.

"You had better make sure that the bylaw goes into effect immediately, Joe. I've seen the gleam in Rob Davis's eyes."

The next day Joe moved an amendment to that effect in council, and it carried. Council also toughened the bylaw by cutting back the 30-day restriction to 25 days. The only regret that I have about the entire exercise was that I didn't start earlier. If I had another month I could have put a sign on every lawn. By the way, I won the new area handily. I don't know if the early signs had anything to do with it but being in the election sign business I have to suggest that they were a crucial factor in my re-election.

I'll be happy to sell you some signs if you need them.

CHAPTER 80

The Sleaze Factor

In 2000, I hit upon an idea that would allow me to generate jobs for the residents of my ward and get political credit for them as well. Job creation doesn't usually fit the profile of a municipal councillor. New buildings and large projects like shopping centres required their site plans to be approved by the city. It's called site plan control. The local councillor had a great deal to say about project approval in his ward. The developer would negotiate the conditions of site plan with the councillor. I would usually call a meeting between nearby residents and the developer to determine what conditions to place on the development. They consisted mostly of things like decorative walls or fences, landscaping, security lighting etc.

In 2000, I negotiated the site plan for a big-box plaza on Wilson Avenue east of Dufferin Street with Mitch Goldhar of Smart Centres. His big-box plazas are not half as smart as he is. He has managed to snap up land at the main intersections of highways right across the country and many in the U.S. as well. I don't particularly like big-box malls because of their car orientation (I call them city destroyers), but suburban consumers love them; they sure are successful.

I first met Mitch when he was starting out. I appeared at the committee of adjustment to seek conditions on a small plaza he was developing on Keele Street. I was on a campaign against pre-cast cement curb blocks; the ones that deteriorate after a couple of years and "uglify" strip plazas. I got the committee to impose "poured cement curbs built to municipal standards." They cost a small fortune.

When we negotiated the Wilson Avenue big-box plaza, I tossed in my "spur of the moment job plan," a requirement to give local residents first crack at the jobs. He agreed to put it to Costco. Why wouldn't they agree? It was to their advantage to have employees live nearby and it cost them virtually nothing. They didn't have to hire anyone they didn't want, but only to look at local talent first. It was to my constituents' advantage to get local jobs, and it certainly didn't hurt my political standing to have secured those jobs. A win-win for everyone. Costco mail dropped this letter to everyone in my ward:

December, 2000
Dear Resident,

Costco Wholesale will soon be opening a new warehouse club on Wilson Avenue east of Dufferin Street (across from the Wilson Subway Station). By agreement with Councillor Howard Moscoe and the City of Toronto, we are informing local residents of employment opportunities prior to jobs being advertised publicly. To apply for a position at this location, please forward your resumé to:

> *Costco Wholesale*
> *North York Employment Opportunities*
> *8495 Goreway Drive*
> *Brampton, Ontario*
> *L6T 5N8*

Since this location will have a pharmacy, we also welcome applications from pharmacists.

Sincerely,

David Skinner
Assistant Vice-president
Costco Wholesale Ontario

So, where's the sleaze in this you ask? Not yet.

The job plan worked so well that later that year we incorporated it into another site plan agreement, this time for a Lowes store opening on Caledonia Road near Castlefield Avenue in my ward. This time, we varied the hiring procedure slightly. Lowes set up a hiring trailer in their parking lot and staffed it with hiring personnel to do the interviews based on the response to the Costco letter.

It was just before the municipal election of that year. In the neighbouring ward, St. Paul's West, there was a hard-fought battle going on between Joe Mihevc and Rob Davis, both incumbents who had held part of the area in the former City of York. We knew Rob as "tricky Robbie" as he was to prove many times over. Rob lived in my ward so he would have received one of the Lowes letters at his home. Rob, without any permission from anyone, immediately reprinted the letter replacing my name with his and distributed it throughout St. Paul's West. I wasn't surprised. He was famous for underhanded manoeuvres. The Lowes people were furious. They were swamped by job seekers.

ROB DAVIS   JOE MIHEVC

Rob Davis was handily defeated by Joe Mihevc. Rob has been desperately trying to get elected again to something for a long time without success.

Good thing too.

CHAPTER 81
At War With the Army

Say what you will about the municipal planning process, it does guarantee public involvement. In fact, we in the North District, mostly North York, went out of our way to ensure public consultation at every stage of the process right down to the site plan; details like the landscaping, public art, fencing and walkways. One excellent example of the results of the process is the Downsview subway station at Sheppard Ave. W. and the Allen Road. It was designed co-operatively and I believe it is one of the most attractive stations in Toronto.

You can imagine my surprise, when I drove along Sheppard Avenue in my ward and noticed a large, sprawling building under construction just a block from the Downsview Station. As the local councillor, I am supposed to know about new building projects in my ward and nothing about this one had crossed my desk.

"What's going on?" I asked the building commissioner.

"It's the federal government," she replied. "They are building a headquarters building for the military."

"So why wasn't my office notified when they applied for a building permit?"

"They don't have a building permit. They have paramountcy. They don't require one."

Paramountcy, it appears, is a principle that is imbedded in the Canadian Constitution. It holds that no order of government can regulate a higher order of government. In other words, neither federal nor provincial governments have to obey municipal legislation, nor does the Federal Government have to obey provincial laws. That's why they don't pay municipal taxes. Traditionally, the provincial and federal governments, when building in a municipality, have voluntarily disregarded paramountcy, paid their building permit fees and gone through the municipal planning approval process. They understood the value of the advice they got from the planners and the public consultation process. More importantly, it was a matter of respect.

This was the first time in my experience that paramountcy had been evoked. This building was being constructed by the Department of National Defence and nobody, but nobody, tells the military what to do or how to do it. They have guns.

Apparently, the military was consolidating several rather ugly military structures around Toronto into a single ugly military structure to house 1,000 full and part-time personnel. Art Eggleton was the minister of national defence. As a former mayor of Toronto, he should have known better, although I doubt if he was aware of the specifics of the project.

TORONTO'S UGLIEST NEW BUILDING OF 2001

If it was done to save money, it was hard to understand how this was going to happen. Even though they ripped off the city for half a million dollars in building permit fees, and the land was CFB Downsview land they already owned, they were still spending

$45 million on this massive, sprawling 33,000-square-metre structure. If the city urban design department had been involved, it might have had half a chance to turn out to be a nice building.

When nobody in the military was prepared to discuss the project with me, I was less than pleased. I issued an invitation to the Honourable Art Eggleton to come to Downsview and receive an award for the project.

TORONTO

The First Annual

"TORONTO'S UGLIEST NEW BUILDING AWARD"

Awarded October 19, 2001 to the Honourable Art Eggleton, Minister of National Defence

The new armouries building at the intersection of Sheppard Avenue West and Yukon Lane is truly an ugly building.

Completed in 2001, it was designed to consolidate the various military facilities around Toronto into a single location and has managed to replace a number of ugly buildings built in the barracks style military tradition with a single, larger, even uglier building.

It is truly amazing that a building, which cost some $44 million, could have been constructed with so little style, without the assistance of the City of Toronto's Planning Department, and with complete disregard for the City's planning process, zoning bylaws and the community. This is truly an accomplishment that only the military could have achieved.

Howard Moscoe

HOWARD MOSCOE
City of Toronto Councillor
Ward 15/Eglinton-Lawrence
Awarded: October 19, 2001
Country Style Donuts - Wilson Heights Boulevard

I called it the first annual Toronto's Ugliest New Building Award. The gala event was held at the Country Style doughnut shop at the corner of Wilson Heights Boulevard and Sheppard Avenue West.

Alas, when the honourable minister failed to show up, the young lady behind the counter graciously agreed to accept the award on his behalf. I made a speech and mugged for the cameras. The owner of the shop threw in a couple of boxes of doughnuts and we dug in and celebrated the event with relish.

The next night, the City of Toronto was hosting its annual architectural awards presentations and reception at the Design Exchange on Bay Street. In attendance were the who's who of the Toronto building and architectural communities. There were some eight awards being handed out for design excellence. With the concurrence of the commissioner of planning, I was given the opportunity of once again publicly presenting the Ugliest New Building Award to Art Eggleton, in absentia, from the podium of the award ceremony.

The national defence ministry soldiered on. Construction continued on the armouries building. That prompted me to bring a notice of motion to council through the community council. I asked council to establish the "Downsview Lands Operational Protocol Committee." Its mandate was to deal with all administrative matters related to the department of national defence lands. Now, the kinds of issues that are normally routine and handled at the staff level required a political decision that had to be approved by council. I knew that, notwithstanding paramountcy, the building would need a municipal address. Normally, that took a routine application to the planning department. Now it required a political discussion, probably the only one this building would ever get. The military may be the best at it, but municipalities know something about red tape too.

The only road entrance to Downsview Park from the east was a private street called Carl Hall Road. The idiots used part of the road allowance on which to construct their DND building, thus closing Carl Hall Road to vehicles from the east. That meant city ambulances from the nearby Dufferin Street station could not service the park from the east, forcing them to travel an extra kilometre or so to service calls in the park. Had the city been consulted, the closure would never have happened.

A couple of months later, I received a call from Kevin Degaust, an aide to Eggleton.

"We need to have a municipal address," he said. "I am told that I have to appear before the Downsview Lands Operational Protocol Committee. Can you put us on the agenda?"

"I'd be happy to put you on the agenda," I said.

"When will the committee be meeting?"

"I'm not sure. It hasn't had its first meeting yet. Perhaps it will meet in three, or maybe six months.

"It would be helpful in the interim if you paid us the half million in building permit fees that you owe"

At this point, Degaust seemed rather agitated. He advised me that Sheppard Avenue was partially built over DND lands and unless I co-operated they would close Sheppard Avenue.

"Go right ahead," I said. "If you want to take the heat from the public, it's your choice. They're my constituents but they're Art's constituents too. Perhaps then the building will get the public discussion it deserves."

Not too long afterward, I received a call from someone who identified himself as a colonel. He advised me that the delay in receiving a municipal number is causing a major headache for the armed forces. The building was the centre for all land forces in Ontario and unless they had a municipal address, Canada Post would not deliver their mail.

"Not a problem," I said. "Tell them to send the mail to Art Eggleton's constituency office. Kevin Degaust will be happy to bring it over. We don't have any record of the building in our files."

The uglification of the building has continued unabated. The landscaping is sombre; not a single flower. It would never have been allowed by our urban design department. It was completed by placing a combat tank at the east and west ends and what appears to be some kind of a landing craft in the centre; all painted a khaki-green. That would certainly be fitting for a military headquarters, but without some kind of a properly designed setting, it looks like some kind of a war surplus sales outlet.

The military equipment is emblazoned with beautifully crafted brass plaques describing its historical significance. I'd like to tell you what they say, but I can't because they screwed that up too.

Remember the controversy surrounding the cost of hosting the G20 summit in Toronto?

CBC News: "The cost of hosting the G8 and G20 summits next month in Ontario now stands at $1.1 billion and further outlays are likely, federal documents show. The price tag includes $160 million for hospitality, infrastructure, food safety and extra staffing. That amount is in addition to the $933-million security bill the Tories revealed earlier this week."

"This might be the most expensive 72 hours in Canadian history," said Liberal MP Mark Holland.

Just before the G20 summit, the entire building was surrounded with a chain-link fence topped with barbed wire. No doubt, they were cleverly tapping into the $933 million squandered on security for the G20 Summit. The fence must have been so intimidating to the hordes of G20 protesters they never ventured north of Bloor Street. It remains today. You can't get to read the plaques because they are protected by a barbed wire fence.

Oh yes, despite their failure to get a municipal address, they did end up getting mail delivery. Canada Post obliged by giving them their own postal code. I'm surprised the army couldn't figure that one out for themselves. The Downsview Lands Operational Protocol Committee has never met.

CHAPTER 82
Playground Dispute

Children love to play. Play is an essential part of growing up healthy. Politicians also love to play, but when they do, it is often unhealthy. The 2000 election was a rough one for Toronto District School Board trustees. Before school opened in September, they had torn down 172 playgrounds at an unbudgeted cost to the board of some $27 million. When the children and parents arrived at school, they found themselves staring at a bed of woodchips where their playgrounds had been.

Why? The board will tell you it was in the interests of safety. The Canadian Standards Association (CSA) released their new safety standards for playgrounds in May of 1998. The board was under pressure to make them "safe," but the standards were guidelines and not mandatory. Even Mike Jones, a civil engineer (retired) who had been the TDSB staff representative on the CSA panel that wrote the standards was shocked. Yes, the new guidelines raised the bar, but they were never intended to be applied immediately. It was expected they would be phased in gradually over a period of time.

"Never, never, never," Jones told a reporter. "Nobody on the CSA committee ever imagined this would happen."

One of the significant pressures being brought to bear on the school board was a directive from the community and social services ministry to daycare centres requiring them to meet CSA standards. Many of the daycare centres shared playgrounds with schools. A lot of the daycare centres were also operated by the City of Toronto. Some, but not all, were at schools. Besides, the city had a playground in almost every park as well. It was a major city issue too.

In a sense, council was lucky. The issue came to us late. That's because Shirley Hoy, our community and social services commissioner, and her staff were locked in a desperate set of negotiations with staff at the community and social services ministry to try and secure some funding to bring our playgrounds up to standard. Bringing city playgrounds to full standard would cost the city $35 million. Negotiations had been deadlocked for some time. Queen's Park, which provides 80% of the day care subsidies, had stopped funding playgrounds in 1994.

Council had the benefit of witnessing the sky open and public scorn dumped on the heads of the school trustees. They were up to their chins in night soil. Toronto Council wasn't about to step off the edge into that cesspool.

We spent the better part of a three-day council meeting railing at the community and social services ministry for mandating the upgrades, but refusing to provide the money. In the heat of passion, I moved the following motion:

"All of the city and daycare playgrounds be re-named 'THE HONOURABLE JOHN BAIRD UNSAFE PLAYGROUND.' We advise the Ministry that when they supply funding, the original name will be restored as each playground is brought up to standard."

JOHN BAIRD

John Baird was the newly appointed community and social services minister in the Harris government. It was his first cabinet appointment. He was still wet behind the ears.

I told the council I would be pleased to make and donate the signs at my own expense. I have a sign business where I make and sell election signs to political candidates. I was stunned when the motion carried by a vote of 25-13. I lost no time in calling the plant and ordered 125 signs to be delivered to my office.

HON. JOHN BAIRD UNSAFE PLAYGROUND

The next day, I dumped 125 four-foot long signs on Shirley's desk. There were 57 centres, run by the city directly that had to be done right away.

When I drove up University Avenue that afternoon on my way home, there was a big smile on my face. As I rounded Queen's Park, I picked up my cell phone, dialed Baird's office. I was greeted by his EA who was obviously upset.

"Why didn't you call and discuss it with us first?" he whined.

"You jerk," I replied, "our staff has been discussing it with your ministry for over two years without result. Nobody knows who John Baird is today. I promise you that by tomorrow morning, everyone in the province will know the name John Baird."

It worked. I doubt if they had to erect more than two signs. By the next week, they had cut a deal for funding the playground replacement with the ministry.

Several years later, I shared a platform with John Baird as we cut a ribbon at Union Station. He had, by this time, been elected federally and was in the Stephen Harper cabinet. We joked about the playground fiasco. He made me promise to find him one of the signs, which at that late date was a tougher assignment than making the signs had been. I was lucky enough to spot one in the North York Mirror office at the City Hall press gallery. It was generously donated by David Nickle.

John Baird later became foreign affairs minister in the Harper government. I can just picture the Russian ambassador staring up at the sign above Baird's desk scratching his head.

CHAPTER 83

Windrows Away

In the early years on North York Council, I had a strong urge to hide under the bed and not go to work whenever it snowed heavily. That's because I knew I would get at least 30 telephone calls that went something like this: "I spent two hours shovelling my *@#% driveway yesterday and last night your &%#@+ snow plough came along and filled it up again. It froze and I can't get to work this morning."

I wasn't the only one. All of the aldermen were feeling frazzled and harassed after each snowstorm. The mayor and controllers didn't care. We were the ones who got the calls. Until I was elected to office, I didn't even know the meaning of the word "windrows," let alone that I had to find a way to deal with them.

There was an enormous amount of pressure on the works commissioner to find a solution. The works department spent a year trying different methods, including separate small push ploughs that would follow the graders and clear the windrows, but that was labour intensive and too expensive. Besides, the equipment we needed was just not readily available in the quantity we required from contractors. In the end, the works department had to invent the equipment that worked best. It was a gate at the end of the plough, a sort of a short blade or scoop the operator lowered when he came to one side of a

SNO-RID EQUIPMENT

driveway and raised it after he had pushed the windrow to the other side. It was tricky to operate, but plough drivers quickly became adept at it especially after they had knocked out a couple of fire hydrants or been thrown to the pavement when the plough hit an obstruction. They called it a "sno-rid."

In 1985, North York invested an additional $119,000 for sno-rid attachments and purchased 26 machines for windrow clearing at the end of March for the next season. The bill for snow clearing in North York went from $1.2 million to $2.3 million. It was worth every penny.

North York was good at providing winter services. Unlike the city called Toronto, the one downtown, North York ploughed its sidewalks. If you lived downtown, the law said you had to shovel the sidewalk in front of your house within 12 hours of a snowfall, and if you didn't you would face a fine of $125. It wasn't that Toronto was insensitive or cheap, it's just that downtown streets weren't built for snow. The suburban municipalities were constructed with 10-foot grassy boulevards. The ploughs had someplace to dump the snow. Downtown, if you ploughed the street the plough would deposit the snow either on the cars parked along the road or on the sidewalk. If you ploughed the sidewalk, you would deposit the snow onto the road.

When amalgamation arrived, those of us from North York knew we would have the fight of our lives to keep both sidewalk ploughing and driveway opening. It was the classic battle between budget misers and service lavishers, only this time the traditional roles were reversed. Downtown councillors were chomping at the bit to cut sidewalk and windrow clearing; North York councillors were gung ho to keep them.

When directly elected Metro arrived, it wasn't an issue because snow clearing on local streets remained with the local municipality. The fight began in earnest in 1998 when the one big, Mike Harris "megacity" happened. By 1999, we were resigned to being melted down into one big city. This was a "cost-saving merger to end duplication," we were told. It's kind of like believing in the tooth fairy. The province had in place a "transition team" that was studying how to put this giant jigsaw puzzle together.

I put the following to council: "Metro Council survey the six local municipalities to see what unique services they would like to see preserved in an amalgamated Toronto."

The motion carried and the data collected, but it was of little interest to the transition team. They wanted to cut, not preserve unique services. What it did was give us the ammunition to slow down the race to the bottom and reach for the best.

Mel Lastman was the newly minted super mayor. When he was North York mayor, he had lapped up the credit for the sno-rid, which he really didn't deserve. Now that he was the super mayor who had been elected on a "no tax increase" platform, his policies became the enemy of the sno-rid. North York councillors had to develop a strategy for retaining these services. Not only were we at the mercy of the downtown councillors who saw them as an easy budget cut, but also those from suburbs that hadn't been offered the services in the first place. If we wanted to save our prized snow clearing policy, our only recourse was to try to extend these Cadillac services (as the penny pinchers called them) to other parts of the city.

We had learned from experience. In the annexation of 1967, when little Forest Hill was swallowed up by the City of Toronto, the one concession promised was they could retain side yard garbage pickup. The good burgers of Forest Hill didn't want their streets cluttered with unsightly garbage cans. The Village of Forest Hill provided its residents with side yard service, where the trash collectors would walk around to the side of their houses, take the garbage to the packer and return the cans to their original resting places. It lasted 26 years, but eventually it was snatched away from them through the efforts of downtown Councillor Richard Gilbert in 1993.

It was a classic battle between rich and poor. Why should the taxpayers of Toronto spend an extra $420,000 dollars to provide the wealthy privileged citizens of Forest Hill better garbage pickup than anyone else? Time had erased the fact that it had been promised to them as a condition of annexation. I recall the public hearings when hundreds of Forest Hill residents lined up at microphones to state their case. I was awed when former Prime Minister John Turner pleaded with council to retain his side yard garbage collection. I'm glad I wasn't on the council that had to make that decision. I would have abandoned my socialist roots and voted with the wealthy. A deal is a deal.

We forged an informal alliance with other, mostly suburban, councillors who were seeking to protect special services of their own. For example, in heavily forested neighbourhoods Etobicoke had mechanical leaf collection. Residents would rake their leaves to the curb and the city would scoop or suck them up and cart them away. In all other neighbourhoods, residents would have to pack their leaves into paper sacks and haul them to the curb for pickup to be taken away and composted.

Robbin Doolittle, in a Toronto Star article wrote: "When leaf collection hit the chopping block, Etobicoke councillors threatened to vote away windrow clearing. Meanwhile, a Scarborough councillor argued their residents deserved a slice of the pie. And while windrow clearing has been extended throughout most of the city, leaf collection never was."

She was right. We allowed mechanical leaf collection to gain a foothold in small areas of the City of Toronto (Baby Point and Scarborough) to secure those votes. Ironically, the cost of specialized leaf collection, which has been called a "luxury service," was about the same $500,000 as the cost of side yard garbage collection in Forest Hill. The gist of the plan, however, was to expand windrow clearing and sidewalk plowing everywhere. We knew that once people in Scarborough and Etobicoke experienced these services they could never be voted away.

In a January 2011 article in the Globe and Mail, Marcus Gee wrote: "Whenever Toronto gets a snow storm, downtown elitists are out in the cold shovelling their sidewalks. Meanwhile, in the hard-done-by suburbs householders can sit snug by the fire while the city does the work for them…. Suburbanites won this perk after amalgamation…. Originally, only North York got its residential sidewalks cleared after a snowfall."

Do I detect a tinge of sarcasm here? Gee goes on to argue that the city could save anywhere from $8 million to $10 million if everyone did their "civic duty" and cleared their own sidewalks. That's not entirely correct. What everyone who takes this position ignores is the City of Toronto had another policy: if a household had nobody under the age of 65 who was physically capable of shovelling their sidewalk, the city would send a crew out to hand shovel it. Toronto's population is aging. If that policy had to be extended across the entire city, it would be far more costly than any mechanical sidewalk or windrow-clearing program.

In any case, I make no apology whatsoever for working to ensure that people in Toronto had the best municipal services possible. It's not grand boulevards and lavish tourist attractions that make a city great. It's the little things like sno-rids that help people live more comfortable lives that define the quality of life in a city. That's what makes Toronto great.

CHAPTER 84

Subways and Art

Most of the world's great cities have acknowledged the importance of creating beautiful subway stations, not only as tourist attractions, but because they have recognized the benefits of having inviting, attractive public places – places that brighten up your day a bit on your morning commute to work.

PARIS METRO STREET ENTRANCE   MOSCOW SUBWAY STATION PLATFORM   STOCKHOLM METRO ESCALATOR

Toronto, when it built the Yonge Street line, had chosen a sort of low ceilinged, mid-century toilet tile motif with each station being of a uniform design; dull grey and uninspiring with all of the charm of a public washroom. Montreal had opted for a subway with flair – large airy open stations with high vaulted ceilings, each station unique.

The drab Yonge line style of station was actually more expensive to build than the attractive Metro stations in Montreal. Rumour has it that what turned the tide for TTC management was the Montreal stations looked more opulent. So for the Bloor line, the Toronto engineers, of course, did the wrong thing and chose to go with the "yech" look, even though it was more expensive. They were afraid they would have to face public criticism if their stations appeared extravagant. One of our riders called it "old grey beard thinking." He was right.

The public didn't like the gaunt design and utilitarian nature of the Yonge and Bloor line stations. Over time, the thinking at the TTC began to shift. "Shift" is probably the wrong word. It was a knock down, drag out fight.

TORONTO SUBWAY STATIONS

You may have noticed that new buildings in Toronto are adorned with works of art. That didn't happen by accident. The planners in the pre-amalgamation City of Toronto had incorporated a public art component into their planning requirements. Buildings above a certain size were required to set aside at least 1% of their gross construction budgets for public art. Public art began to spring up in the downtown core, where new large buildings were being constructed. When the Spadina line was built, there was public pressure to incorporate art, although the tight-fisted management of the TTC was not prepared to spend a single construction dollar for it. They allowed the stations to be individualized, but the art funding was raised largely through public subscription. Each station had its own art installation, most of them done by notable Canadian artists. The public was delighted with the result, but while the hardasses at the TTC were warmed by the public response, they were still not warmed enough to be fully committed to a public art program.

The engineers who run our transit system are eminently practical. They are totally focused on making sure the trains run on time. They don't want to waste money on "art" when it can be spent on brake shoes, and I can understand that. Transit systems in Canada are the most underfunded in the world.

In real life, before I was elected to public office, I was a North York junior high school art teacher. I cared passionately about public art and urged the TTC to apply the planning departments 1% for art policy to the construction budget for TTC projects. By this time, the public art policy had worked its way into the city's official plan and public art was beginning to appear in the suburbs. I knew that unless it was built into the construction mantra of the TTC, it would be a battle that would have to be fought on each and every project and in each and every station.

The notice of motion I tabled at a commission meeting was referred to staff for a report back to the commission. I would have loved to have been party to the back room discussions on this one. When the report came back, it recommended: "For new construction projects, the TTC allocate up to 0.5 percent of the budget for space to which the public has access for artwork and special finishes."

Someone noted that station walls had to have tiles and they would be part of the budget in any case, so that 0.5% was not recklessly extravagant. The policy was approved. It was so wishy-washy that you could drive an Orion bus through it without scratching the side panels. Can you imagine what magnificent subways we would have had if a firm commitment to 1% had been adopted?

In 2008, I approached the commission with a proposal to renovate three stations associated with the major downtown cultural attractions, the Art Gallery of Ontario (AGO), the Four Seasons Opera House and the Royal Ontario Museum (ROM). TTC staff was about as excited as my grandchildren are when I tell them they have to eat their broccoli. Nevertheless, I pressed on. Toronto architect Jack Diamond came up with a magnificent design for the Museum station, but for lack of funds it was destined to become a dusty museum relic. I approached Anne Swarbrick, former Rae government minister of arts and culture, who convinced the Toronto Community Foundation to invest $2 million in the project. It is the only subway station in Toronto to make the Guardian's list of the World's most beautiful Metro station. Alas, the plans that Jack Diamond did for the other two stations are still sitting on the TTC shelf.

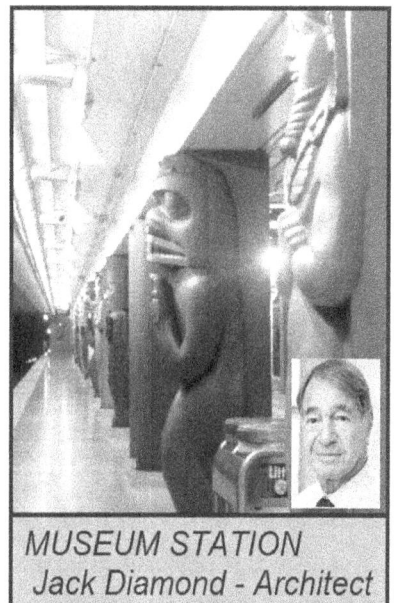

MUSEUM STATION
Jack Diamond - Architect

The low level of commitment to public art by TTC management is illustrated by how they treated existing works of art. "Joy," the glass skylight by Rita Lentendre at the Glencairn station, was taken down at the artist's request because the glass panels had faded after years of exposure to sunlight. The TTC would not spend a dime to replace them.

One of the most beautiful installations on the Spadina line was a neon light installation entitled "Arc en Ciel" at the Yorkdale Station. It was created by Michael Hayden, a Canadian artist who has since

Joy by
Rita Lentendre

achieved worldwide recognition for his light sculptures. "Arc en Ciel" consisted of 158 multi-coloured neon lamps installed in the arched roof of the station, and it created a dazzling moving rainbow effect whenever a train entered or left the station. Over time, water leaks damaged the transformers and rather than incurring the expense of replacing them, the TTC pulled everything out. Michael has told me the cost of repairing the installation would have been less than $1,000. In 1978, after the work was completed, Michael moved to California where he lives and works today. He is best known for his installation at O'Hare Airport in Chicago and is now working on a 350-foot pedestrian tunnel in Cleveland.

When I became chair of the TTC, I vowed that the "rainbow" would be returned to the Yorkdale station. That opportunity came in 2010 when Yorkdale Shopping Centre approached me as the local councillor for help in securing building permits to expand the mall. I signed a memorandum of co-operation with them, which included about $2 million of community benefits, $325,000 of which was set aside for the restoration of the "Arc-en-Ciel."

ARC-EN-CIEL BY MICHAEL HAYDEN (1978)

The project was given approval by the commission that year, yet it has taken more than seven years to work its way through the ponderous TTC bureaucracy. Because of delays and what with the change in the American dollar and rising prices, the cost of the project has ballooned to $800,000. I once asked a developer what is was like working with the TTC. His answer: "I'd rather have pins pushed into my eyeballs."

With the help of Josh Colle, current chair of the TTC, we managed to finally raise the funds and the momentum to push forward. Toronto Council put its final stamp of approval on the project in July 2016.

Since it was first installed in 1978, lighting technology has gone through a revolutionary change. Neon has been replaced by LED lights with computer-controlled pixels an inch apart.

The last time I checked Michael Hayden, the artist, was furiously working on the computer program that will pilot the new installation.

The finished work was scheduled to be installed in October of 2016 and the goal was to flip the switch that turns on the rainbow in mid-November of 2016.

It still hasn't happened. I will spare you the agony of the painful details. It's enough to say that for the past eight years, Michael has been mired knee deep in the mud of TTC bureaucracy. For the first time I fully understand why the Toronto-York Spadina subway extension is $400 million over budget and almost three years late.

As to the "Arc-en-Ciel," in Michael's words, "it will be magnificent." I would add: "someday, hopefully in my lifetime." Stay tuned.

How strong is the TTC's commitment to public art? It has only taken them 60 years to upgrade from "corpse" to "somewhat alive."

CHAPTER 85

Best Kept Secret

The 2003 election was one of my most bizarre. I was up against Ron Singer, a Rob Ford implant who was almost as smart as Rob, but lacked his charisma. I had defeated Singer in the previous two elections, but he was determined to win this one and was rumoured to have canvassed every home in the ward. I canvassed exactly 14 homes.

It all began on Mother's Day 2003 in Madrid. I was attending the International Union of Public Transport (UITP) conference and trade show. A chest pain had started on the morning of the last day and by mid-afternoon had rendered me unable to breathe. I stumbled into a taxi and rushed to the emergency room of San Carlo Hospital where I spent two days in an observation ward.

Fortunately, for me, they found a cardiologist who could speak English, but my poor wife, Gloria, who knew not a word of Spanish, had to fend for herself. Spanish hospitals are far stricter than Canadian ones. They allow 20 minutes a day for visiting (spouse included) and if you think a Jewish deli is noisy, try a Spanish hospital waiting room. Gloria was desperately trying to contact the Canadian Consulate to sort out a glitch in my health insurance, but the nurse on duty would only allow her two minutes on the phone. If anyone can complete a call to a consulate without being placed on hold, they know something I don't. After two minutes, the nurse would keep unplugging the phone.

It wasn't a heart attack. It was constrictive pericarditis. The doctors at the Mt. Sinai Hospital in Toronto suggested it was caused by a virus I may have picked up in Spain. With pericarditis, the lining around the heart swells and impacts on the ability of the heart to function. Eventually, the lining begins to harden like cement. That normally takes several years, but in my case, it all happened in two months. The solution, open the chest and peel out the lining.

The municipal election was fast approaching. If it became known that I had a heart problem, in addition to casting doubts on my ability to function as a councillor, I would have undoubtedly attracted some heavy-duty opposition. The only remedies for my medical condition were heavy doses of aspirin, diuretics to induce the body to eject fluids and the toughest thing of all, stop eating salt. Think of it, no more pastrami, pickled herring, Strub's dill pickles, and Chinese food, everything that I loved to eat.

The only remedy for my political condition was strict secrecy. That was even harder. From that time on, everyone close to me joined the secret service and a strict "cone of silence" fell over my office.

That summer, I was in and out of the hospital as they monitored my condition and adjusted my medication. I could appear to function normally, so long as I didn't exert myself. I could make speeches at council and chair TTC meetings without anyone knowing of my condition, but I could not walk a block without having to rest and catch my breath. It was like walking on eggs.

In August, in the midst of preparing for the upcoming election campaign, I suffered a setback. The oral diuretics stopped working. I had to be admitted to hospital so they could be administered intravenously. Now I was tied to a hospital bed. Ben Rothman, my campaign manager, had to set up the election on his own. My City Hall staff, Irene Sepp, Betty DiBartolo and Maria Rizzo, had the burden of keeping up the pretence that I was still around and functioning normally. Maria had her own election to worry about. She was a trustee on the Toronto District Catholic School Board and running for re-election.

One fortunate thing was all of council's business had stopped when we shifted into election mode. There were no more formal council business meetings to attend or chair.

All calls to my office became conference calls from my hospital bed. To the caller, I was in my office. Betty answered e-mails from my computer as I dictated responses.

Newspaper and radio interviews were accomplished from my hospital bed via telephone and Irene scheduled Ben or Maria to conduct community meetings in my stead. Everything was going smoothly.

And then the axe fell. The Toronto Star phoned to say that because I was the longest-serving incumbent they wanted to kick off the municipal election campaign with a photo of me canvassing in my ward.

"But you have lots of file photos," I said, "Use one of them."

"Not a chance," they said.

After a hasty conference with Dr. Sasson, my cardiologist, I was given a day pass. I got dressed in a suit and tie. Ben picked me up at the back door of the hospital and drove me up to Eglinton Avenue to meet the Star photographer. I shook hands and chatted with customers in the barbershops and on the street near Oakwood Avenue and generally mugged for the camera. As soon as he left, I was whisked back to my intravenous. That set the pattern for the rest of the campaign.

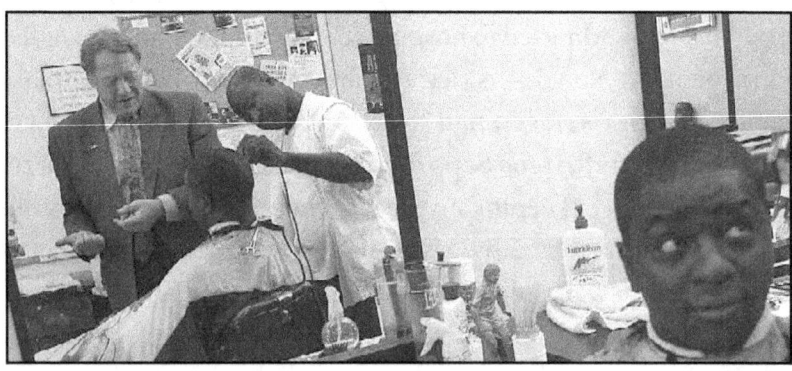

TORONTO STAR

The Toronto Sun called; they wanted a picture.

"Ok," I said. "I'm on the board of the Mt. Sinai Hospital. I have a meeting there tomorrow. I will meet you at 3:00 p.m. in the lobby after the meeting."

"Hey," said the nurse. "Where are you going dressed in a suit?"

"Don't worry," I replied. "I'll be back in 10 minutes. I'm going down to buy a newspaper. I always dress when I go out in public."

I was vice-president of the Association of Municipalities of Ontario and AMO's four-day annual conference was scheduled for the second week of August at the Royal York Hotel – eight blocks from Mount Sinai Hospital. I knew if I didn't show up at the conference, my secret would get out. Furthermore, Sue-Ann Levy, a Toronto Sun columnist, always criticized me for using an "expensive hotel room" for an in-town conference. I didn't want to disappoint her, so I booked a room at the Royal York that I knew I would never use.

Then began my most artful deception. On a four-day pass from the hospital, I would take a taxi to the hotel each morning and return to my hospital bed at about three in the afternoon. On the first day of the conference, Suzan Hall, a fellow Toronto councillor, happened to mention to me she felt too tired to return to her home in Rexdale and come back in the morning.

"I have a community meeting in my ward tonight," I told her. "Why don't you use my room?"

The next night, Councillor Bas Balkisson used the room.

Sue-Ann cornered me at the hotel and said: "So, I see you booked an expensive room at the Royal York again."

"Yes," I replied, "But this year we saved the city money. Three of us shared the bed."

I was released from the hospital at the end of August to join my campaign. Ben sent me out to canvass. I deliberately chose a group of townhouses on Bathurst Street. They had only one front step and would be easy to canvass. It didn't work. I was so exhausted after my second block that I went right back to Mount Sinai Hospital, where I spent 24 hours in the emergency room before I could be admitted again. I never re-emerged until the election was over.

I was scared silly. I normally canvass more than half the doors in my ward during a campaign. I thought for sure being unable to canvass would cost me the election.

I won. Ben said he didn't need me anymore. Next election, all I needed to do was put my name on the ballot and fly off to a Florida vacation.

CHAPTER 86
In Bed With the Lobbyists

This is embarrassing.

Throughout my career, I loathed lobbyists. I spearheaded the thrust at City Hall to establish a lobbyist registry. When staff produced a report that said it would cost more than $1 million to set up a registry, I stormed that I could do it for less than $100 – and I did. I taped a sign on my office door that said if lobbyists wanted to meet with me they had to sign a register. Each month, I would send the list to the clerk to file for public inspection. More than half the councillors bought into the plan. The staff report, of course, was right. My registry was voluntary and after a while it fell apart. A proper registry required checks, balances and controls, and it has to be mandatory. Eventually, council set up a proper registry. We led the way.

Now, after spending a miserable 25 hours in the emergency room at Mount Sinai, a bed became available in the cardiology ward. They wheeled me into a room on the 16th floor. The curtain between my bed and the next was drawn. I could hear the patient in the next bed on the phone talking about the election.

"We're screwed," he said. "Miller is going to win. The lefties are going to sweep City Hall and the next four years are going to be tough."

Gloria gestured for me to be silent. The whining went on for at least half an hour and I must admit I enjoyed every second of it. It was Ivan Fleishman, a lawyer and active lobbyist at City Hall. Finally, I flung back the curtain and there was dead silence.

"Ivan, the walls have ears." I said.

I spent the next week in bed, with Ivan, where we talked about our heart ailments and traded political stories. I can see why Ivan is a successful lobbyist. He is charming, likeable and as full of it as any politician I know.

Ivan agreed to keep my secret. He had as many phone calls as I did and we shared the same line. One day, a call came in and it was my turn to answer. It was Andy Stein, Mayor Lastman's executive assistant.

"Hello, is Ivan there?"

"I'll see if he's in."

IVAN FLEISHMAN

"Hey Ivan, that sounded like Howard Moscoe's voice."

"Yes," he replied, without skipping a beat. "Wasn't it nice of him to visit me?"

An hour later, Bruce Davis, another City Hall lobbyist, walked in to visit Ivan. He did a double take and his jaw dropped. Ivan backed him up to the wall.

"If you mention a word of this to anyone don't bother to show your face ever again at City Hall."

Davis nodded assent.

I once heard a story that hospitals reserve one room on each floor for lowlifes. Now that I've seen this room occupied by lobbyists, lawyers and politicians, I'm sure of it.

By the way, a week after retiring in 2010, I registered at City Hall as a lobbyist.

CHAPTER 87

How Many Nurses Does it Take to Change a Light Bulb?

One of my hospital stays began at a TTC meeting I was chairing. Betty came in with my council agenda and quietly placed it on the floor beside my seat. It weighed about 25 pounds. At a lull in the meeting, I bent to lift it onto the table. The room began to spin, I felt myself falling against the blinds behind my seat and awoke staring up at the ceiling from a stretcher in Mount Sinai's emergency room. All in all, I spent about five months in and out of hospital beds (mostly in), where I witnessed first hand how a hospital ticks.

Almost every time I was re-admitted, I had to spend 24 hours on a stretcher in the emergency room before a bed became available in the cardiac ward. During that long stay, I learned more about the hospital system than I ever needed, or wanted, to know. Each night, I would explore a different part of the building. Eventually, my doctor gave me the key to his office so I could use his computer at night. It was a godsend. I read as much about constrictive pericarditis as I could find. I also began to communicate with a football coach in California, who had gone through the same operation. It was a great emotional crutch. He helped talk me through mine.

We tried to track down the source of the virus. The medical officer of health in Toronto contacted the MOH in Madrid. He, in turn, sent a note out to area cardiologists looking for similar cases. They found only one, a Spanish rock star whose symptoms matched mine.

Because my condition was rare, (it had come on so quickly) almost every cardiologist in the hospital and a whole lot of medical students and interns visited my room. I was determined to find the right surgeon to do the operation. I asked each doctor I met: "If you had to have your pericardium removed which doctor would you ask to do the operation?'"

I then developed short-lists. Three names rose to the top and I picked the one most recommended. He was Dr. Chris Feindel, a cardiac surgeon at Toronto General Hospital, who many said had a particular "feel for this operation." Ironically, the third doctor was the brother of a candidate I had defeated in a previous election, and I certainly didn't want him with his hands inside my chest cavity.

I have built my life around having a healthy disrespect for authority. Any success I've had in politics revolved around my penchant to question the status quo, be it a major societal dysfunction or one of the little things that get under everyone's skin. One day, the bulb above my bed burnt out. I asked the nurse to have it changed. She explained she would have to fill out a requisition and forward it to maintenance.

"So when will I have enough light to read?" I asked.

"It takes about four days."

Now, I can understand why they require a maintenance requisition to change a bulb. Apparently, an orderly had once fallen and injured himself while changing a light bulb.

When the nurse left to get the requisition form, I climbed up, unscrewed the bulb, walked down to maintenance and asked for a new bulb. I knew where they were located through one of my night-time meanderings. By the time she had returned with the requisition form, I had already replaced the old bulb. That prompted a visit from an irate head nurse, who proceeded to chew me out for my improper behaviour.

"If you can't live with my behaviour," I told her, "throw me out."

Back in campaign headquarters, volunteers began to notice my absence.

"Where's Howard?" they would ask.

"He's up canvassing poll 49," Ben would respond.

Election night 2003. It was an amazing victory on two counts. I had won a tough election battle from my hospital bed and David Miller swept the polls to win the city. I had to come out of hiding and leave the hospital to attend my own victory party at Katz's Deli. It was only the euphoria of the win and the support of Gloria that got me through that night. When I talk about her support, I mean that literally. She had to stand behind me and physically hold me up to keep me standing. We also had to appear at the David Miller victory celebration at Harbourfront, where we stood on the stage as David made his victory speech. Again, Gloria had to prop me up. After a few brief media interviews, I was whisked away back to my hospital bed at Mount Sinai. What a night!

During my hospital stay, I was scheduled for several major tests, some at Mount Sinai and some at Toronto General across the road, where the operation was to take place. The tests were scheduled, but what invariably happened was the day before the tests were to occur, I was bumped.

When I looked around me and I spoke to nurses and other patients, I learned that being bumped from a test was a very common occurrence. It seemed being bumped for an average of three days was the norm.

Why? It's because the hospital is paid a per diem (daily fee) by the Province of Ontario for each day a patient is under hospital care. At that time, it was around $900 dollars a day. That fee covers the total cost of a patient's care, including major tests.

When an outpatient comes in for a test, the hospital is paid a separate fee for that service. Therefore, there is an incentive for the hospital to bump inpatients in favour of outpatients. Think about it, every time I was bumped from a test, I spent an extra three days in hospital. That cost the Government of Ontario $2,700. Multiply that by the many thousands of patients bumped from tests and it makes the *ORNGE* ambulance scandal look like chump change. It doesn't just happen in cardiac wards, but almost every other department of the hospital where major tests are scheduled.

That explains why almost every time I was re-admitted I had to spend a full night on a stretcher in the emergency room because the cardiac ward was full. That's one of the many reasons emergency rooms are crowded and why you have to sit there for endless hours waiting for treatment.

The solution seems easy. Take major tests out of the per diem payment and pay hospitals separately for them. In other words, eliminate the incentive for bumping inpatients.

That may sound easy, but I am sure it isn't. I was determined to do something about it. Around a year after I was released from the hospital, I scheduled a meeting with George Smitherman, the then Liberal minister of health. We met in the members' dining room at Queens Park. I knew George from his time at City Hall. He took careful notes.

I know how difficult making a structural change in any government system can be. Every time you try to change the dynamics, there are powerful interests that will lobby against it and hospital boards and administrators are among the most powerful. Nothing changed.

I have the distinction of being one of the few people ever thrown off the board of directors of Mount Sinai hospital. Let me explain. Hospital boards are composed mainly of either wealthy or influential people. They are individuals who are either potential donors or people who are in a position to help the hospital with their skills or influence. The board has traditionally included two members of Toronto Council and the bylaws of the hospital provide for their appointment. Hospital boards seldom make any decisions that the hospital administrators don't lead them to make.

I attended my first meeting as one of the two Toronto Council appointees. David Shiner was the other. We were served a hot lunch. The meeting was chaired by Joe Mapa, president and CEO of the hospital. Most of the meeting was taken up with presentations from hospital staff about what wonderful things the hospital was doing followed by a few questions.

Just before the meeting was about to break up, I raised my hand: "I move that the CEO report to the board on the number of re-direct considerations and critical care bypasses issued to Toronto Ambulance Service this past year." [When an emergency room is at capacity, ambulances are directed to other hospitals.]

"Why do you want to know that?" Mapa asked.

"I'd like to see how our hospital emergency service is stacking up against other hospitals in the city."

The motion carried.

About three weeks later, my staff advised me the head of our ambulance service wanted to meet with me in my office. He and Mapa trooped in together. They wanted to assure me that Mount Sinai's emergency room was on a par with every other hospital in the city.

"Show me the statistics," I said.

"Well, the report has not quite been put together yet."

"So come back when the written report is ready to be presented to the Mount Sinai board and we can talk then," I replied.

There never was a report. The annual meeting was coming up and a proposed amendment on the order paper was to delete the provision for appointing city council members to the board. Apparently, it carried because neither David Shiner nor I was re-appointed. It was a deft move by Joe Mapa. Now I know why they paid him $760,152.83 a year.

CHAPTER 88

Down to the Wire

Another TTC strike loomed in 2005. The negotiators had chosen a remote location to be out from under the noses of the downtown media, although the media seemed to have no trouble finding the place. The setting for negotiations between TTC management and the executive board of the Amalgamated Transit Union (ATU) Local 113 was the Sheraton Parkway Hotel, a plastic, suburban hotel tucked away on Highway 7 in Richmond Hill, east of the Don Valley Parkway. Don't try to get there by TTC.

It was Sunday, April 3, 2005. The strike deadline was 5:00 p.m. The hotel parking lot was filled with TV trucks and it was difficult to negotiate your way through the horde of reporters crowded into the lobby. All of Toronto was waiting to find out if they could rocket to work on Monday morning, or have to scramble to find other means to get there.

It was a particularly ugly set of negotiations. The 8,000 TTC union members were smarting from grievances. In the first place, their pension plan was in difficulty. They had been forced to dip into their pockets for the past five years to make up the shortfall because it was underfunded. It was estimated that it had cost each TTC worker in the neighbourhood of $2,500. This was happening at a time when other municipal employees were enjoying a premium holiday that had been ordered by federal regulators who deemed the CUPE plan to be overfunded. They were expecting to make some of that up in this agreement.

Then there were grievances against management that union members were militant about. One was the penalty against drivers who finished their shifts early. Other issues revolved around shift scheduling, sick day policy, flexibility on clothing allowances and contracting out. It was as much a fight about management rights as it was about money.

The election of Bob Kinnear as union president was an upset victory. He was a 34-year-old upstart who had knocked off Vince Casuti, a long-time stalwart. Bob ran on a "get tough with management platform." The executive board, all of whom got re-elected, had supported Casuti. This was Bob's first set of negotiations and he had to deliver.

A lot was at stake for the mayor too. It was also Mayor David Miller's first set of negotiations. He issued strict instructions that we were not to go over 2%. What we negotiated here would set the pattern for negotiations with police, fire and all other civic workers. Transit was grossly underfunded and we couldn't hope to make up what we negotiated with ATU at the fare box. Riders couldn't handle anything more than a 10-cent fare hike. That's why we stuck with our offer of 2% a year over five years for as long as we could.

There was considerable debate within the management suite at the hotel. Senior staff was prepared to ignore the mayor's directive to get a settlement. I wouldn't let them. They much preferred to give cash rather than cede management rights. A cash solution was a problem for council; ceding management rights was a problem for them.

"Go work on contract language," I told them. "If we have to give them more money we can do that as a last resort."

A traditional way of sealing a deal at the 11th hour was a signing bonus – a cash payment. The advantage of a cash payment was the one-time payment would not be built into future salary schedules. If a signing bonus is required, in the end you have to give it in a way that other civic workers would not be able to demand it.

"Call it compensation for the pension payments they were required to make," I said. "Call it anything you want, but not a signing bonus. Call it a 'red rocket' allowance if you must call it anything."

Normally, negotiations are conducted by TTC staff. They are joined by the chair and vice-chair of the commission as the talks near the deadline. I moved into the hotel on Wednesday, March 30. The strike deadline was Friday, April 1, 2005.

It was a particularly difficult time for me. I had my heart operation a year earlier after the 2003 municipal election. It was the result of a virus I picked up in Spain. It hardened the lining around my heart. The same virus had also attacked my lungs. The lung operation was more painful than the heart operation had been. I had spent the better part of February at Toronto General Hospital recovering from the lung operation. They had to go into my chest cavity and scrape out the barnacles. It had been less than two weeks since I had been released from the hospital. My wife Gloria moved into the hotel with me to protect me from myself. Every so often, she would pull me out of negotiations and force me to nap. It was a secret, which we shared only with TTC senior management

The Friday strike deadline passed and the atmosphere intensified. Kinnear announced that as long as we were still talking, they wouldn't be walking. Negotiations proceeded throughout the day. We were willing to talk contract language, but were unwilling to budge on our final offer of 2.5%, 3% and 3.25% over three years; nor were we willing to consider a cost of living allowance. We were deadlocked. The union team walked out, and it looked like a Monday morning strike was inevitable.

On Saturday night, Reg Pearson, the provincial mediator, called Kinnear and coaxed him back to the table. Negotiations resumed at 8:00 a.m. on Sunday. Reg hustled back and forth between the two teams. It was a roller coaster ride. We made some progress on contract language.

The pension compensation package – the "Red Rocket Allowance" – became a major sticking point. The management and union positions had narrowed. We were offering a payment of $200 per worker per year for three years. They were stuck at $300 per worker per year for three years. We were $100 x 3 years = $300 apart. Downstairs, the media were chomping at the bit waiting for an announcement for the evening news. It was 4:30 p.m. The union walked out.

I telephoned the mayor to advise him of the breakdown. He asked to speak to Kinnear. They spoke privately at 4:15 p.m. I'm not sure what was said. Kinnear claims the telephone discussion he had was not a major factor in his decision. I don't know if it was or wasn't.

I'm told that at this point the union team was divided. Some were prepared to accept, some were not. They gave Kinnear the authority to go down the hall for one final shot. They told him whatever he decided to do they would support him.

Our paths crossed in the hallway: "Do you want a deal or not?" I shouted at Kinnear. "For a couple of hundred bucks, you're going to close down the city of Toronto?"

At that moment, something changed. The deal nobody wanted at 4:30 p.m. became the deal nobody was happy with but could live with at 5:00 p.m. The discussion had shifted to "How can we sell it?" It was almost over.

At the press conference that followed, a tired looking Kinnear made the announcement: "I want to announce to the people of Toronto that there will be full TTC service in the morning. We have reached a tentative settlement with the commission that our executive board will be recommending to our members. It is then up to them to decide whether to accept it or not."

I added my comment: "This is the toughest collective agreement I've ever negotiated. I feel like a member of the bomb squad who half an hour ago was faced with a green wire and a red one. Thank G-d we cut the right wire. It's been that tight."

The media proclaimed the event: Yes, the rockets would roll on Monday morning, but we were not out of the woods yet. Kinnear was right. The package had to be ratified by union members, and even though it was being recommended by the union executive, word on the street said it would be close. It was.

There was a high turnout. Some 6,000 of the 8,000 members came out to vote. The package was approved by a vote of only 60%. A good agreement is one where neither side is happy. Judging from the vote count it was a good agreement.

So why did we get a settlement? The union knew if they closed down the system, they would be legislated back to work. Miller, in fact, had already discussed the situation with the premier and the opposition parties had all agreed to a rare emergency sitting to enact swift back to work legislation. That would mean everything would go to arbitration.

Money wasn't the union's main fear. Arbitrators would come up with some kind of monetary increase that would likely be somewhere between the union's demands and our final offer. In an arbitrated settlement, however, the arbitrators go back to ground zero. What the union feared most was that in arbitration they might lose the other items we had conceded to them. I was right to insist the bargaining team focus on contract language. It was not so much the money as the stubbornness of management that was at the root of their militancy. It was the fear of the loss of non-monetary gains that prompted the settlement.

Of all the things I've done in politics, helping to settle a dispute like this gives me the most satisfaction. I was never much liked by the Toronto Sun. I was thrilled when Sun columnist Hartley Steward, in a piece he called "Kudos to the deal makers," wrote: "While TTC Chairman Howard Moscoe had kind words and effusive thanks for everyone involved, including the mayor, sources say a few bows on his part would not be remiss."

My thanks to the late Hartley Steward, that's what made it all worthwhile.

CHAPTER 89
How Much is a Politician Worth?

The meanest, nastiest, most divisive issue, bar none, is how much to pay politicians, particularly at the municipal level where councils have to set their own salaries and always in public. It brings out the worst in everyone, including the media and the politicians themselves. It becomes a platform from which the dumbest people in politics can grandstand. Think about it. Councillors who have never done a constructive thing in their entire careers can grab a headline by firing off a cheap shot against a salary increase. (Oops! I think I just fired off a cheap shot.) For some, it's the only stairway to a public profile for which every elected official, despite what they might say, hungers.

No matter how much you take, it's too much. No matter how you take it, it's always the wrong way. No matter when you take it, it's the wrong time. Need it or deserve it is never really the issue except, of course, for the politicians themselves. If you support it, you are a greedy bastard who is out for yourself. If you oppose it, you are a hero (even though you get it anyway.) If the increase is approved quietly, without a public melee, it's a "conspiracy" or a "secret deal."

The media love to churn this issue. It's a cheap news story; an easy hit. The great Toronto Council pay raise kerfuffle happened in 2005. It lasted for a full five months and beyond.

A bylaw passed in the year 2000 pegged council salary increases to the rate of inflation. We had already received the 2005 increase of 1.7% at the beginning of the year. Negotiations with our unions proceeded throughout the year and resulted in a settlement that had to be ratified by council in September. The union settlement was a four-year package that amounted to percentage increases of 2.75%, 3%, 3.25% and 3.25%. It was a long-standing tradition around Metro and practically in every other local municipality that after union negotiations were complete the same increases were awarded to non-unionised staff and, in most cases, to elected officials. When the matter came to the policy and finance committee, I made a three-word amendment by adding, "and elected officials." Nobody gave it a second thought; there was no discussion. It was routine.

Until they are ratified, all union settlements are confidential so the report would have come to council as a confidential report on purple paper. Unless someone chose to hold it for discussion, it would be automatically approved. Every member of council had the right to hold the report if they did not agree with any of its provisions. Nobody bothered to hold the item, there was no discussion of it and the policy and finance committee report carried 26 to 9, with 11 members absent.

Once approved, confidential salary reports become public. They can only be re-opened with a two-thirds vote of council. In practical terms, what the amendment meant was instead of the 1.7% inflationary increase they had already received, council members would get an additional 1.05% that year and the same increases that everyone else got for the next three years without regard to inflation. For the first year, 2005, it amounted to a grand total of $800, which we would receive as a lump sum payment.

The Toronto Star led the charge against it: "12.25%," they screamed under the headline: "Sneaky Grab at City Hall."

The Toronto Sun headlined: "Sly City Scarfers."

The Star was even more virulent than the Toronto Sun, which has never ever supported a raise for councillors.

Why was the Toronto Star, which usually shrugged when council raised its salaries, so hopped up? Could it be they were a "Liberal" paper out to discredit David Miller, or did it have more to do with the fact they had a new editor who was itching to make his mark?

What hurt most was in the midst of the on-going debacle, the Star editorially supported Dalton McGuinty when he gave himself and members of the provincial Legislature a 25% pay increase on a base salary significantly higher than ours. That was done by cabinet, without any public debate or discussion. It prompted me to write a letter to the editor, but of course, it was never published.

I long ago convinced myself to deal with the issue of salary increases straight up and take the hit. In my previous career, I negotiated staffing for the elementary teachers in Toronto. As a union negotiator, I was accustomed to not being loved. As a politician, I figured I could publicly support reasonable salary increases for myself and fellow members of council without permanent damage to my reputation; that I was doing enough positive things that would allow my supporters to forgive me for once in a while caring about my own family. The fact that I had been re-elected repeatedly for 32 years proved my stance to be more than just a theory.

The moment the media barrage began, some members of council began to act like deer caught in the headlights of an oncoming truck.

"We were tricked," they claimed. "I wasn't aware I was giving myself an increase in salary!" said many.

Many, including Jane Pitfield, who was running for mayor, were dripping in sanctimony. Michael Walker admitted he had missed the clause. In fact, he was seen on the tape of the meeting urging people to hurry up and vote. That didn't stop him from railing against it. At the next council meeting (November 24), Walker and Councillor Cliff Jenkins tried to get the issue re-opened. They were defeated on a 23-14 vote.

Councillor Case Ootes pegged it correctly when he said: "I find it hard to believe that anyone that voted on it didn't know what they were voting for.... I voted for it and I don't apologize for it."

He was right. Their protestations rang hollow. My response was: "They're admitting their incompetence, their lack of diligence.... They say they didn't know it was happening.... That's a horrible condemnation of yourself, to not understand what's going on in council. Who would elect anyone who doesn't understand what's going on in council? If anyone is upset with the raise, they don't have to accept it."

How much should a Toronto councillor earn? At the time of this debate, it was $85,487. We were actually one of the lowest in the GTA. Mississauga councillors were earning over $112,000 – 31% more than we were.

Royson James of the Toronto Star understood: "They are underpaid. Yes, underpaid."

His quarrel was with the way the raise was taken, not with the quantum of it.

John Barber of the Globe talked about the "we were duped" explanation by some of my colleagues: "It's a better explanation than the alternative.... That they were hypocrites."

The media kept churning the issue. I was dumped on from great heights. The Toronto Star awarded me their not-so-coveted editorial "DART OF THE YEAR AWARD."

Other members of council were signing petitions to try and force the issue onto the agenda. Everyone was getting into the act, pro and con. It was pathetic to read the fear growing in some of my colleagues' eyes. It was time to hoist the white flag. I surrendered. On Tuesday, at the beginning of the meeting, I rose to my feet.

"Madam chair, I rise at the start of today's meeting to withdraw my motion that would increase councillors' salaries beyond the rate of inflation. I do so in the expectation that we can vote on this quickly and so avoid a couple of hours of acrimonious debate."

Everyone breathed a sigh of relief. The vote was 37-3 in favour. The issue was (for now) put to bed.

Beyond the public pressure and the editorial scorn, there were a few reasons I gave up so easily. First, it wasn't worth the aggravation for a measly $800. Secondly, I may have accidentally shot myself in the wallet. What if the rate of inflation over the next three years was higher that the amounts specified? We would actually receive less.

There was a third reason and I'm almost embarrassed to mention it here. Joe Pantalone and I had quietly negotiated an arrangement in this package whereby members of council who had served more than three continuous terms on council would be entitled to receive the same benefit package as members of the Ontario Legislature: benefits for life. That was the real prize. If I were a Catholic, I would have to go to confession for it and I'm sure it would qualify me for the Star's "Dart of the Century." Most members of council to this day don't know that they have it, but they will come to appreciate it after they retire. It is ironic that some of the councillors who were so anxious to give their salary increases back didn't qualify for the benefit package. Bill Saundercook, who served more than nine years, couldn't get it because his service was not continuous. Cliff Jenkins, who I admired greatly for his integrity, was defeated, but did not have the years of service to qualify.

When I retired in 2010, my salary was $95,000. One of my career goals was to make my way onto the Public Salary Disclosure list (the sunshine list). By Ontario law, all public salaries over $100,000 have to be published annually. Thousands of employees of the City of Toronto, a $6 billion corporation that we manage, found their way onto the sunshine list.

Alas, I never made it. But please; hold back your tears. At least I kept my benefits and, best of all, the Toronto Star didn't have anything at all to say about it.

CHAPTER 90

Thinking Inside the Box Outside the Box

For years, transit authorities have griped about the fact that business people get a tax credit for automobile use, but are denied them for public transit.

Tory politicians are passionate about tax credits. In 2006, the Harper Government announced a tax credit for public transit use. It represented a $400 million subsidy calculated on the basis of a 16% tax credit. I suppose the political theory is that once a year, when people toil over their income tax return, they will pause for a moment, turn toward Ottawa and think kind thoughts about Stephen Harper. The announcement had public transit officials jumping for joy.

I have never believed that giving a tax credit for public transit would induce anyone to ride. Tax credits help high-income earners. The poorest of the poor don't pay income tax at all, so a tax credit is of no value to them. Besides, the transit managers decided the administrative burden was too great to give receipts for the purchase of tickets, so the tax credit would only benefit those who could afford to purchase a monthly transit pass. That cut out the majority of riders. Transit managers are high-income earners. They think like Tories.

Why not take the $400 million and distribute it to all riders? So, I advanced a proposal I called an "Instant Tax Credit." It gave an 8% rebate to all riders. It wasn't really a tax credit at all, but hey, if they liked "tax credits" what do I care what it's called. At that time, a strip of tickets in Toronto cost $20. The price would be reduced to say, $18.40. When the strip of tickets is printed, one of the tickets would be printed as a "Federal Tax Credit" ticket. That would be the "free ride," a gift from the prime minister.

I'm a New Democrat, but I wouldn't mind putting a picture of Stephen Harper on the ticket. I believe in giving credit where credit is due. It would be a "political credit." Now riders would think kind thoughts about the prime minister every time they used a federal tax credit ticket or purchased a strip of tickets. The prime minister wouldn't have to wait until tax time for people to genuflect towards Ottawa. His picture would be in everyone's purse, pocket or wallet. If I were Harper, I would have jumped at the opportunity. I would even have put his picture on the transit pass, but it would have had to be smaller than mine.

It was administratively simple. The government simply matches the cost reduction with an equivalent amount to go directly to the transit system. No fuss, no mess, no bother and the Canada Revenue Agency could keep their grubby hands out of it.

CUTA, the Canadian Union of Transit Authorities, said it would take transit system managers eight months to bring in Harper's tax credit. My plan could happen as quickly as they could print tickets. With my plan, they would see an immediate cash flow to help them meet service and generate ridership. No need to involve the provinces in developing extensive formulae for the distribution of funding. Sell X tickets, get $Y. As to the political criticism, let me take the hit.

CUTA was discussing five ways of implementing the tax credit. I had given them a sixth way. I hustled the idea to cabinet ministers, sent it to everyone who I thought might have an interest.

How well was the proposal received? Have you ever seen a transit ticket with Stephen Harper's picture on it? They just weren't capable of thinking inside the box; the fare box, that is.

CHAPTER 91

Kicked in My Canadian Identity

As a former teacher, I have always been aware of the importance of language in determining who you are. I also happen to be a Canadian nationalist. I became increasingly irritated because my computer was constantly telling me I was wrong when I used Canadian spelling. In 2007, I began to raise the issue internally with staff and was provided with a "briefing note" written by the director of information technology.

This is my response to his briefing note:

> John Davies,
> Executive Director
> Chief Corporate Office, Information and Technology
> Dear Mr. Davies:
> Thank you for the briefing note with respect to Canadian English Spell check.
> As I understand your position, the bulk of the software is now being converted to Canadian spell check as a default position, but you are not recommending that the purchase of future software require this as a condition of purchase.
> I thought this issue was settled in 1867 at the time of Confederation when we decided to become a sovereign nation.
> If we believed, as you suggest, that we should not require future software purchases to use Canadian spelling, we might also consider scrapping the CBC and the CRTC requirements for Canadian content in broadcasting. It would certainly be a lot less expensive to import American culture.
> I profoundly disagree with your recommendations and look forward to the debate.
> Sincerely,
> Howard Moscoe
> Councillor, City of Toronto, Eglinton-Lawrence

After two years without seeing any change, in frustration, I wrote this memo to the Government Management Committee. It speaks for itself.

> Saturday, May 02, 2009
> From: Howard Moscoe
> To: The Chair and Members of the Government Management Committee
> Re: Ouch Canada! Canadian Spelling
>
> Attached is a list of 84 words that have been kicked out by my spell-check (appendix i). Every time my spell-check kicks out a Canadian spelling, I feel as if I've been kicked in my Canadian identity. It's bad enough when my American spell-check does it, but it really hurts when it is sanctioned by my municipal government. At present, all of our software defaults to American English. Since 2006, I have been urging our administration to obtain software that defaults to Canadian English. Each time the issue is raised, I am assured the matter will be fixed and still nothing happens.
>
> Yes, there is official Canadian English. It is set by two standards. The first is Hansard, the official record of the House of Commons in Ottawa. All records of the House are required to be in "Canadian English" and this includes all laws and statutes of Canada. The second is the Canadian Oxford dictionary, 2nd ed. (Toronto: Oxford University Press, 2004), which is used by most editors.
>
> It just so happens that while our Microsoft Word does include Canadian English, it always defaults to American English. Is Microsoft of California eroding our language because of some secret American plot to subvert our Canadian identity, or is it because we simply

haven't asked them to produce a version of Word that defaults to Canadian English?

Is it too much to expect all orders of government in Canada, including the City of Toronto, to promote Canadian identity? The Government of Canada is actually one of the worst offenders. A scan of the official Government of Canada website indicates that the word "colour" was spelled the American way 3,000 times. That represents 15.9% of the time it was used. The City of Toronto is not far behind. Our official web site spelled "colour" wrong 8.8% of the time. The Ontario government is far better than most. Its official website only used the American spelling 2.2% of the time.

In a check of eight Canadian spelled words (appendix ii), Toronto again came off second worst to the Government of Canada, which topped the misspelling of Canadian words at 15.1% of the time. Toronto used American spellings 11% of the time, while Ontario was best at 3.6%.

From a scan of the official websites of all of the provinces, it appears only Ontario and Alberta have made a conscious effort to promote Canadian English. On their sites, the American usage was conspicuously low and when it was used, it can be mostly attributed to quoting American publications. Websites like that of Prince Edward Island and Nova Scotia use the American spelling of "colour" 47% and 40% of the time, respectively. B.C. has added a new twist by hiding its usage. When you scan for "colour," it makes no distinction between the American and Canadian spelling.

It costs the city of Toronto countless hours of wasted staff time and lost productivity because hundreds of conscientious employees have to go back and correct, word for word, the American spellings. Yes, Microsoft Word, which the city of Toronto uses, has included spell-check for Canadian English since Word 2000, but you have to adjust the settings each and every time you type something and it often takes as long to do that as it does to go back and correct the misspellings.

The city's policy on these matters is also not clear. It only hints at the use of Canadian spelling. Form 15, report writing checklist from the auditor general's office, states: "Have you checked spelling with more than a spell-check? (Ref: Canadian Oxford Dictionary)"

It stops short of requiring the use of Canadian English and should be amended accordingly.

Recommendations:

1. The City of Toronto contact Microsoft and ask them to produce a spell-check that defaults to Canadian English;

2. Through the normal replacement process, replace all of our software with that which utilizes Canadian spelling for every day municipal business functions;

3. Require Canadian spelling in all City of Toronto reports;

4. Require the use of Canadian spelling in all correspondence both internal and external;

5. Require whoever administers the official City of Toronto website to ensure that it is expunged of all non-Canadian spellings and to henceforth use only Canadian spelling;

6. Advise both the federal and provincial government of the errors on their websites and request that they change them to "Canadian English."

Ouch Canada!

Yours in Government,
Howard Moscoe,
Chair of Licensing and Standards for
the City of Toronto

Has any of this been done? I know the default to Canadian spelling hasn't happened with the City of Toronto computers. As to the rest, check out the federal and provincial websites yourself.

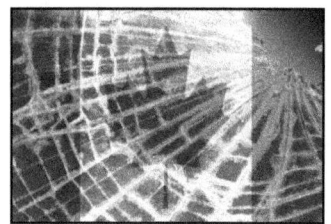

CHAPTER 92
RSVP

The TTC gets invited to many parties, but it is very selective about the company it keeps. When Donna Cansfield was the Ontario minister of transportation in 2006, she threw a lot of parties. Don't get me wrong. It's not personal. She is a lovely person, but she threw a lousy party. Maybe we were just difficult guests.

PARTY POOP #1
Place: Panorama Restaurant, 51st floor of the Manulife Centre, Toronto
Date: Thursday, October 12, 2006
Celebration: Donna Cansfield, Minister of Transportation, smart card announcement. The Province of Ontario will spend $250 million to develop a "smart card" to facilitate easy access to transit systems in the Greater Toronto Area.

The announcement was to award the contract to Accenture, a U.S.-based consulting giant to "develop the hardware and software for the smart card system." Accenture would operate the system for 10 years. It was a leading edge project.

Since the TTC operates 85% of the transit in the GTA, it might have been nice of the province to consult with the City of Toronto before they started down this road.

RSVP: Mayor Miller is unable to attend. His schedule is already full.

RSVP: Howard Moscoe is unable to attend. My response was a trifle less diplomatic.

"I respectfully decline. I'm in the middle of an election campaign. I haven't got time to be at a press conference as a backdrop for the Minister." I added: "If they have $250 million to spend on smart cards, that's nice, that's warm and fuzzy, but I could buy 400 buses with that money. We have to leave passengers on the street. People are being shoehorned into subways."

The TTC learned from bitter experience that the "leading edge" often becomes the "bleeding edge." The announcement advised that "the cards will debut in Mississauga and at Union Station next year and the cards will work across the region in 2010."

It is now 2017 and Smart Cards are just beginning to make their appearance in Toronto. It will take a couple of years more before the system is fully integrated into the Toronto Transit System.

The TTC could have purchased an "off-the-shelf" smart fare system that operates through a cell phone app for a fraction of what they spent to invent one. As it turned out, it is not so smart after all.

PARTY POOP #2

Place: TTC Hillcrest Repair Complex, 1138 Bathurst Street, Toronto
Date: Monday, October 16, 2006.
Celebration: All the great things that Minister Canfield and the Ontario Ministry of Transportation have done for public transit in Ontario; a gas tax announcement.

This wasn't actually a party poop. We attended. After all, the party was being held in our garage. We just pooped all over the party when we got there.

Picture this. There were 20 (or so) buses flanked by operators in spiffy new uniforms lined up in two rows facing each other in front of a speaker's platform – one bus from each of the major transit systems in Ontario. It was a very colourful scene. Some buses had driven a long way to get there. There were buses from as far away as Windsor and Ottawa. The general managers of each of the transit systems were on stage, sitting behind the transportation minister. Adam Giambrone, my vice-chair and I were the only other politicians present. That's because it was our garage. We weren't on the platform. The minister's staffers were a bit nervous about my presence after I had pooped on their party the previous week.

The minister would make her announcement about honouring the election promise to give two cents per litre of the gas tax to public transit systems across Ontario. For the TTC, that meant about $161 million.

Then, one by one, each of the general managers was to troop up to the microphone and announce how he or she was going to spend the money the province had so generously conferred upon them. Gary Webster, the TTC's new chief general manager was to be last to speak.

When I realized what was happening, I told Gary to stand down. I was going to speak in his place. I also told Giambrone, who had been chatting with the minister's staff, to go and tell them of the change in plans. They were adamant that I not speak. Giambrone quietly pointed to the uniformed TTC security staff positioned around the room and said: "Those are our security staff. You are in our garage. What kind of media reaction are you going to get when they close down the garage and order you all out?"

They were skewered.

When I spoke, I graciously welcomed the minister to our facility and thanked her for her support of public transit in Ontario. TTC has long pressed Queen's Park and Ottawa to improve their support for public transit. Even with the additional money from Queen's Park, 80% of the funding for the TTC would continue to come from the fare box. We remained the most underfunded public transit system in North America, if not the world. I told the minister this new partnership was a great first step. I then went on to explain how much farther ahead we would be if the government had simply restored the funding formula the Harris Government had so rudely cut. I then proceeded to provide examples that outlined the money we would have received if this party were held in Vancouver, Montreal, Edmonton or Winnipeg. In each case, it would have been substantially higher than the $161 million they were giving.

"Our ridership is growing by about 16 million rides a year and the TTC is struggling to keep up," I said. "The TTC is facing a massive bill – $740 million – to repair its facilities and replace worn out vehicles leaving little room for expansion of services."

A letter to the Toronto Star from Daniel Kowbell said it all: "It was with great astonishment that I actually found myself in agreement with TTC Chair Howard Moscoe. While other smaller provincial transit systems reacted like Pavlov's dog to Transportation Minister Donna Cansfield announcement of increased funding by the province, Moscoe was quick to point out the realities of said monies coming Toronto's way. While this textbook photo op and glad-handing by Cansfield was contrived by Cansfield to prepare voters for the next provincial election, one must give credit to Moscoe for this golden opportunity to make it known to both Cansfield and the patrons of the TTC that though $161 million sounds like a lot… it is merely a fiscal starting point for the long neglect by past provincial governments."

Needless to say, Party No. 3 was held in a transit garage in Mississauga. I was never invited to any more of her parties. I can't imagine why not.

CHAPTER 93

Big City, Big Snub

No petty pot shots for Prime Minister Harper. When he snubs you, he does it big time. It was November 14, 2006, and the media had gathered at Union Station to hear an announcement from Lawrence Cannon, the federal minister of transportation, about funding for transit security. All of this was a reaction to earlier bombings in the Madrid and London subway systems. I should have been suspicious when Cannon sent Ontario Conservative MP Gord Brown (Leeds-Grenville) to Toronto to make the announcement instead of coming himself.

We had been discussing the security program with the transportation ministry for several months. The TTC had almost finished installing security cameras on all of our streetcars and buses. We were asking for $17 million in total, most of that was to go towards adding other 2,500 security cameras in our subway system. Five months earlier, the government had announced it was setting aside $80 million for transit security to be handed out over the next two years. This was to be round one, $37 million for large transit systems. The second round was to be an allocation for security in small transit systems. There was a federal election coming and public safety and security were high in the Tory election agenda. I had met with two senior bureaucrats from the ministry who were assessing our needs and they were sympathetic to our request.

You would think the money would be distributed according to need. It was. It quickly became apparent at the press conference that it was being distributed on the basis of the need for votes, not security. The TTC carried a third of the transit passengers in Canada. There wasn't a single Tory seat in Toronto and not many likely – lots of potential votes in the 905 though. Based on ridership alone, the TTC should have been allocated $12.3 million.

Here's how the money was distributed: Vancouver, $9.9M; Montreal, $8.5M; GO Transit, $5.3M; Union Station, $4.5M; Edmonton, $2.5M; TTC, $1.46M.

It was a slap in the face. The TTC carried 85% of all passenger traffic in the GTA and got only 16% of the security money.

I hastily pulled our group together and directed staff: "Do not go up onto the stage; do not participate in the photo op."

I was mobbed by the Toronto media.

"It's a spit in the eye... a slap in the face," I told reporters. "This announcement shows complete and utter disrespect for the people of Toronto. It's like handing a bum a dime and saying 'Here, go buy a cup of coffee.'"

I know I struck a nerve. Even the Toronto Sun, which never had a nice word to say about me, backed my position. "This time, Moscoe is right. Rarely does TTC Chairman Howard Moscoe make a valid point in between his bouts of buffoonery [how comforting], but this time he has on a serious subject... security for TTC passengers."

The media conference blew up in their faces. With editorial support from the Toronto Sun (backhanded as it might be), how could I not press on?

I drafted a letter to the prime minister. I advised him: "So that there is a deeper understanding of how big this project really is and how little the federal government has determined Toronto is worth I have designed a sticker to be placed over all the spots where the TTC wants to install security cameras."

I told the media: "I hope the prime minister will in fact have some second thoughts. I'm prepared to put his picture on a transit ticket and whether he's wearing horns or a halo is entirely up to him."

We have the security cameras, but not the money. Then again, in Toronto they didn't get the votes or the seats, so in the end the people of Toronto won.

CHAPTER 94

The Right to Tinkle

Is the right to pee one of the rights granted by the Canadian Charter of Rights and Freedoms? I am not even sure if there is a United Nations Charter that grants it. Yet most would agree, denying a basic bodily function would be like trying to repeal the law of gravity.

In 2009, I was approached by a constituent who complained that Kmart in Lawrence Square Shopping Mall had refused to allow her eight-year-old to use the washroom. A few weeks later, I got another complaint about the same thing happening in a Shoppers Drug Mart.

It's not only because I was chair of licensing and standards for the city that I decided to investigate. I have now reached the age where I can't manage to pass a washroom without using it. I checked out three Shoppers Drug Marts. When I asked to use the washroom, they said that they didn't have a public washroom. They were sorry, but each directed me to a restaurant down the street.

I knew it wasn't true. The Ontario Building Code requires every business to have washrooms for the use of customers. Every architect knows that. They couldn't get a building permit unless they conformed to the Ontario Building Code. I guess the members of the Ontario Legislature had their legs crossed when they adopted the latest version of the Building Code in 1976. They forgot to include a provision that required the business to let anyone actually use the washroom. It looked like businesses everywhere had just arbitrarily decided they weren't going to allow anyone to use the washrooms they were required to provide, and there was nothing anyone could do about it. It seems only restaurants, which had to meet health regulations, were required to keep them open.

How fair is that? Why should the restaurant industry "carry the can" for the retail sector? It's not as if Shoppers or Loblaws couldn't afford to buy toilet paper and soap. They sell the damn stuff. It was time for an amendment to our property standards bylaw that required opening the washrooms that were already there to customers.

When I brought the matter before the licensing and standards committee, the (well, you know what) hit the fan. It seems when I drew my bottom line I was challenging theirs.

"We're clobbering people every which way in Toronto," thundered Councillor Mike Del Grande. "The move will force some stores into expensive remodelling."

Of course, it wouldn't. The washrooms were already there. What Mike didn't tell the committee was that he used to be an accountant for Shoppers Drug Mart.

Gary Sands, who represented the independent grocers and chain drug stores, said the city should come up with some research to show that people actually want store washrooms before we imposed it on businesses.

I brushed this off.

"I don't need a study to tell me that people need to go to the washroom."

The Canadian Association of Independent Business weighed in: "There's no groundswell demanding washrooms. Store owners are usually helpful when someone has to use a washroom, people are understanding; people are people and you don't have to write legislation."

Sure, tell that to the guys at Shoppers Drug Mart or Loblaws.

Have you ever noticed that almost all of the large American chain stores coming into Canada have open, accessible washrooms; companies like Wal-Mart, Costco, and Home Depot. It's not out of the goodness of their hearts. It's because most states have tough regulations. When these companies build here, they are using national template designs that they bring with them. It has nothing to do with their concern for your bodily functions. American legislators have taken care of that for you. Ours slipped up.

The committee voted to adopt the "Right to Tinkle" bylaw with two dissenting votes, Councillors Mike Del Grande and Rob Ford.

"If times were great, maybe I'd consider it, but times aren't great," quipped Rob Ford. "This is not going to create jobs."

Council adopted our new bylaw, but we did build in a compromise. Only stores larger than 3,200 square feet are required to open their washrooms to the public. Why 3,200 square feet? We didn't want to impose it on every mom and pop variety store. The number is for ease of enforcement and comes right out of the Building Code, which says if you are larger than 3,200 square feet you are required to provide separate male and female facilities. That means an inspector doesn't have to go around measuring stores to enforce the bylaw. He can just count the washroom doors.

I hope that Mike Del Grande never has to use a washroom while shopping, but if he does, it'll be there for him. If you ever get the urge and are denied the use of a washroom, call 311 and ask for property standards, and they'll bust 'em.

CHAPTER 95

Reaching Beyond

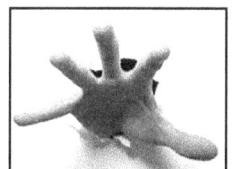

S ometimes, in politics, you have to reach out beyond your jurisdiction and grab for the brass ring. It doesn't always work, but if occasionally it does, it's worth the effort.

GOODS & SERVICES TAX

Municipalities owe a vote of thanks to the TTC, but they don't know it. The TTC won a rebate of the GST for all municipalities and transit authorities in Canada.

If you don't exist, how can you pay taxes? Municipalities have no constitutional status. They are "creatures of the province" and as such, do not exist, at least not as independent entities.

Sound logical? In 2002, the TTC retained lawyer Paul Schabas to take this matter to court.

"The province can't tax the feds and the feds can't tax the province." Schabas said. "Given that municipalities are an extension of the province and they're public and governmental they shouldn't be taxed either."

Schabas filed an application with the Ontario Superior Court of Justice in June of 2002. The TTC was seeking to recover $130 million in GST payments since 1991 when the tax began. Since the TTC was an extension of the province, he argued, it should, like the province, not have to pay GST.

The case had implications for every municipality in Canada. Municipalities at that time didn't pay the full tax. They received a rebate of 55.14 per cent of the GST they paid out. The Federation of Canadian Municipalities (FCM) had been calling for a 100% GST rebate for years. In the GTA alone, municipalities pay about $120 million annually in GST. This was the first time the matter had been put squarely to a court.

It took two years to work its way through the system. The court was about to make its ruling when we were approached by the lawyers for the federal government with a request that we agree to having the matter stayed to give them an opportunity to consider a settlement.

Then, a short time later, Prime Minister Paul Martin made the announcement. Effective 2004, he would accede to the wishes of Canadian municipalities and voluntarily grant them a full rebate of the GST. That announcement put an extra $372 million into the pockets of Canadian municipalities. This would bring their GST rebate for 2004 up to $1.2 billion.

An act of magnanimous generosity as the country headed towards a federal election? Not at all! It seemed the court was about to rule in favour of the TTC. The announcement was a deft pre-emptive manoeuvre on behalf of the federal government. They managed to turn what could have been a devastating loss into a "we love you" gesture. If the court had been allowed to rule, it would have cost the country 13 years of repayments back to 1991, a staggering $5 billion. Not only that, the ruling would have put the matter on the record forever. With a settlement, the prime minister could look like a hero and remain in control of the situation if at some point in the future he needed to roll back the rebates.

Should we have insisted the court case go forward? Was it worth rolling the dice? I'm a gambler, but not with taxpayer's money. Put this one in the win column.

WEEKEND ROULETTE

Why is it, when the price of crude oil rises there is an instant rise in the price of gasoline, but when the cost of a barrel of crude falls it takes so long for that drop to find its way through the pipeline? It seems to me the price of gasoline has more to do with the weather or the day of the week than the price of crude oil.

In 2007, I was chair of licensing and standards for the city. Like most people, I became tired of playing weekend roulette with the oil companies. The price of a litre of gas at the time was around 74.9 cents. It would leap by 10 or 15 cents a litre as the weekend approached. On Monday or Tuesday, it would drop back to say 76.9 cents. What stuck in my craw was that I knew I was being suckered into believing I was getting a bargain; the year before, I could fill up for half that amount.

Which level of government controls the price of gasoline? None, but if there were controls it would be the federal government, not municipalities. In March, with the summer gasoline price spiral on the horizon, I tabled a modest proposal at the legislation and standards committee. It was designed to tip the balance in the favour of the consumer. The city had the right to regulate the hours of operation of service stations. Stations wishing to extend their hours beyond what was allowed had to apply to the city. It was an issue in some residential areas, but for the most part the exemption was almost always granted.

The proposal was that stations wishing to have extended hours would now be required to post any change in the pump price for gasoline 48 hours in advance of the change. That way, a consumer would know about price changes in advance and would buy gas at the low end of the cycle. I reasoned that even if only a handful of stations did it, they would all have to follow suit. The proposal was sent off to the legal department for a report, which would be tabled in time for a public hearing sometime in May or June.

That's when the grease hit the fan. The oil companies churn out media spin faster than you can lubricate a Volkswagen. I would be "interfering with the free market" they blared. When has there ever been a free market in gasoline? The only person who believes there is a free market in petroleum products is the same guy who had a beer with Elvis at the Brunswick Hotel last Saturday night. The only free choice you really have is to buy your gas from Curly, Larry or Moe. How do gas prices at hundreds of locations change in perfect unison? Is it by osmosis, or does it waft forward on the wind?

The influence of the oil companies is awesome. Their spin-doctors went right to work repositioning the issue.

"Proposal could lead to line-ups at the pumps," trumpeted the Globe and Mail. "If a proposal winding its way through council is adopted, Torontonians will find themselves using their lunch hours to line up to buy gas."

"Limit gas station hours at 9-to-5, Moscoe proposes," blared the Mirror.

The licensing subcommittee had recommended the proposal, but after a slew of public speakers lined up by the oil companies spoke at the transportation committee, the proposal was quashed, clobbered and kicked into a grease pit. Chock this one up as a loss. Ouch!

YOUR NEW HOME COMES WITH A STREETCAR

My brother sold his home with a three-car garage in Thornhill and moved into a downtown condo. Within three years, he had sold his cars and was a regular TTC user. I was having lunch with a developer who had a reputation for being innovative. We were discussing the TTC's efforts to get more people out of their cars and onto our system. He told me he was thinking of giving, as a purchase incentive, transit passes to buyers of one of his downtown condos.

A light went on.

The city was reviewing its parking standards. The development industry was lobbying to reduce the parking requirements for downtown buildings "to induce people to use public transit," they claimed. I suspect it had more to do with the fact that the cost of building an underground parking space had climbed to $50,000 or $60,000.

At the time, I was negotiating the terms of approval for two buildings in my ward. One builder agreed to provide a free one-year transit pass to each purchaser as a condition of approval. It worked. It was the carrot that induced people to leave their cars behind and try the transit system. Once they acquired the transit habit, they became confirmed riders.

I began holding zoning applications of condos to amend their conditions of approval.

"Be it resolved that as a condition of approval, the applicant be required to provide each purchaser with a one-year free transit pass at no direct cost to the purchaser."

The motions carried. Councillors who did not support the concept became angry. If you want to do this, make it a policy that is citywide so it applies to everyone equally. The idea was kicked back to the planning department. An added incentive to develop it as a policy, came when a developer appealed the condition to the OMB and it was tossed out.

Council finally adopted such a policy for development applications for buildings containing more than 20 units in transit-oriented areas. As of April 28, 2010, if you constructed a condominium building in the downtown or city centres of North York, Scarborough and Etobicoke; in the central waterfront area; along arteries slated for the Transit City light rail plan, or along avenues as defined by the official plan you had to give each purchaser a free one-year transit pass.

Rod McPhail, director of transportation planning, noted that the cost to the developer would be offset because the policy was being applied in areas that qualified for reduced parking standards. He also cleverly removed it from the reach of the long arm of the OMB by making it a condition of condo registration, rather than building approval. While the policy was not primarily intended to be a revenue raiser, in the first year the policy raised $1,080,694 for the TTC and was promising to raise a whole lot more as the economy rebounded. It was an innovative idea that was being watched closely by cities across North America.

The developers whined, "Unfair cash grab!" The truth was it wasn't such a bad deal for them. The reduced parking standards more than offset any costs. They could purchase the passes at a reduced bulk rate, they were tax deductible and they didn't have to provide them until the condo was sold.

I retired in 2010. Rob Ford was elected mayor. Within two years, the policy was lobbied out of existence. All the contributions the development industry made to political candidates paid off. The winds of political change are sometimes foul.

Put this one into the "nice try" column.

SPURRING A NATIONAL PACKAGING PROTOCOL

Your city has to deal with the mountains of garbage generated each day. We have handled that primarily through our recycling system, but recycling is a second-best idea and very costly. The real answer, of course, is to not generate the waste in the first place.

I bought a cordless telephone set at Costco. When I opened the package, I discovered the set itself occupied only about half of the box. The rest of the package was bolstered by folded cardboard. The big glossy package was a marketing tool designed to give the illusion that you were getting something more for your money. Why do they have to put three layers of plastic around a Barbie Doll, packaging that almost requires a hack saw to remove?

There is a disconnect here. Packaging protocol is the purview of the federal government. Given the influence that manufacturers wield, efforts to regulate packaging at the federal level are doomed to failure. As chair of licensing and standards, I was working on a scheme that might influence national packaging protocol.

Toronto is the largest consumer market in the country. We would, in the interests of waste reduction, enact a bylaw that required every retail outlet over 3,000 square feet to establish a well-signed, well-equipped packaging removal area where customers can remove and leave the packaging. I've tried it. I took a box cutter with me when I shopped at a large retail outlet. Near the exit, I stopped, cut away the packages and left them in a pile beside the trash bin. Some other shoppers stopped to watch and some actually began to applaud. If most customers were encouraged to remove and leave the excess packaging at the store, the retailers would turn to the manufacturers and tell them, "Unless you reduce your packaging, we are not going to carry your product."

Many stores do the opposite. They don't provide bags, but invite you to a select from a pile of empty boxes to carry away your purchases. They are actually inducing you to take their garbage home and dispose of it there.

Would it work? Put this one in the yet to be tested column.

CHAPTER 96

To What End?

Those who travel southbound on the Allen Road are no strangers to gridlock. What to do about the end of the Allen Road has been a lingering local area question since June 3, 1971, when Bill Davis, the then premier, cancelled the Spadina Expressway.

That political decision, heralded around the world as a progressive "city-saving" milestone, has created a throbbing migraine for local politicians. Now known as the Allen Road, this urban artery was truncated at Lawrence Avenue, dumping expressway traffic onto Lawrence Avenue West, an already crowded arterial road. This forced high volumes of traffic with no place to go but down residential streets. The then-local alderman, Esther Shiner, built her political career around fighting to have the Spadina Expressway completed. Her efforts succeeded in getting the road built one leg farther, south to Eglinton Avenue West. In spite of all of her enthusiasm, she could never muster enough support to carry it downtown through Cedarvale as originally planned. Efforts to cope with the flood of traffic dumped from a terminated expressway onto Lawrence Avenue West left a legacy of rush hour "no entry" restrictions on all southbound streets all the way from Bathurst west to Dufferin Street.

ESTHER SHINER

I personally supported the Davis decision to kill the Spadina. As a geography major, I knew how expressways destroy cities. I had seen first hand how the Robert Moses Parkway had destroyed the Bronx. Ironically, as a councillor who later represented a constituency that had been burned by the Spadina decision, I never had to take a stand. Everyone turned to Esther for comment. I was off the hook. On occasion, when I was asked, "Where do you stand on the Spadina Expressway?" I would say, "I never stand on the Spadina expressway. There is too much traffic. It's too dangerous." (Politically, that is.)

I actually hated the Spadina Expressway. My grandmother lived on a street called Roseberry Road. The city expropriated her house – and her entire street – to build it.

When I inherited the ward from Esther Shiner and became the local ward councillor, those no entry signs became a major source of irritation for me. There wasn't a week that went by that someone didn't call my office to complain: "I live on... street. Traffic on Lawrence is a nightmare. Because of those damned no entry signs it takes me an extra half-hour to get home in rush hour. I want them removed."

After more than a year of this, I asked the Board of Control for permission to mail a survey to everyone in the ward south of Lawrence to ask them if they supported removing the rush hour entry restrictions. The area covered was about a third of my ward. When the results came in at about 50% yes and 50% no, I did the politically courageous thing – I ran like hell. I never mentioned the subject again.

With the extension of the Spadina Expressway to Eglinton Avenue, the same local reaction to the traffic happened. City of York politicians met the challenge with a wall of "No Entry" signs for southbound streets along Eglinton Avenue from Bathurst Street to Oakwood Avenue. These weren't just rush hour restrictions but applied seven days a week from 7:00 a.m. to 7:00 p.m.

There was a new twist added: Speed humps. Not just ordinary speed humps, but the mother of all speed humps. West of the Allen Road, humps boxed in every local intersection, even some at dead-end streets. They were so bad and got such an adverse reaction that the city was forced to fill in the roadbed between them, humping entire intersections. I dubbed the local councillor, Joe Mihevc, the most prolific humper in Metro.

East of the Allen Road in Cedarvale, a hump battle raged among the residents forcing the community into two warring camps. I warned then-Metro Councillor Caroline DiGiovanni to stay out of it. It was a local issue. She should have left it for the local York councillors. Alas, she got caught in the crossfire and lost her seat in the 1997 municipal election. It was the Cedarvale vote that forced her out of office.

The battle to extend the Allen Road southward was now over. Metro sold all of the Cedarvale property that had been expropriated to build the expressway and all that remained was how to deal with the stub end of the Allen Road.

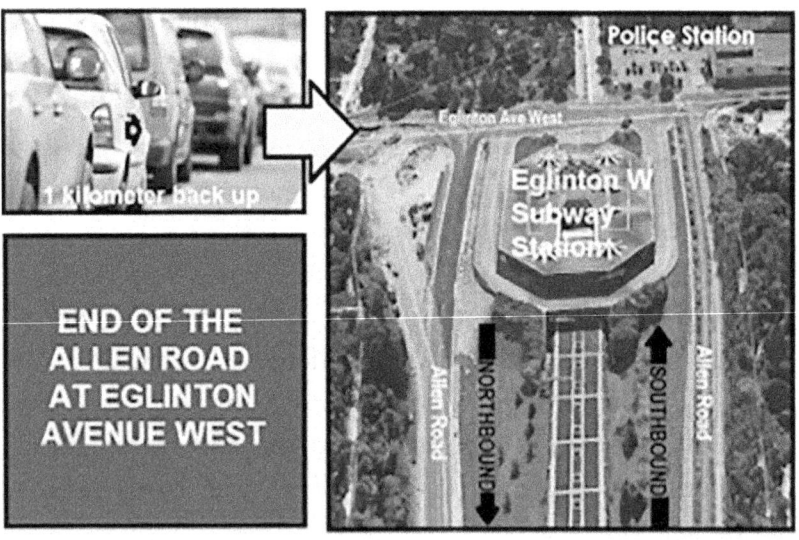

RUMBLE FUMBLE

There were a number of operational problems at the end of the road, including rear-end collisions and speeding cars that had a nasty habit of smashing into the 13 Division police station. It stands guard on Eglinton Avenue at the road end in the path of oncoming vehicles.

I suggested variegated pavement (rumble strips). These are imbedded into the road. You can find an example of them on the eastbound ramp of Highway 401 for northbound traffic onto Highway 400. Transport trucks have a tendency to tip over on the steep highway ramps. The rumble strips automatically wake up sleepy drivers and induce them to slow down.

We installed them at the foot of Allen and they worked. They also woke up the entire neighbourhood all day, all night, every day, every night. Residents' complaints were as loud as the rumble strips. It was only a matter of weeks before we had them torn out and the roadbed re-paved. It was a costly blunder. They were replaced by a flashing sign.

TRAFFIC SCREW-UPS

Around 2005, David Lepofsky, a blind lawyer and disability activist, began to press for pedestrian priority at the foot of the Allen Road. At that time, cars had the right to turn on a red signal off Eglinton to go northbound on Allen. He met with Joe Mihevc (now a Toronto councillor) and traffic department officials on site and persuaded them to change the signals to eliminate the right turn on red provision to make it easier for pedestrians, especially blind ones, to cross and access the subway station. It worked fine for pedestrians, but managed to thoroughly screw up traffic on Eglinton.

As a result, traffic began backing up almost a kilometre from Allen all the way to Bathurst Street and beyond. It became a rush hour nightmare for thousands of motorists jammed onto Eglinton Avenue waiting to turn onto Allen. I represented many of those drivers.

After several meetings with police and traffic officials at the intersection, a solution was worked out that would move traffic without endangering pedestrians. We would cut an extra turn lane onto the Allen Road northbound. After several months of needling Joe Mihevc for having caused the problem in the first place, he agreed to call a public meeting to try the change on his community. The road end was in his ward.

There was a large crowd. They listened intently as the solution was presented. I expected the worst, but to our surprise the meeting broke into applause. Unknown to either of us, since the signal change, their neighbourhood had been inundated by hundreds of cars attempting to escape the traffic jams on Eglinton. Drivers unfamiliar with the local neighbourhood were unaware there was no way out. A permanently re-designed Allen Road end has now been incorporated into the Eglinton LRT budget.

WHO TURNED OUT THE LIGHTS

Lighting was another issue. By 1990, the lighting on the ex-expressway was 30 years old, as were the lights on other Metro expressways. The system needed major repairs. Officials announced they were going to initiate a lighting rehabilitation program and the Don Valley Parkway was going to be given priority. Metro light standards were a unique cobra design.

For more than two years, I had complained about burnt out fixtures and had been told the equipment had been manufactured in Britain and parts were no longer available. After spending several nights on Allen counting lights, I took department officials on a midnight tour and demonstrated that more than 60% of the lights on the ex-expressway had burnt out. That convinced them the Allen should be done first and the repair program should become a replacement program. Until the replacement was done, to provide at least a minimum level of lighting on Allen, the department cannibalised the lighting on the Don Valley Parkway.

SAVE THE ALLEN

Lawrence Heights, the largest public housing complex in Canada, straddles the Allen Road. It was built during the '50s just after the construction of Regent Park. One of the most difficult projects I ever undertook was laying the groundwork for the re-development of Lawrence Heights. One part of that was deciding what to do with the Allen Road. Construction of the Spadina Expressway had bisected the community. Most of the community facilities were located on the west side and were difficult to access by residents on the east side. The divide was reflected in community parlance. Residents spoke about the two halves as the American and the Canadian side. One of the re-development objectives was to unify the neighbourhood.

Early in the redevelopment review, we commissioned a study of "What to do with the Allen Road." Consultants viewed several options that ranged all the way from constructing pedestrian bridges over the ditch to covering over the subway and raising the road to the surface. That option would be financed by selling off any surplus land thus created for development. My guess is none of the "significant change" options is viable because the Allen ditch becomes shallower as it approaches Highway 401.

In the 2006 election, one of my opponents was Ron Singer. He was put up by Rob Ford to oppose me. It was his second attempt to win the seat. In the 2003 election, he worked hard to defeat me and managed to canvass most of the homes in the ward. Canvassing normally works, but in Ron's case, it may have actually hurt him because people got to meet him. Ron Singer was almost as intelligent as his friend, Rob Ford, but with half the personality. I wasn't able to canvass during that election. I won re-election from a hospital bed.

Even though the expressway was in no particular danger, Ron chose to make it his key issue in the campaign, "Save the Allen Road." I'm not quite sure what he was planning to save it from, but fortunately neither did anyone else.

To what end? If there is a moral to this story it is likely to be there is no end. Every political decision results in a myriad of other political decisions, a sort of web that wraps itself around how we live. The one constant is there will be change. Municipal politics is about managing that change, and in a democratic electoral system, it is about building a consensus around how to do that. There is no end. The excitement in municipal politics lies in the process and the satisfaction that comes from knowing you are helping to shape your community.

CHAPTER 97
Sending the Wrong Signals

On November 13, 2010, the night of Rob Ford's election as mayor, the CBC asked me for my comment on how he would perform as chief magistrate: "He won't be able to pass gas without the permission of council," I said.

It was more than just a guess. It was based on his past performance over his 10 years as a councillor. Sure there would be a honeymoon and, in the afterglow of the election, he would quickly be able to make some of the changes he had promised, but that wouldn't last forever. A mayor can't simply demand the loyalty of council. It has to be earned. Rob Ford had never done that and it seemed unlikely he ever would.

Unlike the American system, where a mayor has wide powers conferred by virtue of the office, in the Canadian system a mayor has only a single vote. If a Canadian mayor cannot convince half of the council to go along, there is no place to go.

American mayors in large cities often don't attend council meetings. They only appear when it is time to defend their budgets. Mayors in the U.S., not councils, appoint the senior bureaucrats. After elections, the senior bureaucrats get replaced with the mayor's appointees. Department heads in Canadian cities are part of a permanent, professional swivel service.

A mayor has to command at least a modicum of respect from colleagues. Rob had little of that. In the first place, he was lazy. He hardly ever read his agenda and simply reacted to the titles of reports in a knee-jerk kind of Pavlovian response. That was reflected in the fact that as a councillor, he could only command no more than two or three votes on almost any of his motions. If he couldn't count on the votes of the right wing of council, how in the world could he expect to have the loyalty of the mushy middle, let alone the left? It was only a matter of time before his support as mayor crumbled away.

Rob had a pat set of motions to trot out at budget time. A thousand little "stop the gravy train" cuts, each of them designed to enhance his image. What angered members of council most was that they were geared to making other councillors look bad.

He would attack councillors' office budgets. Councillors are provided with an office budget of some $70,000. It was for expenses, like office supplies, mailings and the cost of sending out newsletters to constituents. Rob made a fetish of spending almost no public dollars to run his office, choosing instead to use his private funds. He tried to out-cheap Doug Holliday, who was by far the most frugal member of council. That is easy to do if you happen to be wealthy. Should public office be accessible only to the wealthy?

Rob made a big deal about refusing to eat the sandwiches brought in when council met during the dinner hour. Instead, he remained at his desk and munched away at the Swiss Chalet dinner he paid to have delivered. He brought his own coffee to meetings. I knew this was a bit of a sham. The board of the CNE met over the lunch hour. A meal was catered for them. I asked the general manager of Exhibition Place if Ford had eaten the meals. It took him two months to get back to me. Yes, he had paid, I was told. I wrote back, "How much?" I was told $5.50 per lunch. If word had gotten out that a meal at the Queen Elizabeth dining room was only $5.50, diners would be lined up back to Union Station with forks and knives in hand. I knew the caterer personally. The cost to the CNE of providing those lunches was at least five times that figure.

Rob conducted an on-going war against councillor's and their so-called perks.

"They get free passes," he would shout. "They're all on the gravy train."

I thought should a member of the board of directors of the CNE have to pay to attend the fair? It's kind of like asking an usher in a theatre to pay to attend a performance.

"And they get free TTC," Rob would yell.

Should a member of the Toronto Transit Commission be riding the system they managed? Should they have to pay to do it?

Rob's rants struck a chord. There are thousands of working people in this city who are struggling to get by. Why should these privileged politicians, whose salaries we pay from our hard-earned tax dollars, ride the TTC free?

"Get off the gravy train!" Rob rode the gravy train theme into the mayor's office.

The most valuable perk provided to each councillor was a Green-P parking card. It allowed for free parking at all city-owned Green-P lots and free access to all street park and display machines.

Strangely, this was one perk Councillor Ford never once mentioned in his tirade against freebies. Could it be because it was the only one he regularly used?

But the thing that angered his fellow councillors most of all was that he continually meddled in everyone's ward. One of the most important roles a councillor played was as municipal ombudsman for the people of their ward. The councillor was the person who would help untangle the red tape thrown up by every day municipal government. The building permit that was delayed, the broken limb of the city tree that had come down in the storm; the pile of trash dumped onto the local park; the clogged street drain; the sewage backup into your basement, to name but a few.

This is the bread and butter stuff that makes your constituents loyal. It's the kind of service that earns you their ongoing support. Rob preached about providing "customer service" as if he was the only one doing it. The problem was he was doing it in everyone else's ward.

"Don't worry," he would say, "if he can't do it, I can fix it."

What made matters worse was he was often doing it on behalf of the candidate who was running against you in the next election. Often times, your role is to mediate neighbourhood disagreements. Sometimes, a councillor has to make judgments about which side was right.

I worked for four years planning the revitalization of Lawrence Heights, the second largest public housing complex in Canada. Rob was right there supporting the side that opposed it. Most members of council resented his interference in projects in their wards. It's not as if he was particularly good at it. Sometimes, a councillor has to say no to a constituent, "You're wrong." Rob constantly demanded staff time and resources to interfere. That didn't earn him the affection of many members of council.

After he was elected mayor, John Tory once asked me: "How do you deal with Rob Ford?"

"That's easy," I said, "don't take him seriously. Treat him as the joke that he is. Make fun of him, it drives him crazy."

In 2009, Rob brought forward to Etobicoke Community Council a petition of 510 signatures demanding that a traffic light be installed at the intersection of Rexdale Boulevard and Tidemore Avenue in his ward. Tidemore Avenue is a short, half-block long, dead-end street that runs north to Rexdale Boulevard. The city budgets annually for some 40 traffic signal installations. It costs $150,000 to $200,000 to signalise an intersection. When a request is made, the traffic engineers undertake a study to determine whether a signal is warranted. They measure things like traffic volumes in each direction and determine whether a signal would have been able to prevent any of the accidents at that location. They then approve signals for the 40 most deserving intersections. Based on the studies undertaken, this intersection would never be eligible for a signal.

This is where the "You scratch my back and I'll scratch yours" protocol comes into play at the local community council. It's legitimate retail politics. If you vote for my unwarranted signal, I'll vote for yours, wink wink, nudge nudge. The only person I have ever known to abide rigidly by the warrants was Doug Holliday. To my knowledge, he never voted for a signal that didn't meet the warrants, but then again if you religiously abide by warrants, who needs politicians? The Etobicoke Community Council recommended the installation of the traffic signals.

Normally, the recommendation would automatically be adopted by Toronto Council. Almost no one reads the community council reports and they were seldom ever held for discussion. I held the item.

Rob Ford was indignant: "Why are you holding my traffic signal?"

"It doesn't meet the warrants," I replied.

When the item came up for discussion near the end of the meeting, I rose to move the following motion:

Be it Resolved That:

1. Council abandon the warrants for traffic control signals in the Etobicoke York District.

2. Each Councillor be allocated one signal per year to be awarded at his/her political discretion.

3. Etobicoke York District be allocated two additional traffic signal allocations to be awarded by lottery.

4   The Director, Transportation Services – Etobicoke York District be directed to undertake a review of all dead-end cul-de-sac streets that flow into arterial roads and develop a plan for traffic signals for these locations to be known as the "ONE For Everyone Plan."

5   The pedestrian refuge median island at the intersection of Rexdale Boulevard and Tidemore Avenue be removed because there are no pedestrians.

6   A sign be erected on Rexdale Boulevard below the signal head advising motorists: "Your car is being delayed because of pork barrel politics in Etobicoke."

Councillor Susan Hall moved the following: "That council delete the recommendations of the Etobicoke York Community Council and adopt the following recommendation contained in the report (April 23, 2009) from the Director, Transportation Services – Etobicoke York District: The installation of traffic control signals at the intersection of Rexdale Boulevard and Tidemore Avenue not be approved at this time as the Traffic Control Signal Warrant is not achieved."

Councillor Hall's motion carried. Alas, because it did, the chair had to declare my motion redundant. Rob had reaped the rewards of 10 years of harassing his colleagues on Toronto Council. It was a foregone conclusion. Before he ended his term as mayor, he wouldn't even be able to get permission to pass gas.

CHAPTER 98

Traffic Congestion is a Hodgepodge of Vested Interests

In the 2014 municipal election, John Tory ran on a platform of easing traffic congestion. That's easy to say, but difficult to do. Since that time, the traffic department has been scrambling to make changes, but that will likely amount to them merely tinkering around the edges. It's a safe bet that by the time the next municipal election rolls around, traffic in Toronto will still be congested. In order to make real change, you have to be willing to make dramatic adjustments, and few politicians have the guts to do that. They did it in London and in Singapore because the officials drew a line around the downtown and said: "You can't drive across this line without paying for it."

In Singapore, only the wealthy can afford to drive downtown. At the same time, both of these cities have first-class public transit so there is an alternative.

CONVENTIONAL WISDOM

When I was a child, I never won an argument with my father because he could always end it by saying, "Because I said so."

One thing that needs to be done is to re-examine conventional wisdoms that everyone takes for granted: Ideas that have been around since Moses was a child. Because I said so, isn't good enough anymore. Here's one example.

"Vehicles parked close to, or blocking, fire hydrants cause serious life-safety concerns. Illegally parked vehicles impede the fire department and other emergency services' ability to access the fire hydrant during emergency situations and put lives and personal property at greater risk." – Report to the administration committee, January 12, 2004.

Nobody has ever questioned this. Let's take a look.

You must leave six metres of space around a fire hydrant. Most large cars are 4.8 metres long, so a car can fit into that space. The shortest fire truck, a pumper, is 10.67 metres long, so you can't fit a fire truck into the curb space next to a hydrant. Is the space around a hydrant necessary when you weigh it against the curb space that it ties up? There are 50,000 fire hydrants in Toronto. Each one ties up a parking space. That's 250 kilometres of curb space or enough space to line up cars, bumper to bumper, from Toronto to almost Windsor or Ottawa. By allowing parking at hydrants, you could increase the number of parking spaces in Toronto by 5%. That would also raise parking revenues, and while that's not the purpose of this exercise, you can buy a lot of fire hose with that money and perhaps even a few more pumpers.

But allowing cars to park at hydrants will block the view of hydrants. Being able to locate a hydrant quickly in an emergency is important. When I was first elected, I received a complaint about a fire on Highway 401 near Avenue Road. When the province built the highway, the planned highway hydrant system was cut from the budget because it was too costly. It was expected fire vehicles would use the local North York street hydrant system adjacent to the highway. But then the province built sound barriers. The fire department couldn't see the street hydrant from the highway. We found a solution: stamp the image of a fire hydrant onto the barrier to indicate that there was a hydrant on the other side, and install a portal though which a hose could be connected to the hydrant. There are solutions that will make fire hydrants visible also.

But cars will block hose access. You can fit a hose over or under a car or between parked cars, but in an emergency, there's always a way. Fire fighters have axes.

Far-fetched? Perhaps, but Toronto has done something as radical before. Toronto and Ottawa are the only cities I know that allow drivers with disabled permits to park in a "No Parking" space. I don't know which Toronto traffic official had the genius to recommend it, but that unusual decision has opened up thousands of parking space to handicapped drivers. Has it caused traffic chaos? Not at all; but I can tell you that as someone who now requires a disabled parking permit, it is a Godsend.

It's time to re-think some of the conventional wisdoms. We can resolve traffic congestion, but to do so we have to tear up the rules and start fresh.

THE RULES HAVE BECOME DISTORTED

The problem with the present rules is they have become twisted and distorted to meet the needs of special interest groups. For example, in Yorkville you cannot move your car in rush hour off the main streets onto the side streets because from 4:00 to 6:00 p.m. all Yorkville streets have been turned into loading zones. That's absurd. The loading zone bylaw has been grossly subverted to serve the private interests of the Yorkville businesses. Most large cities have prohibited daytime loading. It's time Toronto did. In fact, it is the easiest and quickest way to clear main streets during rush hour.

REVIEW CITY BUSINESS PRACTICES

Agents for the trucking companies bring their stacks of tickets to the courthouse and cut deals with the city prosecutors. They are instructed to move the matters through the courts quickly. To the delivery companies, bulk payment of tickets represents the cost of doing business. Tell crown attorneys, "No More Deals." Fight every rush hour ticket. Make the truck drivers come into court to testify. Make the companies think twice about rush hour deliveries. For that matter, why do we allow deliveries at all during rush hours, or even during the daytime? Some cities permit deliveries to be made in the downtown area only after 8:00 p.m. Businesses will adapt if they all have to compete on a level playing field.

TAKE A CLOSE LOOK AT PARKING ON PRIVATE PROPERTY

I would venture to suggest almost half of the fire routes in shopping plazas are not legal. To avoid paying the city to establish a proper fire route, they have simply slapped up signs. There is no bylaw behind them.

There are also thousands of, "Don't park here or we'll tow you" signs with the wrong bylaw number on them because most of those local city bylaws were scrapped. When amalgamation came, they were never harmonized.

REVIEW THE STRUCTURE OF THE HIGHWAY SYSTEM THAT SERVES TORONTO

Highway 401 was originally built as a Toronto bypass. It is now a mid-city highway. There is no longer a rush hour on Highway 401. Daytime congestion is constant. The Ontario Government planned the constructed Highway 407 as a new Toronto bypass. But it was built and operated by the private sector and paid for by tolls (pretty outrageous tolls at that). Have you ever seen a truck on Highway 407? All the trucking is now jammed onto Highway

401. If the same tolls were placed on trucks on Highway 401, they would gravitate north to the 407, which, apart from the Douglas Snow Parkway, is the most under-utilized expressway in Ontario. Right now, Highway 407 is an express route for the rich who can afford to pay to get through the GTA quickly.

Alternatively, you could place tolls on Highway 401 for trucks using the highway during the daytime hours, but allow through truck traffic to travel free on the express lanes only from say 10:00 p.m. to 7:00 a.m.

We could encourage a lot of people who live in Mississauga and Oakville to take the GO-Train by collecting a congestion charge at the Mississauga border for inbound cars along the QEW during rush hour. After all, at that point the highway becomes the Gardiner Expressway, which is supported entirely by City of Toronto taxpayers.

TRAFFIC MAZES

There is congestion on arterial roads because every neighbourhood has constructed a maze of streets, no entry signs and one-way barriers to force the cars out of neighbourhoods onto arterial roads. I once had to print and distribute a map to every resident in the area south of Eglinton and west of Oakwood Avenue entitled: How to Get Home Legally in Rush Hour. Toronto streets were designed in a grid pattern to spread the load of traffic out evenly. If those barriers were removed, there wouldn't be a rush hour that lasted more than an hour, but removing them would be politically painful. Almost every one of those signs and traffic mazes was installed because somebody complained to a councillor. Might it not be better if these barriers were declared inoperable for a defined period, say 4:30 p.m. to 5:30 p.m., and we kept our kids off the street during that time; we could clear the downtown in an hour.

So, what does this all mean? What would I do if I were Mayor Tory?

I would establish a congestion task force with broad community representation, councillors and traffic engineers. They would be instructed to re-build the traffic rules from the ground up starting at zero. The task force would be empowered to examine every issue related to traffic and traffic management, including topics like, how should the traffic regime adapt to the self-driving car? (That's not too far off.) The task force itself won't solve the congestion problem. It will be the community discourse it generates that will allow a plan to evolve. Every traffic issue will be discussed, dissected and debated. The news media will be filled with public dialogue on every facet of traffic management. An informed consensus will slowly begin to emerge. Eventually, it would be presented to council as the city's traffic management plan, be adopted and implemented over a period of time.

Doesn't it seem odd that the City of Toronto has an official plan for almost everything but traffic management?

CHAPTER 99

Farewell

A *Globe and Mail* reporter telephoned me not so long ago to interview me for an obituary she was writing.

"Who?" I asked.

"Mel Lastman."

"But he's not dead," I said. "I saw him in the Bagel World last week."

"He will be some day," she replied.

I never knew they wrote obits in advance. It got me thinking. Why not? If the Globe and Mail can do it, why can't I?

To tell you the truth, I don't want to leave, but alas, we all must. I spent most of my life determined to shape the world around me, so why wouldn't I want to leave on my own terms? Other Toronto politicians have. Thomas Foster, a former mayor who served 36 years on council, made his mark long after he was gone. In his will, he left money to feed the birds. He also left $100,000 for an annual picnic at Exhibition Place for underprivileged children. His will sparked a stork derby that awarded prize money to the mothers of families that could conceive the most children in a decade. There were four stork derbies from 1945 to 1964. When he died, Thomas Foster was buried in a mausoleum inspired by the Taj Mahal.

I'm not interested in the Taj Mahal, but I would like to be buried in my ward. That's not particularly easy because they keep moving the boundaries around. I now have a place reserved in Mount Sinai Cemetery on Wilson Avenue adjacent to the railway tracks that cross Wilson Avenue between Dufferin Street and

Keele Street. Most of my family is there. They are right next to the Sunrise Propane site on Murray Road, where a propane storage tank exploded in 2008. It didn't bother them, though – they were already dead. If they weren't, it would have killed them.

Jewish cemeteries in Toronto are condominium style co-operatives. When the early ones were established before the turn of the last century, the sites were purchased by the community at large and overseen by burial societies. They were then parcelled out in sections to synagogues and a myriad of fraternal, charitable and welfare organizations that supported a largely working-class wave of immigrants that flooded into Toronto. Between 1901 and 1911, Jewish immigration to Toronto had swelled from 3,090 to 18,237. My family belonged to the Canadian Hebrew Benevolent Society (CHBS). Membership entitled you and your spouse to a burial plot in the CHBS section of the Mount Sinai Cemetery.

I began to plan for my final retirement. I didn't have to worry about my funeral. Gloria had pre-arranged and pre-paid all of it. She's great at looking after things like that. The alarm bells began to ring when I got a letter from the cemetery chairman of the lodge.

"The CHBS section of the Mount Sinai Cemetery is quickly filling up," it said. "If you want to reserve one of the few remaining plots, you should contact us right away. You can reserve a plot for $600. Otherwise, you will have to be buried in the CHBS section of the Pardes Shalom Cemetery."

Hey, that's way up Dufferin Street, north of Major Mackenzie Drive. I would have to be buried in York Region. That would be a fate worse than death. In York Region, the arterial roads are landscaped with cement walls. There, they plant lollipop trees, which after 20 years grow into older lollipop trees. Besides, you can't really get around in York Region without a car, and I'm sure I couldn't renew my driver's licence after I reached 100.

After visiting the CHBS burial ground, I picked out two spots and mailed in my $1,200. I wanted to be as close to my parents as possible and there were a number of spots available in the third row from the road. About a week later, I got a phone call from someone who identified himself as the CHBS cemetery chairman: "You can't have those spots. I can give you two in the back row along the fence."

In Jewish cemeteries, that is the row they reserve for people who commit suicide. I had no intention of leaving of my own volition.

"Why not?" I asked.

"The first three rows are reserved for lodge presidents."

It seemed to me that for an almost full cemetery, there were enough empty gravesites in the first three rows to bury presidents for the next century.

After about six months of dickering with the lodge, I telephoned my friend, Isaac Lallouz, for advice. He sits on the board of a burial society. Isaac told me to check recent amendments to Ontario burial regulations.

He was right. In 2012, the Ontario rules that governed the sale of interment rights required the cemetery to place money into a trust account for each gravesite that was reserved. At that time, it was $300 per plot. Were all of the plots they had reserved for presidents backed up by deposits? I doubted it.

I made one last-ditch call to the cemetery chairman.

"Are you aware that Ontario cemetery regulations require a deposit of $300 be made to a trust fund for each plot reserved? I hope that all of those presidential resting places are compliant with the regulations. It would be an embarrassment to the lodge if they were audited by the Bereavement Authority"

"I'll look into it."

Soon afterwards, I received a return call: "Congratulations. We just happen to be creating two new spots in the third row and we have decided to reserve them for you."

I've been fighting bureaucracies all my life. Who could have imagined I would have to do it for my burial site?

I have already ordered and designed my headstone. It is shaped like City Hall with the English inscription to go on the west tower and the Hebrew on the east. Hebrew reads from right to left. The stone is now in storage in the monument maker's shop. I'm happy I don't have to pay storage fees. I am hoping it will be there for a very long time.

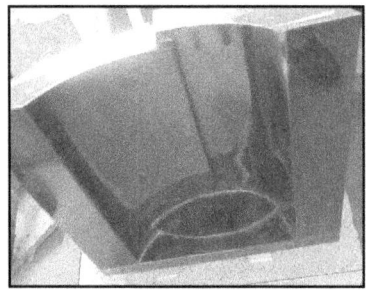

My election sign will be affixed to the rear of the stone, but in keeping with the dignity of the venue, instead of the usual gaudy orange day glow lettering on corrugated plastic, it will be a tasteful brass plaque. I will have to make a few changes to update the sign, like replacing "re-elect."

I have included an e-mail address and told my daughters if they want to participate in my inheritance they will have to take turns responding to my e-mails for at least five years. In addition, they will have to issue at least one press release in each of those five years.

CHAPTER 100
Eulogy

THE LAST WORD [WELL ALMOST]

I'm sorry you came to my funeral. I was hoping to be at yours. Instead of having some rabbi misrepresent me at my funeral, I've decided to do that myself. Have you noticed how nobody bad or evil ever dies? Someone can be the meanest, nastiest son-of-a-bitch in the world and they only say nice things about them at their funeral. For some people, they may have not much to say at all. I don't think I fit into either of those categories.

I flunked my Grade 10 year at Harbord Collegiate. I was a teenage hoodlum who was more interested in my peer group than my studies. Then, fortunately for me, my parents moved. I ended up as one of only four Jewish kids at Runnymede Collegiate and two of them were my brothers. I, of all people, carried the academic reputation of Harbord Collegiate on my shoulders. I didn't know anybody at Runnymede, so when my classmates horsed around in the halls between periods I read the next chapter in the history text. To my amazement, I could answer all of the teacher's questions and, to boot, people thought I was smart. I even won the Grade 11 history prize.

It was then that I came to an astounding conclusion: if you work hard and do some preparation, you can be successful. I never looked back. Ever since that time, I would rather be absent than go into a meeting without having first read the agenda and having thought about what outcomes I wanted. I learned that in politics if you are the one to place the motions, people will be debating your ideas and you can actually exercise some control over the agenda. That's exactly the formula I used to achieve what modest success I may have had.

It's tempting to use this opportunity to bash my enemies. You can't be in politics for 32 years without acquiring your share of them and they almost always come to your funeral, perhaps to gloat. Relax! There is no point in it and certainly no satisfaction if you are dead and unable to enjoy it. I just want to thank both my friends and my enemies for 32 wonderfully exciting years in public office. I loved every minute of it. (Well, almost every minute.)

In 2004, before they wheeled me into the operating room for my heart operation, I told Gloria, "Don't mourn me, celebrate my good fortune. I have had the chance to see and do things that few people have ever had. If it ends here, I'm satisfied." Besides, you know I just have to go before you. (Gloria does the household accounts, which I hate doing and refuse to do).

That was 13 years ago. Every year after that has been a bonus. Gloria: I fell in love with you the moment I saw you across that crowded dance floor in the Saturday night lounge at the YMHA. After that hayride, I was hooked. From your sweet 16 to your 75th birthday, it has been a marvellous adventure for me. Thank you for a wonderful life. You got the short end of the stick. You married a teacher and ended up with a politician.

For my children: Well, you've heard it all before.

For my grandchildren, I leave three bits of advice:

1 – If you can figure out how things work, you can make them work for you.

2 – Have a healthy disrespect for authority. Question everything. Absolute truth is a rare commodity. There are too many "alternative facts" floating around out there. I rush to underscore the word "healthy." But once you have determined what is right, do everything in your power to live by your principles.

3 – Practice Tikkun Olam. I have never been a religious person and I'm not even sure that I believe there is a G-d, but Judaism has a lot of wisdom to offer. Tikkun Olam is a concept found in the Mishna. It translates as "repair the world." Every Jew has a duty to do something to make the world just a little bit better. It is the root of social justice and a principle worth living by. It will make you a "mensch."

By the way, if any of you would like a copy of this eulogy you can have one today. Simply purchase a copy of my book, *Call Me Pisher*, which will be available for sale outside in the lobby after the funeral service, or you can buy it at my shiva at a discounted price. All proceeds will go to my favourite charity, the Moscoe Family Survival Fund. If you buy one today, it will bear a genuine original Howard Moscoe rubber-stamped signature. Who knows? Now that I am dead, it might even be worth something. Alternatively, you can wait a year and pick up a copy for $1.00 at the liquidation store in Kelowna, B.C., where I bought Patty Star's book. You remember Patty, she brought down the David Peterson government.

Why have I written this account? I suppose there is a lot about ego and the need for recognition that drives people to run for public office. Everyone has a basic need to say, "Hey I was here." It's the same urge that prompts someone to spray graffiti on a pristine wall.

Somehow, I think how I lived has been more than to simply mark my spot on the fabric of human existence. Perhaps, someday it will prompt one of my grandchildren or great- grandchildren to stop by and drop a pebble on my headstone. I hope what I have written here helps them to understand where they got their creativity, their drive to succeed, their passion for justice or their cornball sense of humour.

I don't believe there is a heaven or hell, but I am sure there is an eternity. It lies in our DNA.

ADDENDUM
The Moscoe Team

A politician is only as good as the people behind him. I was backed by one of the best teams at City Hall. My office was always a centre of hyperactivity; sort of like politics on steroids. That we were together for so many years is testimony to the fact that we worked as a team, but more importantly, we liked each other. I think I speak for everyone when I say, it wasn't just a job – it was an adventure.

IRENE

I rescued Irene Sepp from the reception desk at the North York Civic Centre when I went to Metro. Her organizing skills were the glue that held my office together. More than that, as head of my intelligence service, she knew everything that happened at City Hall. Irene was a great "schmoozer" and the public face of my office.

IRENE SEPP

She was no stranger to politics. She had been involved in election campaigns since the age of 16. Stan Haidasz, her sister's brother-in-law, had been a Liberal Member of Parliament and she had worked on all of his campaigns. Irene spoke fluent Polish, so she could help me communicate with all of my Polish speaking constituents; both of them. Irene organized most of my fund raisers.

BEN

Ben Rothman came into my election campaign in 1985. He was a parent whose six-year-old daughter, Sara, attended MAGU, an alternative elementary school where I was teaching. Sara is now the Senior Director, Academic Success at the University of New Brunswick. He quietly took over that campaign and had managed most of my election campaigns since.

BEN ROTHMAN

Ben has "been around." As a university student and a civil rights activist, he participated in voter registration drives in Mississippi. In 1967, he went to Israel to study, but instead ended up in the middle of the Six-Day War and organized volunteers. Ben has been a union organizer and has organized NDP election campaigns across the country. In 1972, he served as Assistant to Michael Cassidy, the one-time Ontario NDP leader. At the time, Michael was both an Ottawa City Councillor and MPP. Ben managed his Ottawa City Hall office.

Ben was my polar opposite. He saved my skin by talking me out of some of my crazier schemes or at least persuaded me to modify them. He was calm, thoughtful and thorough and liked by everyone; the voice of reason in my office.

BETTY

Betty DeBartolo came to me when I moved from Metro to City Hall. She was a young intake worker in the community services department. Betty is a "city brat." Her father was a building inspector in the North District and her sister a Toronto property standards officer. She knows the bureaucracy inside and out, but most importantly, she knew how to cut through it.

BETTY DEBARTOLO

In municipal politics, your political survival depends on how well you service your constituents. In our office, once we determined that a constituent had a legitimate grievance, we would not rest until it was redressed. Betty was a pit bull. She would not let go until the problem was resolved. I owe much of my local popularity to her efforts. She now manages the mayor's office in Aurora.

MARIA

Maria Rizzo and I have been friends for years. She was first elected as a North York councillor in 1991 and served two terms. She lost her seat in the 1995 election when the city was re-structured. At that time, she joined my office to handle all my planning, zoning and committee of adjustment matters and continued with me until I retired in 2010.

MARIA RIZZO

In 1997, Maria was elected to the Toronto District Catholic School Board for Ward 5 and has been a trustee ever since. Maria is a passionate advocate for education, community and for social justice.

www.ingramcontent.com/pod-product-compliance
Lightning Source LLC
Chambersburg PA
CBHW071850290426
44110CB00013B/1096